GENERATION
OXY

GENERATION OXY

FROM HIGH SCHOOL WRESTLERS TO PAIN PILL KINGPINS

Douglas Dodd and Matthew B. Cox

Foreword by Mark Mallouk

Skyhorse Publishing

Skyhorse Publishing books may be purchased in bulk at special discounts for sales promotion, corporate gifts, fund-raising, or educational purposes. Special editions can also be created to specifications. For details, contact the Special Sales Department, Skyhorse Publishing, 307 West 36th Street, 11th Floor, New York, NY 10018 or info@ skyhorsepublishing.com.

Skyhorse® and Skyhorse Publishing® are registered trademarks of Skyhorse Publishing, Inc.®, a Delaware corporation.

Visit our website at www.skyhorsepublishing.com.

10 9 8 7 6 5 4 3 2 1

Library of Congress Cataloging-in-Publication Data is available on file.

Cover design by Rain Saukas
Cover photos: Douglas Dodd

Print ISBN: 978-1-5107-2357-3
Ebook ISBN: 978-1-5107-2358-0

Printed in the United States of America

Author's Note

The reader should know some names and identifying characteristics of certain people have been changed in order to protect their privacy. In some instances, I re-created dialogue to the best of my recollection and compressed events to best serve the overall story. However, like most people's memories, mine is selective and at times, flawed. Although I've scoured court motions, transcripts, reports, and conducted multiple interviews in order to create an accurate account of my story, there is simply no way I'm as cool and funny as the guy described between the covers of this book; nor could my friendships have been this strong, my drug-induced highs this good, the sex as wild, the good times as good and the bad times as bad. But this is the way I remember it, and try as I have, I can't describe it any other way.

Contents

Foreword

Generation Oxy is a monument to collective irresponsibility. At several points in the story you will find yourself asking, "How did that happen?"

Of course, at the center of it all was Doug Dodd. It goes without saying that he made some terrible choices. We'd all agree that illegally obtaining thousands of OxyContin pills is reckless and irresponsible. Forming an interstate network of dealers to sell those pills isn't the wisest move. And, in retrospect, Dodd probably should've partnered with somebody, anybody, other than Lance Barabas, a self-destructive, wild man who seems genetically constructed to defy authority in all its forms.

But Doug Dodd's story is not possible without the moral and ethical failings of society's most important institutions.

First, the state of Florida, which from everything I can see, is a lawless swampland. The negligence of state politicians and regulators is astonishing. They enabled, and continue to profit from, the OxyContin epidemic.

There's FedEx, a company that, according to a 2010 US Justice Department report, "knowingly delivered drugs to dealers and addicts." FedEx was indicted again in 2014 for distributing controlled drugs online. No arrests were made.

There's the medical malpractice of doctors who knowingly overprescribed OxyContin and the pharmacists who knowingly filled addicts' prescriptions in the name of greed. Pharmacy giant CVS was indicted in 2010. No arrests were made.

Then, sitting atop of the irresponsibility pyramid, the Sackler family, the owners and operators of Purdue Pharma, the creator of OxyContin. In 2012, the US Justice Department found Purdue Pharma contributed to thousands of deaths by intentionally "misleading the public about OxyContin's risk of addiction."

Of course, no arrests were made.

In fact, in 2015, the Sackler family, founders and owners of Purdue Pharma, were added to *Forbes* magazine's "America's Richest Families" with a net worth of $14 billion dollars.

So when you find yourself asking, "How did that happen?" ...

That's how it happened.

—Mark Mallouk
July 2017

Prologue

The two kids and their crew were making millions of dollars . . . illegally moving OxyContin and Roxicodone pills to a network of dealers spread out across the country—Tennessee, Alaska, South Carolina, New York.

—*Rolling Stone*

It was Saturday night at the Round Up, a popular country dance club located just outside Tampa's city limits. The place was packed with blue-collar workers and drunken southern belles line dancing underneath the disco balls to Blake Shelton's "Redneck Girl" and "Trashy Women" by Confederate Railroad. There were sleeved-out dirty southern boys doing shots at the bar while watching half-naked strippers in Stetsons seductively slow riding the mechanical bull; your typical Florida honky-tonk. My high school buddies and I had been drinking rum and Coke and snorting oxys most of the night. I was seventeen years old and more than buzzed, dancing with a twenty-something raven-haired beauty, sporting a tramp stamp and silicon implants. That might have been why I didn't notice the hulking bouncers pulling my friends off the dance floor until one of the country boys tapped on my shoulder. "You!" yelled the bouncer over the music. I reeled around to see this massive Hulk-like guy in a black T-shirt that read SECURITY on it. "You're outta here!"

He escorted me outside with my friends, and asked for my ID. "Not a problem," I said, and handed him twenty-three-year-old Alejandro James Diaz's Florida drivers license.

The bouncers held the license up and his eyes darted between Diaz's photograph and myself—Douglas Chantz Dodd. We were both thin and roughly five foot eight inches tall with green eyes and dirty-blond spiked hair. Regardless, we weren't twins. "Nah," grunted the Hulk, "this isn't you."

"You're crazy," I replied, as a Pinellas County Sheriff's cruiser pulled up to the club's entrance just behind me.

"We'll see," chuckled the bouncer, motioning to the deputy exiting the patrol vehicle.

Between me, my best friend Lance Barabas, his brothers Landon and Larry, and our buddy Richard Sullivan, our group—which prosecutors would ultimately dub "the Barabas criminal enterprise"—was making millions, shipping hundreds of thousands of oxycodone pills throughout the country. Federal prosecutors would later call us one of the largest suppliers of the ever-increasing oxycodone epidemic. And I had roughly one hundred of the powerful painkillers in a metal vial hanging from the chain around my neck, barely covered by my shirt—a fifteen-year mandatory minimum sentence in the state of Florida.

"Shit," I hissed under my breath. Fifteen years in Florida state prison was not a part of my plans. I slowly glanced toward the group of massive bouncers surrounding my friends and then to the deputy closing in on my right.

The officer noticed my shifting eyes and growled, "Don't even think about it." My fight-or-flight instinct kicked in and my adrenaline spiked. I bolted past my friends and across the parking lot, with the deputy and two of the bouncers on my heels. The pounding of their feet and screams faded into the background as I shot into four lanes of traffic on Hillsborough Avenue, causing a dozen vehicles to swerve and lock up their brakes. I could hear screeching tires, crunching steel, and cracking taillights. But I didn't look back, I just kept running. I raced behind a building, yanked off my necklace, and stashed it in a tree. My heart was pounding, adrenaline surging through my veins as I scaled the chain-link fence of the Oldsmar Flea Market and hid in a maze of rusted storage units.

Within seconds, the sheriff was looking for me in the alley behind the building. "I need a coupla dogs ASAP," he said into his shoulder microphone. The K-9 unit's German shepherds arrived minutes later. They quickly found my vial of oxycodone hanging from a tree branch, and tracked my scent to the flea market. "I've got around a hundred oxycodone," he said into his shoulder mic. More than enough for a trafficking charge. "Get me a helicopter up here, now!"

I had just caught my breath when I heard the K-9s barking and snapping on the other side of the fence—less than a hundred yards away. Then I saw the blue lights of several cruisers at the entrance of the open-air market. They were closing in. So I jumped the back fence and crawled through a muddy field as sheriff's deputies swarmed the market.

That's when I heard the helicopter and saw the spotlight converging on my location. Drenched in mud and sweat, I sprang to my feet and ran into a nearby shopping plaza where over a dozen tractor-trailers were parked. I quickly crawled underneath one and laid between its massive tires.

I called Lance and told him where I was as the beam of the helicopter's spotlight passed over the trailer. "Bro," I whispered while two deputies walked by, haphazardly shining their Maglites underneath the trailers, "you've gotta come get me."

"Sit tight," said Lance; one of his brothers and a friend had been arrested. Another buddy had backed Lance's Dodge truck into a Mercedes and the remaining friends were screaming at one another. It was complete chaos. "But we're coming to get you." He ended the call and told everyone they needed to pick me up immediately. Most of them wanted to get out of the area before they were arrested for trespassing or underage drinking. "Well, we're not leaving him!"

At roughly the same time, several sheriff's deputies spotted Lance on the side of the highway. Due to my and Lance's physical similarities they encircled him with their patrol vehicles, jumped out of the cruisers, and drew their weapons. "Get on the ground!" they yelled. "Get on the ground!"

Lance dropped to his belly as multiple K-9 unit officers approached the area with their German shepherds. A portly deputy jammed his knee into Lance's back and snapped a pair of cuffs on his wrists. "What were you doing in the flea market?" barked one of the K-9 unit officers, while two of the dogs growled and snapped their razor-sharp teeth inches from Lance's face. He could feel the dogs' breath and saliva on his cheeks.

"I wasn't at the flea market!" replied Lance. "I've been here—"

"What're you doing with all them pills?!" snapped the deputy, as he yanked Lance off the asphalt. But the teen didn't respond. "Boy, you're fucking with the wrong officer!" then he shoved him in the back of the cruiser.

Over the course of the next hour—while I waited for Lance to pick me up—I went from sweating and dry heaving to shivering in the cold night air.

As two patrol vehicles pulled into the parking lot across the street, I slyly began to work my way down the shopping plaza, ducking behind bushes and blending into the dark areas, until I made it to a 7-Eleven. I scouted the area and then called Lance's cell for an update. "Who am I speaking with?" asked an official voice on the other end of the line.

"Doug," I replied. "Where's Lance?"

"I've got 'im in the back of my patrol car. But I need to release him to someone. Where are you at?"

"Sir, I'm seventeen years old. How are you going to release him to me?"

"Listen kid," growled the officer, "if you don't tell me where you're at, I'm gonna book your little pal here. What do you have to say to that, smartass?"

"Tell Lance I love him," I chuckled, "and I'll bail him out in the morning." I disconnected and walked into the convenience store covered in dirt and grass, and grabbed a soda out of the beverage cooler. The clerk gawked at me—I was filthy from head to toe—as I tossed some cash on the counter and exited the store. It was after two o'clock in the morning when I called my cousin and said, "Come get me. They arrested Lance." Then I popped the top and gulped down my ice-cold Orange Crush. You know, I wasn't born a drug dealer. I became one.

Chapter One

The Land of Opportunity

Painkiller overdoses . . . exceed the crack cocaine epidemic of the 1980s and the black tar heroin epidemic of the 1970s combined.

—*The Guardian*

I was born in 1988—just after Ronald Reagan declared "the war on drugs"—in New Port Richey, Florida, not far from the Tampa Bay/Clearwater Beach area; it's a small coastal town on the way to nowhere with a stagnant population of around fourteen thousand Floridians struggling to stay lower-middle class. Downtown is peppered with dated strip malls and pawn shops. Lots of fishing boats and packing warehouses. There's no shortage of bars and strip clubs.

I spent most of my childhood running around the playgrounds and trailer parks, barefoot and dirty. Despite how it sounds, I never considered myself poor white trash, although what you're about to read might have you think otherwise.

My mother, Sylvia Drupe, is a functioning alcoholic; a career waitress who loves Budweiser and marijuana brownies. I love her, but she's never exactly been the nurturing, motherly type.

My dad, Douglas Dodd, is everything my mother isn't: mild mannered, conservative, and nonconfrontational. Unfortunately, he's got a thing for waitresses, and as a restaurant manager, it eventually became an issue.

In 1993, I was a skinny little five-year-old kid, oblivious to how fragile my parents' marriage was, when a man approached my mother during her night shift at Chili's. "Ma'am," he said, "you don't know me, but my wife's a waitress at Bob Evans [the restaurant where my father worked], and your husband's fucking her. They're at your house, right now."

My mother caught the two of them parked in our driveway. My dad was nailing Brandy, my future stepmother, in the back seat of our family's Pontiac Trans Am, when my mom yanked open the passenger-side door. "You fucking whore!" screamed my mother, as my dad and Brandy struggled to shimmy into their clothes. "This is the last time, you cheating shit!" she screamed at my father, "we're through!"

Between my father's affinity for waitresses and my mother's addiction to Bud Light, their marriage was doomed. They divorced in early 1993. I'll never forget standing at the front door, barefoot and shirtless in my gym shorts, as the movers loaded the last of our furniture into my mother's U-Haul truck. From the television to the couch, she took it all. We had nothing left. "Dad," I remember saying, "she took the TV!"

"I know, buddy. I know."

Just after the divorce was final, my mother told me, "Dougie, your cheating father only married me because I got pregnant." I was five! Then she clenched her jaw tight and growled, "I could've taken him for everything. Full custody and child support. But I'm not that kind of woman." As far as I could tell, she had already taken everything she could. The truth is she didn't want, nor could she handle, the responsibility of a five-year-old. My father was awarded custody during the week and my mother got me on the weekends. She could barely handle that. Neither of them seemed to be able to afford me.

I went from being a symbol of their loving union to a painful memory of it. They bickered and fought over every dime it took to feed and clothe me. By the time I entered Calousa Elementary School, I had outgrown most of my clothes and all of my tennis shoes. I ended up attending the fifth grade in cowboy boots. They were only an issue during recess. When we played soccer, the boots caused me blisters, and I ended up bruising several of the other kids' shins. My homeroom teacher made several calls to my parents in an attempt to get them to buy me a pair of tennis shoes. My mother told her clothes were my "cheating" father's responsibility— they weren't, but she always said that. My dad turned around and requested my mom split the cost with him, which she refused to do. After getting the runaround for a couple weeks my teacher broke down and bought me a pair of Wilson tennis shoes. My parents should've been humiliated, but they didn't even notice. They were too wrapped up in their new lives.

After the divorce, my mother became a regular barfly for about a year.

She dragged home a succession of losers, but eventually married Gary Park, an alcoholic warehouse laborer. I dreaded the weekends with them. They fought constantly. I remember sitting in my room and crying, listening to them scream late into the night as they threw beer cans at one another. I was eight years old and didn't know what else to do.

In 1998, one of their arguments turned violent. They had been drinking most of the night, arguing about money—they were always arguing about money. My stepfather slapped my mother or she slapped him—depending on who you ask. Regardless, my mother grabbed the phone and dialed 911. When they asked her, what's your emergency, she screamed, "Help, he's going to—"

Gary snatched the receiver out of her hand and told the emergency operator, "Don't bother sending anyone, she'll be dead by the time they get here." Then he yanked the phone out of the wall and started throwing her around, slamming her into the walls and knocking over furniture. The entire double-wide was shaking when I was jolted awake by my mother screaming for help.

By the time I came out of my room they had moved to the front yard; lit by the motion-sensitive floodlights, red-faced and drunk, pushing each other. I exited the trailer just in time to see Gary slap my mom to the ground and kick her in the head with his steel-toed boots. At nine years old, I grabbed a Rubbermaid garbage can and hurled it at my stepfather. The can hit him in the upper back and burst open, sending garbage everywhere.

"Dougie!" screamed my mother while struggling to stand, "get the neighbor!" I ran next door and told them to call 911. When the police arrived, my stepfather was arrested for domestic violence and served with a one thousand–foot restraining order. My mother ended up divorcing Gary and marrying another abusive prick named John Tripper, her third husband, a handyman who grew hydroponic marijuana on the side. My mom's arms were constantly bruised. I remember showing up one weekend and she had stitches running through her eyebrow, along with an implausible story about hitting her face on the bathroom sink. I'm not sure where she found these guys, but she never seemed to run out of them.

I was ten years old when my seventeen-year-old cousin, Eric Dodd, moved in with me and my dad. Dad was working sixty hours a week at Leverock's Seafood Restaurant, and my cousin was selling pot out of the house. One day after school, Eric and I were sitting in the living room playing PlayStation's *Street Fighter* when he asked, "You wanna get stoned?"

"Sure," I replied. I had smoked pot once before, with a girlfriend and her older brother when I was in fourth grade. But this time was different, there was something about lighting up the bowl and sucking in the smoke; the sensation of the THC rushing to my head. The artificial sense of serenity. It didn't take long before I was getting stoned with my buddies before and after school.

On the weekends my mother worked, I would stay with my Aunt Maria. She had recently been arrested in late December of 2000 for selling over a dozen ecstasy pills to a confidential informant and was currently awaiting sentencing. When Aunt Maria wasn't watching me, I would hang out with my sixteen-year-old cousin Roberta. We would go to Dimensions, a popular teen club, and get high, or play on their trampoline and ride dune buggies through the woods.

But once my aunt was sentenced to a year in Florida state prison, and my uncle started working double shifts driving trucks, all semblance of parental supervision disappeared. That house turned into a straight cannabis club with a dozen neighborhood kids hanging around smoking at any given moment.

That's when I first spoke to Kathy Fisher, a beautiful, curvy five-foot brunette cheerleader with a hard body and amazing legs. She had caught my eye at Dimensions weeks earlier. We had shared a couple flirtatious glances, and I got this strange feeling in my stomach. But she was sixteen years old and dating a senior on the football team. I didn't have the guts to talk to her.

My cousin Roberta and her boyfriend knew I was crushing on Kathy hard, so they invited her over one weekend. We were all sitting around the sectional, smoking and grinning at one another. It took me half a dozen hits to build up the courage to talk to her. I wasn't exactly a thirteen-year-old Don Juan, but after about an hour of smoking weed and flirting, we were French kissing and grinding away at each other. Eventually someone suggested the four of us relocate to my aunt and uncle's Airstream in the back yard and "get naked."

Kathy gave me a shy half grin and asked, "You want to?"

I had never wanted anything more in my life. Five minutes later, we were lying in the sleeping area tugging at each other's clothes. I had seen some Internet porn and a couple of *Playboy* magazines, so I felt I had the situation under control. But when Kathy shimmied out of her blue jeans and slipped off her tank top, revealing two perfect breasts, I thought, *I'm totally unprepared for this.*

By the time I was fumbling with the condom and Kathy's panties, my cousin's boyfriend had Roberta completely naked and they were going at it right next to us.

Kathy, who was obviously more experienced than I was, was doing all the right things. Within minutes we were dripping with sweat from the sauna-like condition inside the camper. At one point she pulled her nails across my back and whispered, "It hurts sooo good." I may not have known what I was doing, but Kathy damn sure did. It was everything I had hoped sex would be. But I'm certain my performance isn't among her top ten sexual experiences. Whose first time is?

It wasn't long before we were doing it every Friday, Saturday, and Sunday. I would call Kathy up and say, "I'm gonna be at Roberta's this weekend." I could feel her smiling through the phone when she giggled, "I'll be there."

I wouldn't refer to it as dating—she had a boyfriend. We were more like fuck buddies on those weekends her beau was at football practice or off fishing with his friends. I was a thirteen-year-old stoner getting laid on the regular by a hard-bodied cheerleader with zero inhibitions—life was good. My biggest fear was that my newest abusive stepfather would figure out I was stealing Trojans out of his dresser and hydroponic weed out of the Igloo he kept in the freezer.

Keep in mind that virtually everyone I knew was selling drugs or doing them. Aunts, uncles, cousins, friends, parents, and stepparents. On my mother's side, Uncle Tony was serving an eight-year federal sentence for trafficking marijuana. So, when John's Igloo eventually ran dry, I asked my Mexican buddies Alejandro and Joseph Diaz, "Do you guys have any pot?"

They glanced at one another and laughed. "Yeah," said Alejandro, "we've got some." They walked me out to a detached two-car garage behind their house and pulled back a weather-resistant tarp. The Diaz brothers' stepfather was one of the largest suppliers of marijuana in the Hudson/New Port Richey, Florida area. There, lying on the concrete floor was a large rectangular fifty-pound bale of Mexican brick weed. I had never seen anything so exhilarating in my entire life. "Scrape as much off as you want." *Score*, I thought as I filled up an entire sandwich bag.

Around a month later, on May 9, 2002, several friends and I got stoned on the bus, on our way home from Gulf Middle School. I thought I was so cool pulling out my pipe and weed. It never occurred to me that one of my fellow students might turn me in.

The following day, I was in history class listening to the teacher describe the effects of the Opium Wars.

"The opium epidemic continued virtually unchecked until the 1950s," said the teacher, "when the Chinese Communist Party of Mao Zedong ceased all opium production, forced ten million addicts into compulsory treatment, and publicly executed tens of thousands of dealers."

That's when I noticed our lanky principal walk in and scan the room student by student. I never imagined he was looking for me. "Dodd!" he barked, and pointed down the hallway to the administrative wing. "My office now!"

There was a Pasco County Sheriff's Deputy waiting for me in the principal's gray and tan office. He searched my bag, sifting through my textbooks and notepads, until he found a small amount of marijuana in a Ziploc bag along with a glass pipe. When the deputy pulled the baggie out of my backpack, I thought, *My mom's gonna kill me.*

The principal made me listen to a lengthy lecture on how drugs would ruin my life, while the deputy glared at me. "Marijuana's a gateway drug. You keep it up, you'll be doing heroin before long," he said, sitting behind his desk, pointing a bony finger at me. "It's poisoning your mind; imagine how much better you'd be doing in school if you weren't smoking this crap."

"How much better could I be doing?" I asked with a shrug. "I've got straight As."

The principal gave me a skeptical smirk and pulled up my record on his desktop computer, revealing my 4.0 GPA. "I'll be damned," he grunted underneath his breath. Then he turned to the officer and said, "I'm finished with 'im."

The deputy grabbed me by the wrists and snapped a pair of handcuffs on me, then walked me down the hallway filled with several hundred of my fellow middle schoolers, all gawking and whispering. It was all I could do to hold back the tears. I felt so humiliated and embarrassed. My stomach was turning, and I was a little frightened of what the outcome would be. I knew I messed up and was in for a serious whooping when I got home.

The Pasco County Juvenile Holding Facility was a utilitarian dump with adult-style cinder block prison cells. Once I was fingerprinted and photographed, a deputy asked, "Who do you want me to call, your mother or your—"

"Dad!" I snapped. "Call my dad, please." I knew they would both be angry with me, but I was one hundred percent sure that if my mother didn't kill me, she would thoroughly embarrass me.

My father was more disappointed than angry. On our way home he kept saying, "You've gotta start making better choices, Dougie." But, by this point my stepmother, Brandy, had caught my dad sleeping with another waitress, Debbie—future stepmother number two—so it was kind of hard to take any advice he gave me seriously.

When my mom found out about my arrest, she bitched a little, but what could she really say? My stepfather was growing hydroponic marijuana inside their house.

I was expelled from Gulf Middle School and sent to Schwett-men Alternative School for troubled juvenile offenders. Roughly a month later, the juvenile court judge barked something like, "A straight-A student getting high. That was a pretty dumb thing for you to do, wasn't it?"

"Yes, sir," I mumbled, while staring at the carpet. Then he sentenced me to an intervention program and drug treatment. I had to meet with a social worker twice a week for six months. Plus, I had an after-school curfew and an old-school pager. But it was more about peeing in a cup and keeping my grades up than drug counseling.

My father and stepmother's fights were getting more and more vicious all the time. "You never even loved me," I remember Brandy saying during one of their many arguments. "You only married me 'cause you needed me to take care of Dougie, but I guess he's old enough to take care of himself now," she spat, "so now you're ready to trade me in for a newer model. Is that it, asshole?!"

"I wouldn't say a new model," my dad shot back, "I'd say a better model." Brandy went absolutely ballistic. She moved out shortly after that and took all the furniture. Loaded it into a Ryder truck and drove away with everything. "She took the TV," I griped. "You lost another TV."

"Don't worry," he said, "Debbie's got one." She moved in shortly after, along with her daughters.

Just after my intervention program ended, my father and new stepmother decided to move to upstate New York. Debbie's grandmother had passed away, presenting the opportunity to fulfill Debbie's childhood dream of buying her grandmother's house. She and my father knew it would be a great area to open a bed and breakfast. So, they sold their house in Hudson, packed everything, and moved thirteen hundred miles away. But I refused to go. All my family and friends lived in Florida.

"I can't believe your father's making you choose between your family and friends and him!" spat my mother when she found out about the move. "We both swore we'd never leave Florida. Typical!" She never missed an opportunity to bash my dad. My mother had just kicked out my latest stepfather, and she wanted me to stay with her. At the time, it seemed like a good idea, but it didn't take long before cracks started to appear. After a couple of beers my mother became a pretty mean drunk; she would start complaining about my curfew, my chores, and my music—typical teenager-parent stuff. The truth is, she just liked to get drunk and argue. Hence, the three husbands and multiple restraining orders.

As time went on, the living situation became more and more stressful. On occasion, it was unbearable. In a way, it seemed like my mother's lack of control in her own life manifested itself in her desire to dominate my life. Nothing ever seemed good enough for her.

Chapter Two

Dirty Southern Wrestling

"Better-behaved Cobra emerges as a contender. [Lance Barabas] knows he wants to study psychology and wrestle. His ultimate dream, though, is the Olympics."

—*St. Petersburg Times*

I started Hudson High School in 2003; it was your standard public school building—heavy on function, but light on imagination. Lots of fluorescent lights and low ceilings. Go Cobras! The student body was mostly populated by lower-middle-class kids driving dated pickup trucks and muscle cars. There were lots of rednecks, jocks, and cheerleaders. I met Lance and Landon Barabas the first day of wrestling practice, along with their buddy Richard Sullivan. They were a bunch of blond-haired, blue-eyed, wisecracking rich kids surrounded by a pool of the underprivileged. Despite our differences, we hit it off right away.

We smoked weed between classes, wrestled during the week, and partied on the weekends. It didn't take long before we became inseparable, hanging around after school and carpooling to wrestling practices.

The first time Landon picked me up, he showed up in this huge Ford Excursion. Landon said we had to stop by their house and pick up something. I remember Lance and Landon arguing on the way home about who was going to put gas in Landon's car—a brand-new, fully-loaded Excursion on twenty-inch rims. Landon was driving while Lance was in the passenger seat and they were bickering back and forth like a couple of little kids on why the other needed to fill the tank. Lance said Landon needed to pay for it because he had filled the tank up last time.

"Well, I'm driving and that means you should pay for it," said Landon.

Lance came back with, "Well, get the hell out and I'll drive then."

"I'm not paying for it twice—it's your turn, Landon!"

"Okay, fine," said Landon, "but I don't have any money on me."

"How do you not have any money? Mom just gave you money yesterday! What did you do with it?"

"I spent it."

"Unbelievable, un-fucking-believable. I'm telling you right now Landon, you're paying me back! You're paying me back!" said Lance as he flicked a twenty-dollar bill at his brother.

A couple of minutes later, he pulled the Ford up to Holy Ground, a homeless shelter with multiple commercial buildings and a church. There were two dozen vagrants in tattered clothes hanging around the facility's entrance. "You live here?" I asked.

"Yeah, our mom owns it," laughed Lance, "but we don't live in the shelter." Ms. Barabas was what I would call "redneck rich." She and her boys all drove expensive vehicles, wore designer clothes, and had plenty of money, but lived in a double-wide trailer in front of the facility.

Regardless of our economic differences we were a tight group of friends.

Lance, "the Little General," was a control freak. Since the age of ten, he had been running around his mother's shelter, telling grown men to make their beds in the morning, and screaming, "Bed time!" at night. Then he would flip off all the TVs and lights. I loved him like a brother, but he was an alpha-male gun nut with a big mouth, a Napoleon complex, and ADHD. To top it off, he didn't like to take his Adderall, which was the only thing keeping him somewhat under control.

Lance's older brother Landon was a "Pretty Boy" with Captain America good looks. He thrived on attention and was so vain he couldn't pass a reflective surface without looking at himself. He would have carried around a compact if we'd let him, the narcissist.

Then there was Larry, the oldest of the Barabas brothers, Larry "the Lineman," was a massive four-hundred-pound football player who had blown off a full scholarship to FSU to stay close to his family and high school sweetheart.

And of course, our buddy Richard. His goal—in preparation for his future career as a porn star—was to sleep with as many women as possible. He was rumored to have contracted multiple STDs and had been dubbed "Hazardous" by Hudson High's female student body and "Shit Dick" by me and Lance. A wild child and a big drinker to say the least.

Regardless of how it sounds, they were a great group of guys. But as close as we were, I always felt like the odd man out. Their families owned restaurants and bars, assisted living facilities, and homeless shelters. They had all the options in the world, and I was struggling to survive on the Pasco County free-lunch program.

The Hudson High School wrestling team consisted of roughly two dozen members, spanning twelve weight classes, between 103 pounds and 265 pounds. Lance and I fluctuated between the 119- and 125-pound weight class; Landon and Richard both wrestled at the 172-pound weight class.

We practiced Monday through Friday, from 2:30 p.m. until 4:00 p.m. We worked out and dieted all week long. If we weren't preparing for the upcoming season, we were going to football games or mixed martial arts (MMA) matches.

Sometime in mid-2003, the four of us were at the University of South Florida Sun Dome watching a couple MMA fighters smash it out in the octagon. The place was packed with thousands of pumped up *Muscle & Fitness* types wrapped up in tight T-shirts and tribal tattoos, cheering as the fighters slammed one another onto the bloody mat. We were all drunk on beer that Richard had bought with his older brother's ID, gawking at the models holding the round card high above their heads and prancing around in their bikinis and body glitter.

Richard was hitting on these two platinum blonde cougars in their late thirties or early forties by playing dumb and shy. He told them he was a sophomore at the University of South Florida and one of the women was actually buying his bullshit act. Between rounds, Richard went for more beer and she turned to Lance and said, "Your friend's a real cutie."

"Yeah, he's a great guy and all the chicks at our high school say he's hung like a horse," replied Lance, trying to suppress a grin. "But if you don't wanna be shelling out two hundred a month for Valtrex the rest of your life, I'd make sure he wears a condom." She scrunched up her nose and reared back. We all burst into laughter.

Minutes later, the reigning champ took down the contender using a double-leg take down and we were all screaming how "sick" that was and chattering about fighting in the UFC someday; all except Richard, who couldn't figure out why he was getting the cold shoulder from the cougars. Lance turned to him and said, "After graduation, you and Landon should try out for the UFC trials."

"Fuck that! Two years from now I'm gonna be shooting bukkake and giving pearl necklaces, not rolling around with some sweaty UFC fighter."

About two months later, the arguments with my mother started to escalate. At one point, I came home after wrestling practice—slightly after my 7:30 p.m. curfew—and she was waiting for me at the front door with a Budweiser in her hand. "Where've you been?!" she screamed, and went on a twenty-minute rant about "My house!" and "My rules!" That was no big deal; I had heard it all before. But when she screeched, "I hate you! I wish I'd never had you!" I said, "I'm done."

At the time, I was fifteen, and I knew that my living situation was abnormal and would only get worse. I called my dad the following day after school and we talked about the ongoing issues with my mother. I told him I couldn't take it anymore and I was thinking about moving in with him.

He was remorseful about the situation with my mother but ecstatic about me coming to live with him. Weeks later, my bags were packed and I was boarding Delta Airlines. Final destination: New York.

I moved in with my father, stepmother, and three stepsisters in Richfield Springs, a rural Podunk town upstate. It was the northern equivalent of Hudson, Florida—not a thriving metropolis. I enrolled in Richfield Springs Community School, which encompassed kindergarten through twelfth grade, and immediately joined the football and wrestling teams. I started dating Susan Artum, a petite brunette with a great body and Angelina Jolie lips. But I spent most of my time with my new stoner buddies Bobby—a sophomore in college—and Andy—a high school dropout. They were running a large-scale weed operation in the middle of the woods, growing fields of marijuana—tons of it. We would sit around, smoking a bong, and process the harvested weed.

I ended up skipping a postseason football game that the school claimed was mandatory and they axed me from the wrestling team. Richfield Springs has a policy that states if any student doesn't finish out a season in one sport that they would be banned from participating in any other sports for that school year. They felt it would be more educational if their students were roaming the streets instead of participating in structured school activities.

It really tore me up, but I eventually got over it. My grades dropped to Bs and Cs, and I started partying all the time. I got into the full swing of the grow operation, and it wasn't long before I was selling bags of pot right out of my school locker.

It was about that same time that my puppy love relationship with Susan turned into full-blown true love. My first love. We were inseparable. If we weren't cuddled up watching movies together or on a four-wheeler adventure in the thick wilderness, we were on the phone talking.

In hindsight, though, we weren't right for each other. She needed constant attention, and it could sometimes be exhausting. She also had a handful of guys chasing her, vying for her affections, and I couldn't be with her every minute.

While I was smoking blunts and falling in love in upstate New York, Lance "the Little General" was down in Florida and went off his meds. As a result, he ended up cursing out his science teacher because she asked him to stop talking in class. Then he slammed a door in her face—it came close to knocking her out cold—and almost got himself charged with assault and expelled from Hudson High. But Ms. Barabas talked the teacher out of pressing charges and talked the school board into limiting her son's disciplinary action into a month-long suspension. Several weeks after he returned to school—still refusing to take his Adderall because he complained that it made him feel tired, unsocial, and too focused on schoolwork—Lance got into an argument with his physical education teacher and yelled, "Motherfucker, I'll blow your fucking head clear off!" That didn't go over well.

After that, the principal told Ms. Barabas her son would have to take Adderall daily, "or find another high school to terrorize."

Once properly medicated, Lance leveled off, stopped arguing with his teachers, and pulled his grades up. He started focusing on wrestling, and college recruiters started watching him.

Sometime in late 2005, I was supposed to meet Susan at a house party, but when I got there she was gone. Someone told me she and this guy Mike had been making out at the party, and they had left to go back to his house. I went nuts.

An hour later, when Susan walked in with Mike, I scooped him up, slammed him on the ground, and started pounding on him. It took four football players to pull me off him.

Susan spent the next several weeks begging me to take her back. She started calling a dozen times a day. Sometimes she would sneak into my room in the morning, get naked, and slip underneath the covers. Other times she would ride the bus home with me from school. Her strategy was to stalk me into forgiving her. Her constant presence only made things worse. Just the possibility of Susan in bed with that guy, moaning in ecstasy, pissed me off. I knew she was really drunk that night, but I didn't care.

She was my first real girlfriend, and I was utterly crushed by her betrayal. I moped around like a sick puppy. I couldn't eat or sleep. I couldn't look at her. It was pathetic, and eventually I decided I couldn't be in the same school with her anymore.

I moved back to Florida and picked up in the middle of my junior year at Hudson High. I moved back in with my mother and her new boyfriend, this one a cokehead. After a couple of months, he graduated to smoking crack and my mom kicked him out.

Lance picked me up that first weekend to go spearfishing. He asked me, "How was New York?"

"It sucked! The whole state's filled with Yankee whores."

"What?" He laughed. "As opposed to all the nice girls in Florida?"

It never felt so good to be back in the Florida sunshine. It was beautiful in New York, but nothing beats spearfishing, jet skiing, or going to the beach every weekend. I'm a Florida boy at heart. Between Lance and the guys, and all the "nice girls" in Florida, it didn't take long before Susan slipped to the back of my mind. Eventually, she and the pain faded altogether.

Chapter Three

Ground Zero

"The toll our nation's prescription drug abuse epidemic has taken in communities nationwide is devastating, and Florida is ground zero."

—Obama's drug czar, Gil Kerlikowske

I re-enrolled in Hudson High roughly halfway through my junior year, just in time to sign up for the wrestling team. Unfortunately, when I asked my mother for the registration money she informed me, "The only thing I'm required to do is keep a roof over your head and food in the fridge. You wanna wrestle, you can pay for it yourself." And my dad told me, "That's your mother's responsibility, not mine."

So, while my buddies were tag-teaming cheerleaders and going mudding in their new trucks, I went to work forty hours a week as a fry cook at Mike's Dockside, a seafood restaurant down the street from my mom's house. But once I started receiving paychecks, my mother demanded money for the utilities and gas. "Isn't that part of keeping a roof over my head?" I asked.

"I've got a mortgage, Dougie!" she griped, while sucking down a Bud Light. "This is my house, my rules." I'd heard it all before.

It was an impossible situation. As soon as I made any money, my mother came with ways to take it. She didn't want to do anything for me. I had to have my seventy-five-year-old grandmother take me to get my driver's license. My mother wouldn't do it. In order to get school supplies and clothes, I started buying weed from my Mexican buddy Alejandro and another buddy Leon, who had premium hydro; and selling it to my fellow students and co-workers out of the back of the restaurant where I worked. Eventually, I got a job at Hooters as a short-order cook and started supplying half the long-legged, big-breasted waitresses in the place.

After a couple months, I had saved enough to buy a Honda Prelude my Uncle Tony had for sale. He seemed a little shocked when I counted out $3,500 in rumpled fives and tens. Fresh out of federal prison for trafficking marijuana, he picked up the wad of bills, placed it against his nose, and inhaled the aroma. "Here's your first lesson nephew," he said with a grin, "don't ever keep your weed and cash together." My lips parted slightly in shock, but before I could deny it was drug money, he asked, "Your mother know about the vehicle?"

"No," I scoffed. "She wouldn't even take me to get my license—grandma had to do it."

Uncle Tony shook his head and tossed me the keys. "Christ," I remember him saying, "what kinda mother won't take her son to get his license?"

When my mother saw the Honda she was furious. "How'd you get the money for it?!"

She had been demanding money out of my paycheck since I'd started working, but she had also found a half pound of hydroponic weed in my safe weeks earlier—she knew what I was doing. "You know where I got the money," I responded.

By the beginning of 2006, my life had become one long music video. I had my own car, and I was with several girls on the regular. There was Bethany, a gorgeous brown-eyed brunette member of the ROTC that used to give me hand jobs in algebra during the teacher's lectures—to this day, x times 2x equals $2x^2$ gives me a woody. And there was Juliana, a pale, thin, Goth chick with licorice black locks who loved to do it in my car in the student parking lot after school—180 degrees of sweaty Honda sex. But the girl I was really into was my longtime friend, Jennifer's best friend, Kristina Williamson. Kristina was a five-foot-five-inch dirty-blond sophomore cheerleader with a tight body that made my mouth water every time I looked at her.

As much as I liked Kristina, I could never seem to commit to her, or tell her I loved her, or trust her. I never saw the point. "It's only a matter of time before one of us fucks over the other one," I used to tell her. "Why make it official?"

I remember lying in bed with her after a punishing twenty minutes of fornication, dripping with perspiration and panting with exhaustion. Kristina looked over at me and said, "I know you don't trust me. You don't trust anyone. But I'm not your mother, ya know." But they were *all* my mother, and I didn't trust any of them. Between my father's infidelity and my mother's mental brutality, I'm not sure I believed in love.

Familial bonds required me to love my mother, her parenting forced me to despise her, and her addiction caused me to fear and pity her. But nothing, it seemed, would allow me to escape her. And I think Kristina knew that.

I was acing my classes during the week and partying with Lance and the guys every weekend. We would all meet at Alejandro and Joseph's double-wide—along with around a hundred other Hudson High students. The Diaz brothers' acre-sized lot would be packed bumper to bumper with pickup trucks and muscle cars.

We would move all the living room furniture outside and have wrestling matches with sixty kids drunk on Hunch Punch (a bunch of cut-up fruit like apples, pineapple, grapes, and watermelon in a big cooler with fruit punch and about five bottles of flavored vodka and Everclear in it) and Jell-O shots crammed into the trailer, cheering us on. It was a bunch of sweaty southern boys pulling double-leg takedowns and hip tosses on one another, then body slamming each other on the carpet and wrestling until someone ended up in a headlock or a rear naked choke, forcing them to tap out. It was more like a scene from *Fight Club* than your typical high school party. There were always a few real brawls and lots of drinking.

You could usually find two or three cheerleaders high on opiates or ecstasy making out in a bathroom somewhere and a dozen drunken jocks guzzling down Solo cups full of beer. Sometimes the crowd would swell to over two hundred students dancing around bonfires and in the back of pickup trucks. The cops didn't usually show up until after midnight.

Around ten o'clock on February 10, 2006, I was driving home and smoking a joint when a Florida state trooper noticed that—like an idiot!—I didn't have my lights on. The trooper pulled behind my

Honda and flashed his blue and whites. My heart was pounding as I nervously flipped the joint out the window. The ember shot into the night and disappeared as I pulled to the curb.

The trooper was in his early forties. The John Wayne type. Typical southern law enforcement. He leaned into the driver's side window, flared his nostrils a couple times, taking in the lingering aroma of weed, and grunted, "I smell marijuana. You been smoking?"

"No, sir." I made a scene of sniffing the air a few times and said, "I don't smell anything."

"Well, I do." Then he told me that gave him probable cause to search my vehicle. He immediately found a Ziploc bag with half an ounce in the center console and arrested me. My first thought was, *My mom's gonna kill me.* Then he stuck me in the back of his cruiser and returned to my Honda for a more thorough inspection. While he was digging through my trunk I slid the cuffs up my forearm and twisted my torso just enough to work my cell phone out of my front pocket. I tried calling my mom at home and on her cell, but they both went to voicemail. So I called my friend Jennifer, explained the situation, and said, "You've gotta find my mom and get her to pick me up."

The trooper took me to Land O'Lakes Juvenile Detention Center, photographed me, and told me to take a seat in the waiting area. I sat in one of a dozen molded plastic chairs and wondered if Jennifer had tracked down my mother. Two hours later, she showed up with Kristina and my mom, who was drunk. Her speech was slurred and she reeked of alcohol and cheap perfume. The officer on duty only begrudgingly allowed her to sign me out.

Once we were in the car, my mother began berating me from the front seat, while I sat quietly with Jennifer in the back seat.

"One of these days you're going to end up in fucking prison, you little jerk!" screeched my mother while periodically sipping out of a plastic cup. "You're a pothead just like your uncle!"

"Oh yeah?" I snapped. "What've you got there, vodka?"

"It's fucking water!" she growled, glaring at me.

"Well, you haven't been drinking *that* all night."

She suddenly swirled around, lurched over the seat, and began punching and slapping me as Jennifer and Kristina screamed for her to stop. Eventually they got her to calm down. Then my mother pulled out her cell and called her brother. "Anthony," she slurred into the phone, "your nephew got caught driving around with half a pound of weed." She thrust the cell at me. "Here, talk to your uncle!"

"What the hell's going on?" he asked, as I took the phone.

"It was only half an ounce, Uncle Tony."

"Half an ounce? Well, what's her problem? That's nothing."

"What do you think? She's drunk."

I remember catching Kristina's eyes in the rearview mirror. They were filled with pity and embarrassment for me. I hated my mother for that.

When we got home, Mom started screaming at me. It got so bad I took my dog and went to stay with Alejandro and Joseph. They were older than me and had their own place. Alejandro was a senior in high school who sold pot and his brother graduated the year before and now laid block for a living. When I came home the following day, my mother had changed the locks. I had no clothes or money. No big deal. She did crazy shit all the time. I headed back to Alejandro and Joseph's to camp out on their couch, and continued going to school and work.

Roughly six weeks later, I was called out of class to my counselor's office, a drab, windowless room with cheap particle board furniture. My mother was sitting in a grey aluminum folding chair, nervously tapping her foot and looking distraught. "Where've you been?!" she snapped, as I walked into the room. "I've been worried sick about you!"

"What're you talking about?" I asked, glancing between my counselor and mother. "You changed the locks."

She glanced at the counselor, and said, "That's not true. I would . . . I would never do that."

"Right," I scoffed.

She and I shot a couple sarcastic comments back and forth and my counselor interjected, "Doug, you're only seventeen. You're going to have to go back."

"Absolutely not," I said, staring him in the eyes. "I haven't missed one day of school since I left and I'm an A student. I work full time and I can pay my own bills." I turned to my mother and said, "There's no way I'm coming back."

"Huh," she grunted. "We'll see what the judge says about that," and she gave me this creepy mischievous grin.

I later found out my mother went straight home and wrote Juvenile Court Judge Walter L. Shaffer a letter stating I was out of control and she desperately needed help with me. She then asked him to impose the stiffest punishment possible in order to teach me a lesson. That included moving back into her house.

I never understood why she went to such extremes to make my life so hard. One minute she wanted me around, the next minute she didn't. The truth is, my mother was struggling to get me under her thumb. Even if I had obeyed her every whim—between her alcohol-induced mood swings and the losers she dated—she was never going to be happy.

She treated me like a toy yo-yo, constantly pushing me one way and pulling me back. I don't think she even knew what she wanted. For the longest time, I thought it had something to do with her being adopted into a hard-nosed Italian family with four older brothers and an abusive father. It wasn't until years later that I was told she had been diagnosed with a borderline personality disorder.

Around a month later—on April 28—I was standing in the same beige-and-tan juvenile courtroom where I had been sentenced three years earlier, when I was in middle school. It smelled like feet and teen desperation. My mother was sitting behind me, feigning concern and support, when Judge Shaffer entered the courtroom. He was a plump conservative-looking white guy sporting a traditional black robe and white comb-over. "Mr. Dodd," he barked, "I've reviewed your juvenile court record and I'm baffled by your lack of respect for our state's drug laws." He told my mother he had read her letter and agreed "wholeheartedly" with her. The judge then looked back at me and growled, "You're lucky to have a mother that loves you this much!" It took everything in me not to scream, "You're joking, right?!" He then suspended my license for one year, gave me three months of drug counseling at Pathfinder Treatment Center, which included random drug testing and nine months of probation. "And I'm imposing an immediate after-school curfew to be served at your mother's residence for the duration of your probation."

All that for a misdemeanor!

When we got home I went to my room and slammed the door and cranked up my radio. My mother flung open the door, unplugged the radio, and said, "My house, my rules. Don't play with me or I'll make your life a living Hell."

"I don't want anything to do with you!" I said in a very serious and stern voice as I stared back at her.

My mother turned around and called the Pasco Sheriff's Department and told them I was no longer welcome in her house. Twenty minutes later a deputy knocked on my bedroom door and said, "Pack up your stuff."

I loaded up my car again with my stuff and the officer followed me to my grandmother's house. She lived about twenty miles outside Hudson, in the middle of nowhere. Grandma was my father's mother; she was a sweet seventy-five-year-old widow and an absolute angel. So sweet it took me awhile to get used to it. The first week I stayed there she kept trying to give me lunch money and do my laundry. I kept telling her, "Grandma, I've got a full-time job and I can fold my own clothes." But at least once a week I would come home and my bed would be made and the carpet vacuumed. I told her, "you're not my maid," but she kept doing it.

I had been taking care of myself for so long it freaked me out, but Grandma was just being maternal—more so than my own mother had ever been.

Living with her was the perfect solution; when I first moved in, Grandma was dating a guy ten years her junior, and she would stay at his place most nights. I don't even want to know what was happening over there. When she was gone I had the house to myself. Eventually, her boyfriend died—probably from exhaustion—and Grandma went into mourning. But eventually she snapped out of it, met a retiree in his seventies on the Internet, and started staying at his place several nights a week. Between bingo, casino cruises, and long walks in the park with the new guy, I had the place to myself again. Even the nights she stayed at home, I hardly noticed. Grandma would go into her room, close the door, and turn off her hearing aids. She couldn't hear anything without them.

Not my music, not the door bell, nothing.

The court-ordered rehab was a breeze; a couple days a week, I attended group drug counseling classes. About a dozen of us watched videos, listened to lectures, and spoke with a counselor. She was a really nice lady, and I have no doubt she graduated with honors from some prestigious university, but it was obvious she had never been an addict. Listening to her speak about addiction was as dry and clinical as reading straight out of a textbook. She just couldn't make a connection with any of us.

I, on the other hand, was making some valuable connections. One guy stood out to me when he shared his stories. With his body language and the way he answered questions, he came across to me as someone who could get things done. A year later, that guy ended up being one of my biggest suppliers.

As a result of my 2:30 p.m. curfew, I ended up hanging out a lot with my cousin Julian, who lived down the street from Grandma's. We spent most of our time watching movies and getting wasted on oxycodone pain pills, a semisynthetic opioid used for managing severe acute or chronic pain. It's available as Roxicodone for breakthrough pain and in a controlled-release form, known as OxyContin. Unlike marijuana, opiates are out of your system within a couple of days, making it easy to avoid my weekly drug test. Quick and easy.

That was ground zero for me; sitting on my cousin's couch popping painkillers for the first time. The warm, soothing sensation of the oxycodone rushing through my veins, relaxing and loosening every muscle fiber within my body, was overwhelmingly euphoric. The opiates washed away the anxiety and nervous tension of being a teen—a pharmaceutical escape from my dysfunctional life. Nothing had ever felt so good.

I knew a couple dozen people that took Roxicodone 30 milligrams and OxyContin 20, 40, and 80 milligrams, on a regular basis. In 2006, "roxies" and "oxys" were becoming the drug of choice in central Florida, from high school students to business professionals. Everyone was taking them.

Maybe a month into my probation I was kicked back on my cousin's sofa playing *Halo* on Xbox—in an opiate-fuelled bliss—and I started thinking, oxycodone is semi-legal, easy to use, abundant, and very popular. I turned to Julian and asked him if he could hook me up with a hundred pills. "Sure," he said. "I've got a connect I'll set you up with."

My cousin's "connect" turned out to be an old, tatted-up, pot-bellied biker. I was a little nervous meeting this guy. He was a crazy-looking SOB who lived in a single-wide trailer in a dirt lot behind the auto body shop he worked at, and he had two Dobermans that looked like they were ready to rip someone apart. The guy was a pothead with prescriptions for both Roxicodone 30s and OxyContin 80s, but he hardly ever took the roxies because the oxys were managing his back pain. I bought a hundred Roxicodone 30s for $8 per pill, hoping to sell them for $12.50 per pill over the next few weeks.

After a while my grandmother loosened up. I was doing well in school, wrestling, and had no problems with probation. She eventually allowed me to go out from time to time. The following

Saturday night—I didn't have curfew on the weekends—I was at Lance's with around ten other guys. We were drinking and playing poker—Texas Hold 'em. One friend's older brother Matt was there and I knew he was into pills. So I asked him if he knew anyone that wanted to buy some painkillers. "Yeah," he said with a laugh, "me. What do you have?"

I dug the pills out of my pocket and handed them to him. "They're roxie thirties."

Matt flipped them around in his hand and said, "I'll take 'em."

I sold him thirty tablets for $12.50 a piece. He told a couple of people and I told a couple of people. Three days later the rest were gone. It was too easy.

My buddy Angelo connected me with a married couple that had prescriptions. Another friend, Ethan, got me another script. Miles, a guy I had met at the drug rehab treatment center, knew a couple of guys with prescriptions, and Thomas had four scripts from four different doctors. My cousin Tony Jr. gave me a bunch more guys with scripts. Within a few weeks I had over two thousand pills coming in per month. I started selling them for $15 per pill or ten-packs for $120. I made almost five grand the first month.

My new business venture was based on the great demand for oxycodone and the correspondingly high prices the pills could command. And for that I could thank pharmaceutical companies like Purdue Pharma. The drug itself had been around since the 1920s and has been prescribed for decades with few adverse effects—and certainly no national epidemic of addiction to opioids.

The problem started in the late 1980s. Purdue's patent for MS Contin, a morphine drug designed and marketed to cancer patients, was about to expire, which would allow their cash cow to be gobbled up by the competition. They needed a new, exclusive drug. One that could replace or outperform MS Contin.

In 1996, Purdue introduced OxyContin—containing a twelve-hour controlled-release formula—and their marketing department kicked into high gear. One tablet, twice a day, providing "smooth and sustained pain control"—that was their pitch. There was only one problem; it wasn't true. In more than half of the patients prescribed OxyContin, the drug wore off after only eight hours. Despite Purdue's own research, the company continued marketing the drug's twelve-hour duration.

They pumped hundreds of millions of dollars into advertising. They expanded their sales force to over six hundred reps and began pitching doctors on the virtues of prescribing OxyContin twice a day. They offered doctors complimentary weekend junkets at luxury hotels and expensive meals. They gave their sales reps massive bonuses and trips. The company even went so far as to create a medical textbook to "educate" the newest generation of doctors on their miracle drug. That textbook listed oxycodone as a moderate-potent opioid that can be prescribed with relative safety to patients; it paid little attention to addiction or overdoses.

Some doctors raised concern about patients' complaints that the drug wore off hours before their next scheduled treatment. Purdue's response was a simple one—increase the dosage.

Over the next decade three things happened in the United States. One: Purdue's profits shot up from $400 million to over $3 billion annually. Two: oxycodone prescriptions, for products from a variety of pharmaceutical manufacturers, increased substantially. Three: opioid addiction in the United States increased tenfold.

Even when the Drug Enforcement Administration (DEA) eventually indicted three of Purdue's top executives for "mislabeling" the drug, which finally put a stop to their aggressive marketing campaign, the executives only got a slap on the wrist.

By then, the damage was done. An estimated two hundred thousand people have lost their lives to oxycodone overdoses since 1996 and nearly ten million Americans are currently addicted to some form of oxycodone; making it the most abused pharmaceutical drug in US history.

Of course, my friends and I knew nothing about this history at the time. We were just looking to have some fun and make some good money.

Chapter Four

Swamp Challenge Champion

"Bigger's not always better on the mats. [At] Saturday's Swamp Challenge... Hudson had four winners: Douglas Dodd (125), Tony Germano (152), Devin Brown (171) and William Bentley (189)."

—*Tampa Bay Times*

Around the same time things started to take off for me, in June of 2006, Lance "the Little General" and "Shit Dick" Richard graduated Hudson High. Lance got a scholarship to Cumberland University in Knoxville, Tennessee—the same university where his older brother "Pretty Boy" Landon was wrestling. But Lance was so lovesick over his high school girlfriend, Tiffany Sutler—a big-breasted, spunky little brunette softball player with sexy freckles—that within three months he dropped out of Cumberland and moved back to Florida. They fought constantly, but Lance was hooked on her.

Richard—whose parents could have easily paid for him to go to any university—moved to San Diego with two other guys. He wanted to live the "California dream" and pursue his adult film career.

Richard thought it was going to be all tits and ass, but it was a lot harder to break into the porn industry than he had expected. He went on several interviews with low-level adult-film talent agents, directors, and producers. It's my understanding that the bulk of the interviewers told Richard that industry novices seldom start their careers with heterosexual films. Most pay their dues starring in several dozen homosexual films to build up credibility and a body of work. Richard has always maintained he wouldn't demean himself by "acting" in gay porn and that's the reason he had such a hard time. But I wouldn't be shocked if there were a few guy-on-guy DVDs out there starring Richard. Not that I'm judging. Regardless, during his quest for stardom, Richard's funds ran low and he ended up taking a job as a carpenter—just like Jesus, had the Messiah been a wannabe porn star.

Sometime in late 2006, over corn flakes and skim milk, Richard came across an ad on Craiglist: "adult film talent wanted." He jumped on Interstate 5. Two hours later he was sitting in the waiting room of a nondescript production studio with four other budding adult film stars, each waiting his turn and ogling the casting agent's tanned hard-bodied blond assistant. She had the look of an aging porn star that had seen it all before; smacking on her gum and flipping through a *Variety* magazine. She ignored Richard and the other beefcakes.

An hour later the assistant told Richard, "He'll see you now," and led him into a plush office with decent furniture, a large desk with an assortment of headshots stacked at the corner, and a couple of guest chairs. In the far corner of the room was a king-sized bed, covered in plastic and surrounded by lights and camera equipment. It all looked very legit.

Richard took a seat and the casting agent, a tall, thin, middle-aged guy wearing a silk shirt unbuttoned to his navel, said, "So, why do you want to work in adult films?"

"Well, I like having sex with women, and I think I'm pretty good at it, so . . ." The agent went on to ask several more questions that I'm certain Richard answered with the grace and poise of a seasoned male bimbo. Eventually, the agent came to the conclusion the eighteen-year-old was perfect for the project. But he needed Richard to audition.

"You'll get the standard industry audition rate of two hundred and fifty dollars, of course." He pulled out a contract and asked Richard to read it over. "It's all standard stuff. I just need to video you, so I can show the producer and director what they'll be working with. I'm sure you understand."

"Of course," said Richard, nodding like a plastic dashboard bobble head, while scribbling his name on the contract without reading any of it. A major mistake on his part.

The agent called in his assistant to work the camera and told Richard to strip down to his birthday suit. Richard assumed he would be working with some young female costar, but the agent tossed him a tub of KY Jelly and said, "We'll be videoing you masturbating in order to gauge your girth and the consistency of your ejaculate." Richard wasn't deterred. This was his big break. So he climbed on the plastic covered mattress, got on his knees, squeezed out some lube, and started stroking it. He seductively opened his mouth in ecstasy and moaned for the camera as KY squirted and dripped on the plastic.

Periodically Richard could hear the assistant and the agent discussing his performance from behind the camera and the glaring lights. Every once in awhile the assistant would pop her gum and the agent would blurt out something like, "You're a real pro, work the head more . . . nice," and "You're doing great, tiger." Like a seasoned adult film star Richard never stopped yanking and pulling at himself. He pulled out all the stops for the agent.

Unfortunately for Richard, every time he was about to burst the agent asked him to change positions or pose for a still shot; dragging the masturbation session out for around thirty minutes. Eventually Richard popped like a champagne bottle.

As he was getting dressed Richard overheard the agent tell his assistant to "label this one Derrick." Then he turned to Richard and asked, "You sure you're eighteen?"

"Yes sir."

"Great." He told Richard he would be in touch, handed him $250 in sticky cash, and practically pushed him out of the office.

Over a month later, Richard still hadn't heard from the agent, and the phone number was disconnected. He was eating lunch at work, feeling cheap and violated—not in the good way—when he decided to look over the contract he had signed. He quickly skimmed over it and noticed the name of a popular California-based gay porn site—CollegeHunksUSA.com.

In a panic, he called Lance back in Florida, and asked him to pull up the website. Sure enough, on page two, under the name "Derrick," Richard was posed naked among a dozen other eighteen- and nineteen-year-olds, jacking off for the camera. "Be honest," he asked. "How bad is it, dude?"

"It's bad Derrick," laughed Lance, "it's bad." Richard begged Lance not to tell anyone about the site. "Come on bro," said Lance, "you know I wouldn't do that to you."

Lance called me immediately. I had just started my senior year at Hudson High; between Lance and myself we disseminated the site's address to every chick Richard had dated in high school. Within days the site went viral among the female student body, who relished his stroke of bad fortune.

These were the types of guys I was dealing with, lovesick maniacs and sexual deviants.

While Richard was getting duped in California I was busy trying to make the state wrestling finals.

I. Loved. Wrestling. To me, wrestling was the sport of all sports. I trained hard to prepare for a match, but no matter how tough my training partner was, once I got into that circle on the mat it was just me against my opponent. My success at that moment was dependant solely on my preparation and my performance. Most people don't realize the tactics that go into wrestling. There are three different primary starting points, with every move having a countermove or reversal. Strategizing for a match was a ritual I loved.

Luckily, wrestling came naturally for me. I was always a smaller kid who hung out with the older crowd, so I got messed with a lot and had to learn how to defend myself. Plus, my older cousins were all tough guys who, at one time or another, used to wrestle or take some kind of MMA or karate classes.

Looking back, it was tough to balance wrestling and partying. Tournaments were held early Saturday mornings and my phone would be blowing up on Friday night with requests from

Lance and the guys to come out of the house. Except for taking a few college courses, Lance wasn't doing much of anything. He had no job and no direction, other than hanging out and having a good time. I knew I couldn't go out the night before and show up in the morning prepared for the tournaments. They didn't care. Wrestling gave me something to focus on and work towards. It was structured, which I actually enjoyed and at the time desperately needed.

Lance used to come up to practice and go through my routine with me. We would do calisthenics and weight training, run bleachers and do wind sprints. He wasn't much help at the meets; all he would do was hang out with the coach and talk crap from the sidelines.

At this one tournament, held at Berkley Prep—a private school where all the kids had trust funds and matching BMWs—Lance was no help at all. The gymnasium was packed with over two hundred spectators including Jennifer and Kristina. I easily pinned the first guy I wrestled in a rat-tail match—a match where you wrestle for a ranked spot in a bracket in an individual tournament. My second opponent was a thick-necked kid from Indian Rocks Beach High School and he looked intimidating. Lance was standing on the sidelines with me and I asked him about the kid. He had wrestled him several times the year before. "He's nobody," said Lance, with a dismissive wave, like he was swatting a mosquito. "He's weak, bro. You've got him."

That kid slammed and rolled me all over the mat. For two minutes each over three periods I got jerked and yanked around like a helpless puppy, while Lance laughed the whole time. The kid never pinned me, but he eventually won by fifteen points.

"What the fuck Lance?!" I griped, out of breath and panting. "You said he was nobody!"

"What'd you want me to say—the guy's a badass and you don't have a prayer? He's a two-time state runner-up bro. I knew he was gonna kick your ass!"

"You could've given me a heads up!" I won my third and fourth match; beat the last guy with an ankle pick takedown, and pinned him in a cowcatcher. I took third in the tournament.

In December, Lance's older brother "Pretty Boy" Landon came home from college for Christmas break, and Lance, Landon, and Alejandro all came to the Christmas Tournament at Gulf High School. I beat the first four guys hard and fast, slamming and pinning them, one after another. But when my fifth opponent stepped onto the mat I thought, *Oh shit!* She was a thick, 125-pound brunette from Chasco High School—not a bad-looking chick.

Lance and Landon leaned into me and said, "You lose this match and your kids are going to hear about it. We'll never let you live it down."

"Relax, I've got this," I said. But I didn't. She was so flexible I had a hard time trying to pin her. She kept squirming and twisting out of my holds. The worst part was Lance and Landon screaming the whole time from the edge of the mat. "Come on sugar britches, pin 'er already!" and "Stop playing around sissy boy, pin 'er!"

I was trying to be respectful and this chick was literally trying to take my head off. I eventually got her in a headlock and won the match and went undefeated at the tournament.

In late January or early February—I'm not sure which—I went undefeated in the Land O' Lakes High School Swamp Challenge.

I finished out the wrestling season as a regional qualifier, district runner-up, all conference, and one match short of the state championship. Thirty-one wins and six losses, with the majority of individual team-ranking awards. It was a good thing they didn't do any drug testing for high school wrestlers back then.

Sometime in early 2007—I'm not exactly sure of the date—Kristina and I were on our way to a party and she pulled out a couple one-milligram Xanax bars. "You shouldn't take those," I said. "Not if you're gonna be drinking." Kristina got absolutely wild when she mixed alcohol and Xanax. She would lose all impulse control and start flirting with other guys and making out with other girls. Or get drunk to the point of blacking out. I always ended up being a babysitter when she did Xanax. "Seriously," I said, "I'm asking you not to take 'em."

She shot me a *Mind your own business* glare and popped the bar in her mouth. "Relax."

"Oh that's just great Kristina. That's great."

There were nearly a hundred high school and college students at the party, including my cousin Pete. He was an average-looking Italian with dark features and lots of body hair—he had a full beard at fourteen years old. A little Abe Lincoln. Everyone was dancing and drinking—including Kristina. It didn't take her long before she was stumbling around hugging everyone, yanking beer bottles out of people's hands, and yelling, "I wanna drink!" Your basic sloppy drunk. I spent most of the night keeping her in my peripheral vision, but I wasn't concerned. She was hanging with my cousin and he knew Kristina and I were together. Plus, he had a steady girlfriend. No big deal.

Some time around ten o'clock I lost track of her. She wasn't answering her cell and her car was gone. I got this really bad feeling in my gut, so I asked someone to swing me by her house. When I got there her car was parked half in the driveway and half on the yard. Most of the lights were off in the house, but the front door was unlocked. So I walked in, shot down the hallway, and into her bedroom. It was dark, but I could clearly make out movement underneath the blanket on the bed. I yanked off the covers and sure enough Pete and Kristina were half-naked and all twisted up. She was so busy going down on him she didn't even notice me. But Pete did. The sight of them together was gut-wrenching. I couldn't even speak. I just stumbled out of her room and down the hallway.

Pete caught up to me in the front yard, wearing nothing but his jeans. "Bro, you're not mad at me are you? It's not like she's your girl. Right?" I couldn't even answer him. I just got into the car and told my friend, "Go, just go."

The next morning I woke up and Kristina was sitting on the corner of my bed sobbing, begging me to just hear her out. She had made a mistake. She was drunk. She was so sorry. "Please give me another chance. Please!"

I remember looking at her and saying, "I told you it was just a matter of time."

I'd be lying if I said we never hung out or had sex again, but I certainly didn't forgive her, and I damn sure didn't trust her. Not that I ever had.

Maybe a week after I caught Kristina with my cousin, I started seeing a couple different girls. There was Amber Stevens; a former cheerleader who had graduated Hudson High the year before—a thin African American girl with gravity-defying features. She was a freshman at Pasco-Hernado Community College and an aspiring model with a thing for white guys. There was also Kenna FitzGerald, a dirty-blond cheerleader with a sweet body that used to give me the most enthusiastic blowjobs in the boys' room during lunch.

By this point I was wholesaling oxycodone to almost a dozen guys. Angelo, a buddy from high school, bought roughly a thousand a month, and Ethan typically got several hundred to sell to his fellow students at Hillsborough Community College. There was Eddy, a local dealer, who usually needed about a thousand pills. And my first roxie customer, Matt, was always good for a couple scripts a month.

Lance even started asking me for fifty to one hundred a week. But he wasn't selling them for the money, at least not at first. He was selling them to feed his habit. For every two pills he sold he got to keep one. I wouldn't say he was hooked on them, but he liked them. We all did.

By the end of my probation I had saved roughly $60,000 in cash by selling oxycodone. I used some of it to buy a fully loaded pearl-white Jeep Cherokee Laredo. However, the bulk of the money was sitting in my safe. I knew it wasn't a good idea to just leave it there, so I asked my Uncle Tony what to do with the cash. "It makes me nervous leaving it at Grandma's house."

"Lesson number two nephew: don't ever keep all your money together," he said, while shaking his head at my clumsiness. "The last thing you want is the local cops or the DEA finding all your cash." He suggested I bury some of it in the backyard or put it in a safe-deposit box, and leave the rest with a family member. "But not your mother!"

We celebrated spring break of 2007 at Daytona Beach. "Pretty Boy" Landon and "Shit Dick" Richard flew in. Lance "the Little General" and I rented two suites at the Hilton—a multistoried hotel on the beach with all the amenities. First class all the way. Female students from Gulf High School were on the floor above us. Half of the floor below us was filled with students from Hudson High, and our floor had a bunch of rich girls from River Ridge High. The hotel was overflowing with high school football, basketball, and baseball players. Wrestlers and track stars. Lots of peppy cheerleaders and giggling socialites. Girls. Girls. Girls.

We spent the first few days drinking and laying around on the beach and the first couple of nights rolling on ecstasy and hitting the clubs. On day three, we spent our time watching some of the national cheerleading competition, along with a thousand other spring breakers. Pom poms and school spirit, spandex and body glitter. Hot teen girls in tight outfits. It was everything a cheer competition should be.

That night we had a small party in our hotel rooms with half a dozen girls from River Ridge High. There were a bunch of chicks getting drunk and snorting coke. According to Richard we had slandered him with every decent-looking chick from Hudson to Gulf High. "You two cock-blocked me so bad I'm willing to fuck anything at this point."

"We're not cock-blocking you, Richard," laughed Lance. "We're saving lives!"

Richard got so desperate he started hitting on what he called "dogs" and "boozy bitches," and eventually picked up a tough-looking girl from River Ridge High. A five-foot-ten-inch tall specimen with broad shoulders and five-o'clock shadow. She played football in the PAL league as a tight end! Richard sweet-talked her into taking a shower with him. A minute later, he had her naked and moaning for more.

Landon used his driver's license to pop the lock and Lance and I slipped into the bathroom. I snapped one or two pictures of Richard and his football player in the shower. They were soaking wet and screaming for us to get out.

After another hour the party dialed down and started to break up. People started hooking up and meandering back to their rooms. Sometime around midnight two girls banged on our door, screaming something about their friend overdosing and having a seizure!

Lance and I rushed down the hall and there was a girl I had met at the party earlier, lying on the floor with her eyes rolled back in her head and foaming at the mouth. She was "fishing out," jerking and twitching. Every girl in the room was crying. I turned to her friends and said, "Call 911!" But no one moved toward the phone.

"Do something!" they kept saying. "Do something!"

We wiped her face with a wet hand towel and I tapped her on the cheek a few times but she was unresponsive. I was about to go for the phone myself when her eyes fluttered and she looked up at me. A minute or so later, she whispered, "I'm fine," and smiled.

I only mention the episode because the following morning she showed up at our suite to thank me and apologize. "I'm epileptic," she said. "Sometimes I have seizures when I speedball."

Mixing coke with oxycodone obviously did not agree with her. "Then why do it?"

"I like the high." She grinned shyly. Then gave me a half shrug and asked, "You don't have any more coke, do you?"

"You're fucking crazy," I said and shut the door on her.

We spent the next couple of days drunk and stoned, laying on the beach and chasing girls. It was one of the best times of my life.

Around the same time, Barack Obama and Hillary Clinton had begun campaigning for the Democratic nomination and everyone was speculating on who would win the primaries. "I'm telling you, bro," said Lance, "either one of those two becomes president and they're gonna strip us of our right to bear arms." Lance wanted me to buy a handgun, an assault rifle, and ammunition before it was too late. He already owned a Glock .45, a Bushmaster AR-15, and a Remington .308 sniper rifle.

"You're never gonna need those things, they're a waste of money."

"It's now or never, bro," he grinned. "I've got two words for you: zombie apocalypse."

"Oh, well that makes sense."

We went to a gun store somewhere in Tampa. The place was packed with weapons display cases containing a cornucopia of domestic handguns and rifles. Shelves were stacked with ammunition, tasers, and targets. Lance loved the place. He leaned over the glass case and pointed out one weapon after another. "Let me see this one," he would say to the guy behind the counter, "let me see that one."

By the time Lance was done handling half the guns in the store I felt obligated to get something. I had gone target shooting at the gun range, and we were always riding around on back trails on four-wheelers and shooting stuff. I bought a Sig Sauer 9 mm with an extended clip for around $500, a Smith & Wesson MNP

(Military and Police addition) short barrel AR-15 all decked out for almost $2,000, and a bunch of ammo. Lance was more excited than I was. But I have to admit, it was a badass gun.

We took Lance's Dodge Ram 2500 out to the middle of the woods to an area known as "the pits" to try out our new toys. The place was nothing but mud and sand surrounded by dense pines and oaks. There were a couple of burned-out cars and some rusted-out laundry machines. Every kid at Hudson High knew the place.

Lance pulled out his sniper rifle. While I set up a neat row of aluminum soda cans on the front fender of an abandoned Ford, he set up his Remington and bipod. He lay down on a beach towel, lined up the sights, and took several shots at the cans from around one hundred yards away. Lance popped a hole in the car's doors and actually hit two of the soda cans. I had never fired a .308 caliber rifle before; Lance did mention, "It's got a lot more kick than the AR-15."

I lay on my belly behind the bipod and lined up the sights on a Cherry Coke can, slowly squeezing the trigger. The rifle cracked and recoiled, smashing the edge of the scope into my brow. I felt a thump and everything went black for a second, but it didn't really hurt. I felt some sweat trickle down my nose and Lance said, "Bro, it split you wide open."

"Nuh uh." I glanced down at the blanket and saw a small puddle of blood forming beneath my head as it dripped off my nose. "Fuck!"

I put pressure on it while Lance loaded up our stuff, but it didn't stop bleeding. "Face it, bro," he said. "You're gonna need stitches."

In June 2007, just days before graduation, my dad flew down from New York. He and one of his buddies unexpectedly stopped by my grandmother's house the morning of the ceremony. I was smoking a honey Dutch cigarillo when I heard the doorbell; I looked out the peephole and saw them standing on the front porch. *Shit!* I put out the blunt and sprayed some air freshener, but when I opened the door my dad immediately asked, "What's that smell?" and his buddy Rick asked, "You got anymore of it?"

My dad frowned in disbelief as I pulled out a bag of hydro. Rick—a real stoner—pressed the weed to his nose and inhaled. "This is some primo shit." He turned to my dad and said, "We've gotta smoke some of this. Come on."

My dad shook his head in irritation as I rolled a fat blunt. For my sake, he acted appropriately disappointed. But when Rick passed my dad the joint he took a deep pull on it. As he exhaled, he started coughing, and we all shared a grin.

A couple minutes later Rick noticed my rifle case in the corner of the room.

"What's that?" he asked pointing to the case with his chin.

"An AR-15." I snapped open the hard plastic rectangular case and handed him the assault rifle while my dad stared at me in shock.

Rick checked to make sure the magazine wasn't in, pulled the slide back to check the chamber was clear, and sighted the weapon like he knew what he was doing. He turned to my dad and said, "This is a twenty-five-hundred-dollar weapon," and my father shot me a *What is going on?* look.

"I got a good deal on it," I snapped weakly.

"You got anything else?" he asked, as Rick placed the AR-15 into the case. I showed them my Sig Sauer 9 mm, Smith & Wesson .22, and a four-prong taser, roughly $3,000 in weapons. My father was not pleased. "What do you need all these for?"

"Nothing," I replied, nervously laughing. "Lance and I like to go shooting sometimes, that's all." I could see my dad's concerns bouncing around in his head. Between my toys and the new truck, I was obviously making and spending a lot of cash.

He started shaking his head. "What the hell's going on Doug, where's all this money coming from?"

I stared at him for a couple seconds, thought about telling him I was mowing yards and trimming trees on the weekends, and for a split second I even thought about telling him the truth. But instead I said, "Come on, Dad, don't make me lie to you."

That night, I graduated with honors and received the Principal's Scholarship. My dad, a couple cousins, an uncle, and both my grandmothers, Grandma and Meme, were there among the sea of proud parents and friends. I remember looking out at the crowd as I waited in line and thinking maybe I would see my mom. But she wasn't there. I'm not sure why I thought she would be at my graduation; she had never come to any of my wrestling matches. I did see Lance and the guys. They were laughing and waving as I ambled across the stage, fucked up on roxies.

The day after graduation my grandmother forced me and my dad to have lunch with my mother. "Your father hardly ever comes down to Florida."

"Come on Grandma, I don't wanna see her," I whined while stomping around my bedroom in protest.

"Douglas!" she snapped. "She's your mother; you're going!"

We ended up meeting at an Applebee's restaurant around 11:30 a.m. My mother was slightly late. Typical. I hadn't seen her in months. When she walked up to the table I thought, *Holy shit! It's Sharon Stone in Basic Instinct.* She was wearing too much make-up and a tight little skirt and top. Completely age-inappropriate. To top it off, she was sporting frosted tips and a new set of saline breast implants. "Jesus," gasped my father, "you smuggling a couple of cantaloupes under there?" Then he said something about her being top-heavy.

She gave him a flirtatious little grin and stuck out her tongue. "Cut it out, I just got 'em." While we ordered she told us her new boyfriend had bought her the accessories. He wasn't a fan of the flat-chested, twelve-year-old-boy look she had been sporting. Then she made a crack about my dad's newly shaven head and the fact that he had gained some weight.

"Debbie actually cooks," he replied, referring to his new wife.

My mom shot him a nasty look and feigned irritation, but they were actually enjoying themselves. She put away some alcohol, but overall she was on her best behavior. Everyone was. It was almost like our once-happy family had reunited, though there had never actually been a happy family to begin with.

When I got back to Grandma's she stopped me in the living room and asked, "Well, how'd everything go?"

"We didn't have to call the cops" I shrugged. "So better than the last time they were together." I think she was hoping for more.

Chapter Five

Hillbilly Heroin

"Florida doctors became the most prevalent buyers in the nation of the highly abused painkiller oxycodone . . . known as 'hillbilly heroin.'"

—*Orlando Sentinel*

I had never thought much about what I'd do after graduation. My parents had never suggested college and they damn sure hadn't mentioned paying for it. It wasn't until my grandmother asked, "Are you going to USF [University of South Florida] or Pasco-Hernando Community College?" that I even thought about the prospect of going. I had always assumed I'd be getting a job at a gym as a personal trainer, or something like that.

"Grandma," I remember chuckling, "I'm not going to college."

She pinched her brow together and scrunched up her nose in irritation. "You graduated with honors didn't you?"

"Yes ma'am, but I—"

"You're going to college!" she grumbled. Then she reminded me I was living in her house—just like my mother used to. She patted me on the back and gave me a kiss on the cheek and I got the impression the discussion was over. My grandmother could be as hard as coffin nails and as soft as butter when she wanted to be.

Shortly after that, maybe a couple months after graduation, Lance and I enrolled full time at Pasco-Hernando Community College and started taking business management courses. For a community college, PHCC's campus was sweet—lush lawns, well-maintained landscaping, lots of oak trees and pines, and two ponds.

Around the same time, "Pretty Boy" Landon came down for summer break.

He, Lance, and I were at Clearwater Beach playing volleyball, listening to music, and doing pills. "You know," said Landon, as I handed him a couple roxies, "these things are going for almost a dollar a milligram in Tennessee." Lance and I locked eyes for a split second while Landon popped the pill into his mouth.

"You think you could sell some of 'em?" asked Lance.

"Fuck yeah, my buddy Justin will get rid of 'em." Landon told us there was such a huge demand for oxycodone, anybody and everybody with a back problem in Tennessee was driving down to Florida to get a prescription for roxies and oxys. "Some of these pillbillies have scripts at two or three pill mills," he said grinning. "Justin calls it hillbilly heroin. They love it."

I fronted Landon two hundred Roxicodone 30 milligram pills just before he left for Knoxville. A couple days later, Lance told me his brother had sold the roxies for almost $4,000 and he needed more.

It was our first day of class and Lance couldn't stop talking about it. "This is huge," he whispered to me, as the professor went over the syllabus. "Can you get five hundred roxies?" I nodded while scribbling down some information the professor was writing on the dry erase board, hoping Lance would shut up. Unfortunately, his ADHD was in full bloom and "the Little General" simply couldn't contain himself. "Have you done the numbers?" he whispered.

Of course I had done the numbers. I could easily buy roxie 30s for $7 per pill and sell them to Landon for $18 per pill—five hundred pills came to $9,000. "It's a profit of roughly fifty-five hundred dollars. I'll split it with you."

On our way to the parking lot, I told Lance I would have the roxies by that night. "But I'm not driving 'em up to Tennessee with you."

"Don't worry about it," he said. "I'm gonna ship 'em FedEx." Between electronic sniffers and the random x-raying of packages, I didn't think shipping the pills was a good idea. But you couldn't tell Lance anything. "We'll stick 'em in something like ah . . . like ah . . . "

"Pill bottles." There were hundreds of cheap vitamins on the market.

We went to our local GNC store. The walls and aisles were stacked with shelf after shelf of health supplements. Neat little rows of pill bottles, containing a variety of different size and color pills. They were perfect. We grabbed a couple of vitamin bottles, half a dozen protein bars, and several *Muscle & Fitness* magazines. Then we went back to Lance's house. We carefully peeled off the vitamin bottles' seals, dumped out the contents, stuffed five hundred oxycodones into the bottles, and re-glued the seals. I wrote a letter from Landon's mom to her son; telling him how much she loved and missed him—stuff my mother would never say—and Lance, using an alias, sent the package via FedEx to Landon's Cumberland University student mail box in Tennessee. The next day Landon got the pills, and he sold them for over ten grand.

Landon then went to a Knoxville Toys "R" Us, bought a teddy bear, gutted it, stuffed the bear with our cash, and overnighted it to his brother in Hudson. We tracked the shipments all the way to the door—it was that easy. A week later Landon needed one thousand roxies, then it was two thousand. Then he asked for three thousand pills and, at the time, I couldn't get that many.

We were sitting at a plastic booth inside Pasco-Hernando's cafeteria, inhaling cheese fries and sucking down a couple sodas before having to race to our next class. "I've only got about ten people with scripts, and they can only get refills once a month, except for Thomas," I said. "I'm practically out for another two weeks."

"Fuck!" snapped Lance, and his eyes started darting around frantically looking for a solution. "I'll bet Jimmy can get 'em."

Jimmy Cage was dating a friend of Lance's girlfriend. His mother was a lieutenant with the Tampa Police Department, his uncle was a DEA agent, and Jimmy was a known drug dealer. When he was eighteen years old he had been busted for conspiracy to traffic cocaine and ended up doing around a year in state prison. When he got out, Jimmy went straight back to dealing . . . everything. Weed, opiates, methamphetamines, cocaine, steroids. You name it, Jimmy could get it. His toys filled up his entire yard. He owned a Corvette, a thirty-foot power boat, and a Nissan Titan. Everything Lance and I wanted.

He started selling us two thousand roxie 30s every other week, for $10 per pill, which wasn't cheap, but we needed the pills.

Between Florida and Tennessee, we were easily clearing $40,000 a month—that's a lot of teddy bears.

That night Angelo's girlfriend Amanda threw a party at her house in Beacon Woods, a lower–middle class subdivision in Hudson. Amanda's mother, Tania, was a divorced ex-stripper turned hairstylist in her late thirties or early forties. Fake tits and frosted tips. She liked cocaine and teenage boys. One night she got drunk with Richard, Landon, and a buddy of mine from Gulf Middle School named Randy, and they ran a train on her. I was absolutely terrified of her. She was constantly flirting with me and telling me I should "stop by sometime."

"I'm good, Ms. Brooks," I'd say. "But thanks for asking." When I was around her, I always felt like a gazelle in the sights of a lioness.

Lance and I were standing in the living room, watching a couple dozen of our friends drinking and half dancing to Kid Rock singing "You've Never Met a Motherfucker Quite Like Me." Lance was chattering on and on about the cost of roxies and oxys, shipping the pills, how important it was to have a good group of guys. "Tight, you know?" he said. "People we can trust. Guys like us, you know?"

"Uh huh," I grunted as I noticed this redhead from River Ridge High School. She was bobbing her head while drinking a Michelob Ultra and periodically glancing at me.

Tall and thin with an amazing ass.

"We're gonna have to get more pills . . . a lot more."

"Who's the Testarossa?" I asked, motioning toward the redhead across the room.

"Serenity," he replied. "I think her parents are members of Greenpeace, or they're in the Peace Corps or something." I asked

Lance if he had ever dated her during one of his and Tiffany's many breakups. "Nah." Serenity could tell we were talking about her, she kept sneaking glimpses at us and grinning. Perfect teeth. "Richard nailed her a couple years ago."

"Fuck!" I barked, and the smile faded from her face. As far as I was concerned any chick "Shit Dick" had slept with was radioactive; on the order of Three Mile Island or Chernobyl. Toxic. "She's scorched earth."

"So use a condom."

"Can't risk it."

My plan was to save a half million dollars by the time I got my BA and quit. "If it's working," Lance asked, "why would you quit?"

Because, according to my Uncle Tony, I told him, inevitably everyone gets caught. That is unless you have a reasonable goal and exit strategy. "But even then there's no guarantee."

"Half a million," snorted Lance. "No. I'd need more than that to quit. I'm gonna need way more." For Lance, it was more than just the money, it was about being a big shot. He wanted a finely tuned organization of opiate distributors throughout the country.

He wanted to be the next American Gangster. The Scarface of pills. The founder of the Lance Barabas Criminal Enterprise. But I didn't have those aspirations.

"Look," I said, "I don't mind helping you get the pills, but I don't want anything to do with that other stuff. That's on you."

"Pretty Boy" Landon was already putting together a network of Cumberland University wrestlers and college students in Knoxville to distribute the painkillers to dealers. He was ordering more pills every week. We were buying scripts from friends of friends, but it wasn't enough.

That's when Lance and I met Justin Knox for the first time. He was moving the bulk of the pills Lance was shipping to Tennessee. Lance and Landon had rented a townhouse for the summer and Justin drove down from Knoxville in his new yellow Hummer H3 to hang out at Clearwater Beach for a couple days. The guy was also a standout wrestler at Cumberland University. The combination of steroids and human growth hormone had transformed Justin's five-foot-eight-inch frame into two hundred pounds of twisted rebar. He was a beast.

We went to the Comedy Club near downtown Tampa, a converted red brick cigar warehouse with concrete floors and a two-foot-high stage surrounded by a crowd of drunks and hecklers. We were chewing on Buffalo wings and chips when Justin asked me and Lance, "Can you get me more oxys?"

The majority of what we had been shipping were Roxicodone 15 and 30 mg tablets. People were less willing to give up their Oxy-Contins. Lance glanced at me as the crowd around us erupted into laughter. "We'd have to get 'em directly from the pill mills," I said. "People that need 'em won't give up their oxys."

Justin leaned into us and yelled over the crowd, "Oxys are where the money's at. I could move ten thousand a month, easy."

"We got you, bro," said Lance, glancing at me and nodding like we were in complete agreement, like we already had a solution. "We'll figure something out."

That's when I came up with the idea of "sponsoring" people, to become "doctor shoppers." Doctor shoppers are patients who go to doctors' offices solely to obtain pills and often visit more than one doctor to obtain multiple prescriptions from several doctors. I called my cousin Tony Jr.—Uncle Tony's kid—and Brad, a friend of a friend who owned a tattoo shop, and told them to keep an eye out for people with back problems. "I'll pay for everything," I said. "But I get the roxies and the oxys. All of 'em." That's roughly $1,200 for an MRI, around $500 for a first-time visit to the pill mill, plus whatever their prescriptions cost, which could be anywhere between $220 to $270 for the Roxicodones and between $630 to $1,260 for the OxyContins. A potential investment of nearly $3,300. "And I'll pay six dollars for the roxies and twenty for the oxy eighties." Oxy-Contin 80s were where the money was.

"Fuck yeah!" said Thomas, when I called him, "I'll find some people for you." He already had his own MRI and prescriptions from four different doctors, so I started with him. Within a week he had gotten me two prescriptions for 240 Roxicodone 30 mgs and 120 OxyContin 80 mgs.

While this was happening, my cousin Tony Jr. hooked me up with a guy named Steven Schultz who had already had an MRI. We met at an Arby's fast food restaurant so I could question him to make sure he would qualify for the OxyContins. He had radiating pain down his left leg and loss of sensation and weakness in his limbs. "I've got a herniated disk," he said, slurping down a Coke. "I'm actually in a lot of pain."

"Perfect!" I laughed, Schultz's face scrunched into a scowl. "Sorry, you know what I mean."

I dragged him to M.D. & More and Doctors R Us and waited in the parking lot while Schultz went into the pill mill and complained about his back pain. An hour later he walked out with the scripts for roxie 30s and oxy 80s. Then we shot over to the Walgreens

Pharmacy where he got his scripts filled and I paid him $1,400 for roughly $8,500 worth of oxycodone.

Then there was Freddy, a guy with degenerative disk disease, and Renaldo, who had a bulging disk. Tony Jr., Brad, and Thomas were bringing me more and more people all the time. Lumbar hyperlordosis and scoliosis. Sometimes they wanted the money and other times they wanted half the pills. Some of my doctor shoppers were business professionals and others were straight junkies.

I once sponsored this guy named Trent, a bone-thin cokehead with a bulging disk. He was often twitchy and always paranoid. He needed to pay his mortgage or he was going to lose his house. I shuttled him around for a week, holding his hand through an MRI and two pill mill appointments.

Kenna was with me when I dropped him off at a CVS pharmacy to fill his scripts. We were sitting in my Jeep when Trent walked through the automatic doors with a bag full of oxycodones. He glanced our way, scratched his neck as his eyes twitched around the parking lot, and took off running, darting across two lanes of traffic. "Ohmigod!" snapped Kenna, "he's taking off with your stuff!"

As he disappeared into the woods behind a McDonald's all I could think was, *There goes thirty-three hundred dollars.* "Fucking junkie!"

My doctor shoppers' pharmacists got to the point where they had seen me so many times they started letting me pick up the scripts myself. Class II narcotics. Certain pharmacists would actually call me up and let me know, "Your prescriptions are ready to be picked up." They weren't even my pills!

At the end of the summer, Landon moved back to Knoxville. But a couple months later, he came back to Florida with Danny and another guy from the Cumberland wrestling team. They were both dealing pills for him in Tennessee. That night we were all partying at Prana's, a trendy four-level multi-bar dance club near downtown Tampa. The place was jumping with heroin chic wannabe models and college girls hustling drinks out of metrosexual corporate lawyers and stockbrokers. Everyone was dancing to Rick Ross's "This Is the Life" and Drake singing "Money to Blow," having a blast.

Over drinks, Danny mentioned that he had people in Alaska that could move five thousand Roxicodones or OxyContins per month. "And the prices are higher there than in Tennessee," he said. "Oxy eighties go for a hundred dollars per pill up there."

Danny's guys in Anchorage flew into Tampa around a week later. We set up some anonymous Gmail accounts and bought two prepaid cell phones to use for business. Lance overnighted them five hundred oxycodones the first week, then one thousand, and then, two thousand.

Sometime in late July or early August of 2007, I was at Alejandro and Joseph's place for poker night. They had it almost every weekend. A couple of tables with twenty-dollar buy-ins and around $200 pots. There were about ten guys smoking cheap cigars and drinking domestic beers.

At 10:30 p.m. Ashley Cutter and Karen Reynolds—two cheerleaders from Hudson High—showed up. They had been at a beach party most of the night and they were looking for somewhere to crash. By twelve o'clock the poker game was over. The winners and the losers cleared out and Alejandro and I were left sitting on the living room sectional with Ashley and Karen. We smoked a blunt while Alejandro and Ashley flirted with each other. They weren't dating each other or anything, Ashley was just the type of chick that liked to get drunk and wild; five-feet-five-inches tall with dirty-blonde hair, and a sweet set of lips.

Karen and I ended up stuck out on the couch listening to Ashley and Alejandro grunting and moaning. Karen was cute, but she was also dating one of my friends, so I wasn't about to try anything. We ended up crashing on the floor wrapped up in a blanket and couch cushions with our arms and legs all over the place. Uncomfortable as fuckall. Around four in the morning Alejandro left to serve community service hours for a disorderly conduct charge from a few months earlier. About a minute later Ashley tiptoed out of his bedroom wearing a T-shirt and panties. She knelt beside me and whispered in my ear so Karen couldn't hear, "You're up; come in the bedroom."

I was half-asleep and mumbled, "Wha . . . why?"

"I wanna do it." She said, as she gently stroked her hand across my stomach.

No further explanation was necessary. She and Alejandro weren't dating, therefore she was fair game. But I asked anyway. "What about Alejandro?"

"What about him?" she asked, pulling me into Alejandro's room.

Maybe a week later, I was sitting at a heavy wooden table in PHCC's library, surrounded by the stacks and cute coeds. I looked out the window at the ducks moving across the still waters of the campus pond. Everything was calm and peaceful. That's when I got the call on my cell from Kristina. "So, what's this I hear about you having sex with Ashley?"

"Where'd you hear that?" I said, as if it were an outrageous lie.

"She's telling everyone you two did it at Alejandro's." I mumbled and stammered out something unintelligible, but I didn't deny it. Kristina growled, "You slept with her, didn't you? Please tell me you suited up."

I'm actually a big believer in using condoms. But I hadn't worn a rubber with Ashley. "I . . . it was four o'clock in the morning." Why I felt the need to explain myself to Kristina, I don't know. She wasn't my girlfriend. However, we were sleeping together. I sputtered out, "I didn't have a—"

"You're disgusting!" she screamed out of my cell. She was so loud that several students turned and glanced at me. "Ashley's absolutely got an STD. She's a whore!" This was coming from the same chick that I'd caught with my fucking cousin! "You're dirty. I'm gonna tell everybody you're dirty." My mind immediately jumped to how hard of a time we gave Richard and I instantly became terrified I'd be known as "Shit Dick Doug."

"All right, Kristina, calm down." Students were now unabashedly staring at me, and I whispered, "I don't have an STD." More students turned toward me, shaking their heads and grinning.

"I'm never sleeping with you again!" she yelled and the line went dead.

As irrational a conversation as it had been, Kristina brought up some very good points. Ashley had made the rounds. I'm not judging her; I'm just saying. So I drove down to Spring Hill Health Care Center the next morning and asked to be tested for "the works. Everything."

"Everything, huh?" asked this librarian-sexy female doctor in her late thirties, sporting a white lab coat and wire-rimmed glasses.

She was girl-next-door hot with no makeup. "Have you had unprotected sex with a questionable party?" I explained my situation and the doctor tried unsuccessfully not to grin. "I'm sorry," she chuckled. "I'm not laughing at you. It's very common for someone to get tested after unprotected intercourse."

"Then what's so funny?" I asked, as she drew several vials of my blood and passed it to a frumpy nurse.

"It's just . . . " She grinned at me, "I've never had a male patient come in before, that's all."

A week later, a Care Center nurse called and told me my results were in. Sitting in that little white room waiting for my test results, every unprotected sexual encounter I'd ever had raced through my mind—even hand jobs. By the time the doctor walked in I was sure I had something. "You're fine, Mr. Dodd." She handed me a couple condoms and said, "Stay that way."

I texted Kristina as soon as I got back to my grandma's house. "The results are negative. No STDs." She called me a couple hours later and said, "You're still dirty. I'm never gonna sleep with you again."

I had Kristina in the back seat of my Jeep within a week of my test results, dirty or not.

Sometimes I was able to buy five thousand oxycodone a week and not have one problem. The next week so many things would go wrong I'd be lucky to end up with 240 roxies. My doctor shoppers would forget to go to their follow-up appointments and their prescriptions would expire. Or they would start using the pills and suddenly they wouldn't want to sell all the painkillers. "I'll take half and you take half," they would say. Sometimes they'd end up in rehab or get arrested.

I would love to say that the Barabas Criminal Enterprise ran as smoothly as a new Bugatti, but that's not the case. Lance's ADHD created several problems, the worst of which was Lance's recklessness. He couldn't seem to grasp the concept that there were literally thousands of law enforcement personnel actively battling the war on drugs. They're well funded, well trained, and absolutely ruthless.

One of the many reckless things Lance did on a daily basis was talk openly about drugs in public, among friends, and on the telephone. He would make a half-assed effort to conceal the discussion using a rudimentary street code for oxycodone easily breakable by anyone with a lukewarm IQ. Roxicodone 30 mg tablets were blue, so they became "blueberries," "blues," or just "berries." OxyContin pills were orange at the 40 mg size and green at 80 mg, so they were ingeniously known as "oranges" and "green apples." "Bro," he'd say over the phone, "I need a thousand oranges." Or he'd say, "Can you get me five hundred green apples?"

"So, what?" I'd ask. "Are we supposed to be in the grocery business?" and I would hang up on him. He was constantly doing stupid shit like that; simultaneously incriminating himself and whomever he was talking to. Narcotics officers aren't stupid.

It's not like we were farmers.

I told Lance over and over that talking on the phone was the worst thing he could do. Face to face was the safest way. If that wasn't possible I made sure to use track phones (anonymous cheap prepaid phones), but Lance wasn't as careful. He was oblivious to the fact that there were actually rules and guidelines of things not to do. In his mind he was invincible. George Jung, Frank Lucas, Tony Montana.

When Lance wasn't saying incriminating things over the phone, he was threatening some poor dealer or doctor shopper. It got to the point some would refuse to deal with him. But the thing that bothered me the most was Lance's need to prove what a big-shot drug dealer he was. He bought one of his brothers a dirt bike and the other one a Carolina Skiff boat. He just gave it to them. We would hit a strip club and Lance would spend half the night shoving twenties and fifties into the dancers G-strings and buying all the boys lap dances. We would go to some bar and he'd spend $1,500 buying everyone drinks. But when it came to paying me for the product, he always came up short. "I don't have enough cash to buy 'em," he'd say. "You'll have to front me."

"What're you talking about?" I recall asking him. "Landon just FedEx'ed you a ten-thousand-dollar teddy bear two days ago!"

"Bro, between my lease and some other stuff, I'm broke."

"If you hadn't pissed away two grand buying everyone drinks at Parana's last night," I growled, "you could pay me."

"What're you so pissed about, bro? You'll get it next week."

I tosssed him the painkillers and snapped, "I'm sick of financing your fucking lifestyle." He never did get his money straight. Lance had every dime spent before the cash ever arrived.

It didn't take long before the little town of Hudson wasn't good enough for Lance. He transferred to Hillsborough Community College and rented an apartment with a couple other guys. Within a few months, that wasn't good enough either, so he leased a half-a-million-dollar place in Victory Lofts, a trendy luxury high-rise surrounded by skyscrapers in downtown Tampa's Channelside District. This newly developed funky industrial area nestled up against the Florida Aquarium and the Port of Tampa, surrounded by lots of shops, restaurants, and bars, and was decorated with newly planted palm trees and historic streetcars—urban living at it's best.

Lance's loft was an open floor plan with twelve-foot ceilings, exposed ductwork, and polished concrete floors. Stainless steel appliances and granite countertops completed the package. The apartment was right next to Raheem Morris, the head coach of the Tampa Bay Buccaneers football team at the time. Lance blew a ton of money on furniture and electronics.

My first time visiting the loft, Lance took me out onto the balcony, overlooking the port. We were watching a cruise ship depart for the Western Caribbean or someplace, and Lance asked, "What do you think, bro?" He had a grin racked across his face, ecstatic with his trendy new place. "Well?"

He was hooked on opiates and throwing around money. "I think you're gonna get us caught," I replied, as I looked out at the dark, choppy water of Tampa Bay.

"You're overreacting," he said. "Everything's fine."

A couple weeks after I got a clean bill of health from the Care Center, around 11:30 p.m., I was at my grandmother's house. I'd just gotten out of the shower and my cell rang. "What're you doing?" asked Cindy, this chick I'd been flirting with since high school. She'd been one grade ahead of me during school and constantly out of reach. Now, she was at a party down the street and bored. "Can I come over?"

"Aw, I was about to go to bed, but—"

"Perfect," she giggled. "I'll be right over."

Five minutes later we were in my bedroom tugging off Cindy's blue jeans and blouse, nibbling and kissing. What I remember most about Cindy was how loud she was. Lots of moaning and deep breathing. I kept sliding my fingers into her mouth trying to keep her quiet. "You've got to keep it down," I hissed at one point. "My grandmother's in the next room."

"I thought you said she's almost deaf."

"Almost deaf. *Almost.*" This chick was a screamer. The last thing I needed was for Grandma to lecture me because she overheard Cindy squealing.

After that night, I started seeing Cindy on and off. Nothing serious, just casual sex. It pissed Kristina off, but at that point I didn't care.

Here's where it gets interesting. In late October, Alejandro and I went to a friend of a friend's Halloween party. There were roughly fifty high school kids and college students dressed up as everything from Frankenstein to Sputnik. Everyone was dancing to Armin van Buuren and Basement Jaxx, Cindy wasn't there, but her younger sister Melinda was; a tall, thin brunette cutie with a nice ass and the perfect proportion of breast. Not too much, not too little, they were just right. We'd graduated together, but she was always kind of shy and awkward. I'd never really noticed her until that night. She was wearing hot pink knee-high boots with spiked heels, fishnet stockings, a tight miniskirt, and corset. Whiskers and a ponytail. A sexy little kitten with a riding whip. *Whoo-peesh!*

"You supposed to be a dominatrix or something?" I yelled over the music.

"I'm a naughty kitten," she smiled and popped me with the whip. *Whoo-peesh!* I asked her what was up with the whip, and she meowed into my ear, "If you're a good boy, I'll show you later." This was not the shy little girl I remembered from second period Spanish class.

We spent the next hour dancing, drinking, and flirting. We did a couple lines of oxycodone in one of the bedrooms and Melinda asked, "You still seeing my sister?"

"Does it matter?"

"Not really." A couple minutes later we were making out. Someone yelled, "Cops!" and I saw the flashing blue and white lights coming through the windows. Everyone was drunk and underage, so they immediately scattered. We slipped out the back while a couple of Pasco County sheriff's deputies were walking through the house telling everyone to "clear out, the party's over."

Melinda and I ended up back at Alejandro and Joseph's place with Alejandro and some chick he'd met at the party. Joseph worked nights, so I pulled Melinda into his bedroom, unbuttoned her pink corset, tugged off her knee-high boots, and unzipped her miniskirt. "You can never tell anyone about this," whispered Melinda as she slipped out of her G-string and slinked onto the bed.

"I won't."

She wrapped her long legs around my waist, and grinned. "She'd be so pissed." Deep down I think Melinda wanted Cindy to know. Sibling rivalry. It wasn't the best sex of our lives but, as they say, sex is like pizza—even when it's bad, it's still pretty good. She didn't complain.

Maybe a week later, Lance and Tiffany stopped by my grandmother's house to pick up something—probably some pills. We were sitting in the living room and Lance asked, "Alejandro says you hooked up with Melinda the other night?" I glanced at Tiffany and the little gossip's brow shot up. I shrugged, but didn't answer. "Come on, bro, did you hit that or not?"

"I'm not going to say."

"Why?"

I motioned toward Tiffany. "Cause, your girl is friends with Kristina and she's got a big mouth."

"Please," spat Tiffany with an exaggerated roll of her eyes. "I'm not going to tell her." Then she went into this long explanation about how she'd known me "way longer" than she'd known Kristina. "I've known you longer than Lance. I won't say anything." She leaned forward and held up her hand and said, "Pinkie swear."

We locked digits and I spilled my guts out about Cindy and Melinda. When I was finished Tiffany had a look of disgust on her face and Lance couldn't stop grinning. "Sisters," he chuckled. "Nice." That little bitch Tiffany went straight to Kristina and told her everything!

Several days later I was at my buddy Mike G's party with Ethan when Kristina waltzed up to me and barked, "You're a filthy pig. Ashley, Cindy, and now Melinda?!" "That's so nasty. You're dirty."

"Stop saying that." I tried to explain that I'd worn a condom, so technically I hadn't actually touched the sisters, but it didn't seem to matter.

"Seriously? I'm never sleeping with you again."

And that's when I started hating Tiffany.

Chapter Six

The Town is Dry

"Cardinal Health shipped enough oxycodone to pharmacies in Sanford, Florida, [to] supply a population eight times its size."

—*Bloomberg BusinessWeek*

The Drug Enforcement Administration (DEA) is responsible for curbing our nation's ability to obtain illegal narcotics. However, despite the abuse of oxycodone, the drug is not an illegal narcotic. It's simply controlled. In fact, it has many legitimate uses. But it is the "controlled" aspect of controlled substances that can put the DEA in the ironic position of increasing rather than decreasing drug abuse.

Using their registration and licensing system, the DEA can determine the amount of controlled substances being manufactured annually. If they conclude that there isn't a legitimate national need for a specific drug, the DEA can limit the pharmaceutical companies' production. As a response to the amphetamines epidemic of the 1970s and the abuse of methaqualone, or Quaaludes, in the 1980s, the DEA cut the manufactures' production up to 90 percent, largely eradicating the problem.

That's not what happened with oxycodone. Largely due to pressure from the pharmaceutical industry lobby, the DEA allowed production levels of that controlled substance to rise year after year. Between 1996 and 2007, they signed off on a twenty-fold increase of oxycodone and nearly quadrupled the production of hydrocodone.

They did occasionally bring the hammer down on a few companies who pushed things too far. Cardinal Health is a health-care company that specializes in pharmaceuticals and other medical productions, and in November 2007, the DEA suspended the controlled substance license of their Lakeland, Florida, distribution center for illegally selling large amounts of oxycodones and hydrocodones to several Internet pharmacies. The problem for us was that Cardinal serviced over 2,500 pharmacies in Florida, Georgia, and South Carolina, so that closure caused an immediate shortage of opiates.

Maybe a week after the suspension Lance and I went into a Walgreens to grab a script with one of Lance's sponsors and the clerk said, "We're out."

Neither Lance nor I had ever heard of a drug store running out of drugs. At first it struck us as funny. "Well, when'll you have 'em?"

"Could be next week," replied the clerk with a shrug. "We just don't know." They got the pills in the following day, but it was obvious Cardinal Health's suspension was going to be a problem. And within a week the cost of roxies shot up from $.70 to roughly $3.50 and oxys jumped from $10.50 to around $12.50. The availability slowed down to a trickle and the street value spiked.

It was only a couple dollars, but a couple dollars times ten thousand to twenty thousand pills a month is significant. The money was leaving our pockets and going right into the pharmacies. They stopped accepting insurance because they were contractually obligated to bill the insurance companies the pre-shortage prices. Instead, they started hoarding the few painkillers they had for their cash customers, and telling anyone with insurance, "we're out."

We were getting call backs from pharmacists saying, "We'll hold the oxycodones for you, but you've gotta pay cash," which was the only thing we had. The DEA suspension slowed us down and created problems. It was a basic economic dilemma for supply chain management. The demand for the product outweighed our supply.

Jimmy's inexhaustible supply was cut in half and Landon was screaming for more pills in Tennessee, as were Danny's guys in Alaska. Despite the shortage we were still picking up a couple dozen customers' prescriptions from pharmacies on a weekly basis, but it wasn't enough to meet the demand.

Lance "the Little General" was barking orders at everyone and flashing his Glock .45 every chance he got. At one point, a sponsor was running late for work and couldn't make a drop of roughly five hundred oxycodones. Lance got on the phone with the guy and told him, "If you don't get me those pills, I'm going to drive down to your job and put a bullet in your fucking head—got it?" But he was all talk, he never acted on anything.

When I heard about it I called him up and said, "What the fuck Lance, do you wanna get arrested?!"

"I'm sorry bro, I just got in my feelings. We need those pills!"

"I don't give a damn. If you don't settle down I'm going to choke you the fuck out!" It was one pep talk after another with this kid.

The pharmacies were running out of oxycodones so often that I started waiting in their parking lots for the delivery trucks. I would eat my meals, make calls, and study there. For a few weeks there I was practically living out of my Jeep like a vagrant, that's how bad it was.

Tampa was so dry we started buying up pills all over Florida—1,500 in Orlando, a thousand in Plant City. It didn't really matter what they cost because the markup was so high.

In most states it was a dollar a milligram, but in Alaska an OxyContin 80 mg sold for as much as a hundred bucks per pill. There could be a 300 to 400 percent markup by the time it hit the end consumer.

The dry spell left us so desperate for oxycodone, I started making mistakes. My cousin Roberta's roommate Albert, a skinny Puerto Rican drug dealer, supposedly knew a guy—we'll call him "Guy"—who had robbed a delivery truck right behind an Eckerd Drugs. He ended up with five hundred Roxicodones, four hundred OxyContins, and two thousands hydrocodones, and he only wanted five grand for the lot. I had bought several hundred 100 milligram morphine tablets from Albert before, so I knew him, but he was sketchy at best. If we weren't desperate for the pills I would have never dealt with him. "Cash," said Albert. "And it's gotta be tonight."

Like an idiot I blew off an accounting test and drove north to Brooksville with Albert and his pregnant girlfriend. After roughly an hour's drive we pulled into this makeshift dirt road mobile home park filled with shitty 1970s single-wide trailers. It's the kind of place where houses had wheels and vehicles didn't. The trailer we were supposed to meet Guy in was the worst of the bunch, with cracked multicolored paneling and broken windows. The inside was worse than the outside. It smelled like cat urine and weed and was completely empty with the exception of orange shag carpet and a recliner—your basic drop house. Albert's buddy, an obvious crackhead, was sitting in the recliner when we stepped inside. He never got up. He never even asked Albert's pregnant girlfriend if she wanted to sit down.

Twenty minutes later Guy banged on the door. He was a Jamaican with thick dreads. Everyone squeezed into the trailer. He looked me up and down, sized me up, and asked, "You got da money, mon?" with a slight island ascent. I flashed the five grand wrapped in a rubber band and the Jamaican nodded. "I'll get the pills, mon."

He turned to leave and whipped back around with a black Glock 9 millimeter. Albert's girlfriend immediately started to scream, "Awh! Awh! Awh!" Which honestly scared me more than the sight of the gun.

"Shut up, bitch!" snapped the Jamaican. Then he started yelling for everyone to get against the wall. His hand was shaking so much I was afraid he might shoot one of us by accident. My adrenaline shot up and my heart began pounding so fast it felt like one continuous vibration. Albert and his buddy were yelling, "What're you doing?!" and "What's going on?!" as the Jamaican patted us down. While he was digging the cash out of my pocket and snatching the gold chain off Albert's neck I was thinking, *I can't believe I blew off accounting for this.*

He pushed the barrel of the Glock to my temple and growled, "You stick your cracker head out dis trailer and I'll blow it the fuck off!" And the look in his bloodshot eyes told me he wasn't fucking around. Then he popped open the door and vanished into the night.

Albert's buddy immediately bolted into the bedroom and reappeared with two revolvers, about the same time we heard a car's engine start. He slapped one of the guns into my palm and said, "Let's go!" I wasn't about to go after a gun-toting Jamaican for $5,000. "Fuck that!" I dropped the weapon on the kitchen counter and told Albert and his girl to get in the truck, "I'm leaving."

I was more upset about the fact there were no pills than losing the cash.

By late December everyone was begging for more and more opiates.

Jimmy came up with a connect in Miami who had 1,500 Roxicodone 30s and 2,000 hydrocodone 1,000 milligrams—a semisynthetic opioid used to treat moderate to severe pain—for an outrageously low price. "I've got a guy down there who works in a CVS or something," said Jimmy. "He wants thirteen thousand dollars even." Those pills were easily worth $45,000 in Tennessee or Alaska. "But someone's gotta go get 'em."

So I shot down to Naples and across Alligator Alley to Miami. By the time I got to South Beach, it was eight o'clock in the evening. I met up with the pharmacy tech curbside in front of the Delano hotel and bar. He was the nervous nerdy type with black-framed Buddy Holly glasses and greasy hair. Sure enough, he had four 500-unit white plastic jugs of hydrocodones and a Ziploc bag filled with Roxicodones in the trunk of his car. We swapped out the cash for the pills. I zipped them up tight in my duffel bag, and we parted ways. No big deal. A completely benign transaction.

I only mention it because of the woman I met at the Delano Hotel's bar; it was this trendy open-air liquor garden with dark wood floors and marble counter tops. The place was littered with modelesque escorts and wannabe trophy wives, GQ lawyers and aging bankers. Dim lights and sushi. The atmosphere reeked of techno music and new money—not exactly what I was used to.

Using my fake ID, I ordered a twenty-dollar Jack and Coke at the bar, and used it to wash down a roxie 30. That's when I noticed this sexy blond in her late twenties wearing a naughty Catholic schoolgirl outfit—plaid skirt, white blouse, and leggings—sitting two stools down, and making eyes at me. "You got one of those for me?" she asked, with a giggle and a hair flip—we'll call her Catholic Girl. I'm not even going to pretend to remember her name.

I slipped a roxie onto the bar, ordered her a Jaeger Bomb, and asked her what she was doing out so late on a school night. She gave me a mischievous grin and said, "Looking for someone to tie me up and spank me. You up for it?" *God I love South Beach!*

Twenty minutes later, I was in her bedroom surrounded by Gothic décor—lots of leather and dark wood furniture, mixed with Catholic icons, and a two-foot-high crucifix hanging above her bed. She was pulling at my belt and zipper, while I was snapping off her Victoria's Secret thong and bra. She whispered in my ear, "Not my heels." Seconds later she was on her back, missionary, with her legs around my waist, digging her stilettos into my ass cheeks and thighs. Jesus stared down at me from the cross as Catholic Girl raked her nails across my back and pulled my hair, which I didn't like, but I wasn't complaining—she looked *that* good. As for what followed, well, there are numerous reason I can't get into it—some of them embarrassing, others borderline immoral, and a few potentially illegal. What I will say is Catholic Girl had some odd fetishes, and we both had plenty of sins to atone for.

Two days later I was back at the Spring Hill Health Care Center sitting on an examination table covered by antiseptic wax paper, praying. *Please don't give me the same doctor,* I thought. *Please! Please! Please!* That's when she stepped into the room and immediately exclaimed, "You were here four months ago!" I suddenly felt like my grandmother had caught me masturbating. Immoral and unclean. "What happened?"

"She had a Catholic schoolgirl outfit on Doc—I figured I was safe!"

"Well," she asked, while snapping on a pair of latex gloves, "what changed your mind?"

I shrugged. "I'd rather not say, but . . . it went tragically wrong."

She plunged a needle into my forearm with all the sensitivity of a rapist and started lecturing me while my blood filled up a glass vial. "Did you know there are over seven hundred thousand new cases of gonorrhea—the clap—in this country every year? It causes burning during urination and yellowish green discharge from the penis." She stopped, looked me in the eyes, and said, "And you can get it from vaginal or oral sex." *Ohmigod!* I thought, *Not oral sex!* Then she told me chlamydia caused pain during sex as well as penile pus. Syphilis caused external genital and mouth sores. *Mycoplasma genitalium* caused nongonococcal urethritis. I didn't know what that was, but it sounded horrible.

I'm pretty sure that's when I mumbled, "Geez Doc, she had a Catholic school girl outfit on."

She squeezed her eyes into slits and growled, "Then there's pubic lice and scabies. *Human papillomavirus* is carried by a quarter of all women—"

"What? Twenty-five percent?!"

She nodded her head. "HIV, which is still potentially deadly," she said with a sigh. "One in three people have herpes, which causes painful genital sores and it can't be cured. One point three million people in this country have hepatitis, causing scarring of the liver, cirrhosis, liver cancer, and chronic infections." Then there's chancroid, a genital ulcer disease, methicillin-resistant *Staphylococcus aureus*, and *Lymphogranuloma venereum*. I almost threw up when she told me what those caused. Then she snapped off her latex gloves, tossed them in a biowaste box, and said, "We'll call you when your results are in." She stomped out of the examination room.

For the next week or so, the slightest discomfort warranted an inspection of my manhood for anything out of the ordinary. I had several sleepless nights searching the Internet for the symptoms of hepatitis and syphilis.

A week later, I was back at the Care Center to get my test results. "Negative," said the doctor, staring at the lab report. She actually looked disappointed; like she was hoping I had caught chlamydia or gonorrhea, just so she could gloat and pump me full of penicillin. She handed me a couple condoms and said, "Use 'em."

The oxycodone supply was so limited and prices were so high that every once in awhile one of my doctor shoppers would figure out their scripts were worth more than I was paying for them. Despite our agreement, they would start selling to some midlevel dealer or selling the pills themselves.

I remember arguing with this one doctor shopper for twenty minutes about our agreed upon price. "It's not enough," he kept saying over and over, even though I paid for his MRI and pill mill appointments. "I can get more selling 'em myself."

"True," I replied, over and over again. "But you could also go to prison for it too. This way you make two thousand dollars a month and you only have to deal with me." He begrudgingly sold me the pills—roughly 240 roxies and 120 oxys. We had the same fucking argument every month.

While I was struggling to scrape together pills in Florida, Richard was across the country in California fighting to break into the porn industry and losing the battle.

On December 15, 2007, Richard, Noah, and Eli—two other guys from our hometown who also wanted to give the California dream a try—were at a San Diego State University frat party; roughly a hundred students crammed into a house, guzzling down Busch beer and dancing to 3 Doors Down and Limp Bizkit; a bunch of sorority girls and frat boys hoping to get lucky. The way I heard it, some Latin guy's girlfriend was slutting around at the party and her boyfriend showed up. He created a scene and the frat boy throwing the party threw the boyfriend out. Of course, his girlfriend stayed.

The boyfriend came back around 2:30 a.m. with a dozen of his buddies, who looked remarkably like Mexican gang members. Shaved heads and prison tats. The party crashers were politely asked to leave by a couple preppy frat boys, which didn't go over well.

A dozen of the fraternity brothers pushed the party crashers out of the house and into the front yard. Maybe one of the Mexicans threw a punch or a student spit in someone's face—who knows? What I do know is when the brawl broke out Richard was in the living room diligently working on talking some unsuspecting coed out of her panties. In the middle of a giggle hair flip she glanced out the window and gasped, "Ohmigod, your friends are fighting!"

Richard immediately bolted out the front door and dove into the sea of bodies. Crashers and students were pushing and punching one another. Richard smashed some guy he didn't recognize fighting with Noah. His fist connected with the guy's cheek, dropping him like a marionette whose strings had been cut. He then jumped on another crasher and quickly got him in a headlock. That's when the gang members decide to turn the fistfight into a knife fight.

Suddenly some coed screamed and Richard looked up and saw a couple students stumble out of the crowd covered in blood. That's when Richard felt what he thought was two quick punches to the lower back. Within seconds he felt the blood gushing down his back, ass, and legs. There was another scream and Richard saw some guy stab Noah through the palm of his hand while Eli got stuck repeatedly in the side and ribs. The crasher slipped out of Richard's hold and plunged his knife into Richard's gut. He hit the ground and heard the sirens as the crashers took off running.

By the time the ambulance showed up, Richard, Noah, and Eli were heaped together on the lawn covered in mud and bleeding from multiple holes.

They were taken to Scripps Mercy Hospital where surgeons worked through the night cutting and stitching the trio back together. Richard underwent exploratory surgery. They yanked out his organs and determined he had puncture wounds in his stomach and liver. One of Eli's lungs had a hole in it and there was extensive damage to his spleen, which the surgeons removed. Noah had to have some stitches and they sent him home. He didn't lose anything, which was nice. But he'll never be a pianist.

Around a week later Richard's dad flew him back to Florida. The day he got back Lance and I showed up at his dad's house. Richard was lying in bed, surrounded by surf posters and sports trophies, shirtless with a blanket pulled up to his hips. Clear surgical tape was stretched across the scar that spanned from his navel to his sternum.

"Fuck!" gasped Lance with all the tact of a sledgehammer. "They gutted you like a fish, bro." Then he leaned forward a couple times in a mock-wretching motion and put his hand over his mouth. "Sorry, bro, I just threw up in my mouth a little bit." Richard shot him a *Thanks, asshole* look and Lance half snorted half laughed, "I guess this is it for your porn career."

Richard didn't catch the sarcasm. "Yeah," he sighed. "I'm ruined." Richard started to drone on and on about how his lifelong dream had been snuffed out. Lance rolled his eyes as Richard talked about his budding adult film career. "I was so close."

"What career?" laughed Lance. "You yanked the skin off it for thirty minutes and blew some nut for a gay porn site. That's hardly a career."

"I was waiting for some very promising call backs. What're *you* doing?"

"Me?" snapped Lance. "I'm a dope boy, I'm living the dream." He genuinely believed that, too. Lance told Richard about the money we were making and offered to hook him up with a doctor once he was all healed up. He looked at Richard's midsection and laughed. "With a Frankenstein scar like that, you're guaranteed to get the max amount of pills!"

Chapter Seven

State of Florida Mandatory Minimums

"Florida has among the toughest mandatory minimum laws in the nation. . . . A person convicted of trafficking a weight of oxycodone that amounts to about 44 pills faces a mandatory minimum sentence of 25 years in prison—with no time off for good behavior."

—*Gainesville Sun*

Just before the end of 2007, I stopped by Uncle Tony's welding shop in Tampa. I needed him to hold $20,000 for me. Somehow we ended up talking about one of his friends' sons who had been selling oxycodones. "He got charged with trafficking," said my uncle as I slipped the cash onto his desk. I nodded, not the least bit concerned. Why would I be, I didn't even know the kid. My uncle stared at me for a few seconds, took a deep cleansing breath, and ran a hand through his hair. "He got fifteen years for one hundred and fifty pills—the mandatory minimum."

I remember a cold chill running through my veins and I'm certain the blood drained from my face. At that very moment, I had roughly one thousand Roxicodones sealed up in two vitamin bottles sitting in the back of my Jeep. "Fuck." I whispered, "fifteen years?"

I had heard the term "mandatory minimum" before, but I'd always assumed it applied to large-scale drug traffickers moving truckloads of cocaine or heroin across international borders. Not intermediate drug dealers slinging a couple dozen painkillers.

Under Florida statute, the minimum penalties are determined by quantity ranges based on weight, not by dosage. As a result, a person could have oxycodone pills whose combined dosage is less than the minimum amount, but, because the pills are particularly heavy, the person would still be guilty of trafficking in oxycodone instead of simple possession.

Depending on the manufacturer, the weight of each pill varied drastically, regardless of the dosage. Purdue Pharma's OxyContin 80 mg weighed considerably more than Impax Laboratories' oxycodone 80 mg controlled-release. However, both contain the same amount of oxycodone. Therefore, twenty Purdue OxyContin 80 mg, containing a total of 1,600 milligrams of oxycodone, weighing roughly .2 grams would trigger a state of Florida three-year mandatory minimum while twenty-six Impax Laboratories' oxycodone 80 mg controlled-release containing a total of 2,080 milligrams of oxycodone, weighing .15 grams would be a simple possession charge.

I quickly began memorizing the weight of each manufacturer's pill per milligram. From Mallinckrodt Pharmaceutical's Roxicodone 30 mg to Actavis's oxycodone 30 mg and Purdue Pharma's

OxyContin 80 mg to Impax Laboratories' generic oxycodone controlled-release 80 mg.

I knew all the oxycodone manufacturers and the minimum mandatories: four to thirteen grams of oxycodone is a three-year State of Florida mandatory minimum prison sentence; fourteen to twenty-seven grams is a fifteen-year mandatory minimum sentence; and twenty-eight grams up to twenty-nine grams is a minimum of twenty-five years. Over twenty-nine grams—life! I could ramble them off depending on the dosage or weight, as well.

Lance couldn't stand it. We would be at his place shoving a hundred Purdue Pharma OxyContins into a vitamin D bottle, I'd look at him and say, "This is a fifteen-year mandatory minimum." Or he would ship a FedEx package containing a couple *Men's Health* and five vitamin bottles packed with four hundred oxycodones made by Teva Pharmaceuticals; and I'd tell him, "That's a mandatory minimum of twenty-five years."

"Stop telling me that shit, bro!" he would yell. "You're pissing me off!" I wasn't all that worried about getting caught at the time. I just liked fucking with him.

On the last Saturday night in January 2008, Lance and I were with a bunch of other guys at Ybor City, an area of Tampa founded by cigar manufacturers in 1880. Located just northeast of downtown Tampa and Channelside, it's the kind of place that's jumping every weekend, and most of the action happens on 7th Avenue, where the former yellow and red brick cigar warehouses and factories have all been converted into sexy nightclubs and trendy entertainment venues, restaurants, and theaters. Gaslights and streetcars line the avenue. It's Tampa's version of Bourbon Street.

We were there for the Gasparilla Pirate Knight Parade and the place was packed. Shoulder to shoulder drunks. Pirate float after float, travelling down 7th Avenue with throngs of spectators on the sidewalk, screaming and waving at the pirates on the floats hoping for beads and coins.

The legend goes that José Gaspar, or Gasparilla, a naval officer turned pirate, plundered ships in the Gulf of Mexico and along the Spanish Main from the late 1700s until 1821, ultimately wrapping himself in chains and throwing himself overboard rather then be captured. It's a myth that Tampa has been celebrating for over one hundred years, with one hell of a parade.

There were drunken women flashing the pirates from restaurant balconies as the floats crept by. Cannons pounding away as the krewes waved from their ships. The night air was filled with music and the smell of puke and beer.

We watched the whole thing from an outdoor patio bar. The beer was free-flowing and we took shots off an ice sculpture. Landon and Noah, a buddy he had graduated with, were crushing up oxys and snorting them; Chris and Travis were drinking Busch Beer and flirting with a couple high school hotties; and Lance and I were popping pills and doing shots of Patron every time a pirate fired a cannon.

Lance had arranged for us to meet up with some girls at the Round Up, a country dance club located just outside the city limits. Around ten o'clock he yelled, "We gotta go!" over the deafening crowd. "The girls bro. We gotta hit the Round Up!"

I got in using twenty-three-year-old Alejandro James Diaz's Florida driver's license. But I hadn't been in the club for thirty minutes before Lance got caught trying to get in using his older brother's ID. That's when the bouncer tapped me on the shoulder and barked, "You! You're outta here!"

A minute later I was running through traffic with one hundred oxys hanging around my neck and a dozen deputies on my trail. I ditched the pills, jumped a couple fences, and hid from a helicopter.

Twenty minutes after that, the deputies mistakenly arrested Lance, thinking he was me. Once the sheriff got him in the cruiser he started drilling Lance about the pills they found in the flea market. "Boy, them pills, that's a trafficking charge," he said from the front seat. "You know what that means? Huh?"

"How would I know?" replied Lance, the cuffs digging into his wrists, "I don't sell pills."

The cop awkwardly twisted around to face the teen, flashed his MagLite into Lance's dilated pupils, effectively blinding him, and scoffed, "You damn sure take 'em."

Luckily, Lance hadn't been caught with his older brother's ID—Chris had. Nor had he been in the club when the deputy arrived. And he never admitted any knowledge of the oxycodone. So all the sheriff's deputy could do was call Lance's mother and tell her to meet him at the border between Pinellas and Pasco County— State Road 54.

An hour later, he yanked Lance out of the cruiser. "Next time," warned the deputy, as he took the cuffs off, "keep some ID on you." He gave Lance a little shove toward his mother's truck. Ms. Barabas then turned around and bailed out Landon and Noah, and my cousin Tony Jr. picked me up at a 7-Eleven around three o'clock in the morning.

Not long after the Round Up incident, in mid-2008, Lance and Landon dropped off two parcels—one destined for Maryville,

Tennessee and the other Fairbanks, Alaska—at the UPS Store in New Port Richey. Nearly five hundred oxycodone in total. The next day the packages disappeared from the UPS tracking website. Lance called, but no one in customer service seemed to have an answer. The packages were just . . . gone. As we later found out, from a report by Deputy John Sharpe, "The packages were opened by UPS personnel and were subsequently seized by the Pasco County Sheriff's Office as evidence."

Deputy Sharpe had seized the shipment, but due to Lance's alias—Lance Attaway—the narcotics officers investigating the incident couldn't track the packages back to him. A couple days later, the manager of the UPS Store contacted Lance on his prepaid cell and told him they had located the packages, but Lance needed to stop by and sign something before they could reship them.

"That doesn't sound right," I said to Lance on our way to the store. "I'm not going inside there. I'll bet you there's a fucking narcotics squad waiting for you." Lance just shook his head and rolled his eyes like I was an idiot. I told him, "Two hundred and seventy four roxie thirties and over two hundred oxy eighties, that's a mandatory minimum of twenty-five years!"

"Whatever, bro."

When we pulled into the parking lot I started glancing at the sea of vehicles neatly lining the strip mall's asphalt lot. Toyota. Ford. Dodge. Dodge. Nissan. Chevy. They were all empty. Then I spotted a black Ford Expedition with tinted windows and two narc types sitting inside. Crew cuts, clean-shaven, and angular features. Both had that permanent pissed-off law enforcement look on their face. "Stop!" I snapped, and Lance pulled into a parking space. "Look! Look!" I frantically jabbed my finger at the officers. "Let's get outta here."

"You're so fucking paranoid," he griped, "it's not even funny." He took a hard look at the officers, and said, "They're just a couple of guys." But he didn't sound nearly as cavalier as he had sounded earlier. We both scanned the lot for additional officers while Lance mocked me for being overly cautious, in his words "a pussy." Then he noticed two other guys that had "undercover" written all over them, sitting in a dark-grey sedan, watching the entrance of the UPS Store—three spaces away from us. The color drained from Lance's face.

"Still think I'm paranoid?" I said, my eyes never leaving the sedan's passengers. "Let's get outta here."

"No . . . no, that's not proof." Those pills were worth roughly $12,000. We argued about it for a couple minutes, but Lance wouldn't walk away. "There's only one way to be sure," he said. Then he slipped his hand in his pocket and pulled out his prepaid cell. My heart was thumping away as Lance called the UPS manager and told him, "I know the cops are trying to set me up. Put 'em on the phone."

The manager didn't even try to deny it. He just took a couple seconds to think about it, and said, "Call back in five minutes. I'll get 'em."

Seconds later—three spaces down—one of the undercover officers received a call on his cell, he said something to his partner, and exited the sedan. When he stepped into the UPS Store Lance turned to me and laughed, "That was close."

Lance wasn't the least bit concerned four undercover Pasco County narcotics officers had nearly ambushed us. On the way back to his place all he could talk about was the $12,000 we had lost.

That night Lance and Richard went out and bought special-ly designed Pringles potato chip cans with hidden compartments in the bottoms. They stuffed them full of several thousand oxyco-dones, bought some real Twinkies and Orange Crushes, and threw the grocery bag full of snacks into the trunk of Richard's new lim-ited edition Chip Foose Ford Mustang 5.0.

Richard started making a biweekly trip to Tennessee up Inter-state 75, "the Oxycodone Express." During one of his first runs he got pulled over and searched leaving Knoxville, which freaked him out. He started asking for $1,500 per trip. So Lance asked me and I told him, "There's no way I'm driving across state lines with two thousand pills in my truck. You do it."

Lance and Landon started taking turns making the trips. A few weeks into the new arrangement, Lance met his brother in Knoxville and they decided to go out partying the night before they were supposed to head back home. They got so fucked up on oxys Lance couldn't drive home the following morning. "What's the big deal?" asked Landon. "Drive home tomorrow."

"I have a test tomorrow," whined Lance. Sometime around noon Landon decided to drive his kid brother back to Tampa. They grabbed a handful of pills and headed down I-75 in Lance's Dodge 2500. After a few hours of listening to the hypnotic sound of tires on pavement, with more than a few opiates coursing through his veins, Landon dozed off at the wheel.

Lance, who had fallen asleep earlier, was jolted awake by the *Thump! Thump! Thump!* of tires hitting asphalt speed bumps. "What the fuck!" he screamed at the sleeping giant. Landon snapped his head up and swerved back onto the main thoroughfare.

"Shit! Shit!" yelled Landon. "Fuck, I fell asleep. Fuck! Sorry, bro," he said, rubbing his eyes. "I'm good, I'm good." Lance ranted about how stupid he was, but he eventually fell back asleep. And so did Landon. A minute later Lance woke up to *Thump! Thump! Thump!* Landon snapped awake. "Shit! Sorry, my bad. I'm good, I'm good." Lance asked his older brother if they needed to switch places, but Landon insisted it wouldn't happen again. "I'm good, I promise, man."

Ten minutes later he drifted off again. This time when Lance woke to the sound of *Thump! Thump! Thump!* he was being thrown around inside the truck's interior as the vehicle fishtailed all over I-75. "That's it!" screamed Lance. "Pull over!" They swapped seats and Lance popped a couple roxies, giving him a temporary rush. Twenty minutes later, he was jolted awake by the *Thump! Thump! Thump!* of the speed bumps again. "Son of a bitch!"

Landon started screaming at Lance, instigating a shoving match while going eighty on the highway. They ended up pulling into a rest stop and exchanging blows like a couple of crackheads fighting over the last rock. Eventually they passed out in the Dodge.

A few days after Lance got back to Tampa he decided it wasn't worth the hassle and started shipping the pills again, alternating between FedEx and UPS.

Lance and I had a fundamental difference of opinion when it came to shipping practices. Statistically, I felt it was safer to ship more pills in fewer parcels, thereby reducing the likelihood of the packages being discovered through random screenings. "Less shipments equals less seizures," I'd say, over and over again. "We should—you should be shipping one large package a week, max!"

"No fucking way!" he'd snap. Lance felt shipping three or four small parcels per week was safer. "So what if they seize one every once in a while; they're not gonna catch us." He would rather lose four or five hundred pills than two thousand.

By this point Lance was buying more scripts than I was, and the money was really coming in. We didn't have a jet boat or a new Corvette like Jimmy, but we had WaveRunners, four-wheelers, dirt bikes, and new trucks. And we were having a blast.

Our weekend partying was spilling into the week. Clubbing was turning into a ritual, and picking up girls at the bars was as easy as ordering a drink with a good fake ID. The money and drugs were changing everything.

Around the same time, I stopped by my maternal grandmother's house one Saturday for a family dinner, and my mother was there. We hadn't spoken in months, and I wasn't looking to change that. I drove there in my Jeep Grand Cherokee and dressed in Affliction and Ralph Lauren. I was about halfway to the front door when my mother rushed out of the house with a glass of wine in her hand and her arms outstretched. "How's my baby boy doing?" She hugged me, looked me up and down, glanced at my Jeep, and said, "You're doing so good, Dougie, I'm proud of you."

"You're kidding, right?" She never whispered one word of encouragement when I had made second team all-conference and was in the paper, finished one match from the state championship, or graduated with honors, but now she was proud. There was no way my mother didn't know how I was making my money. It's not like I had a nine-to-five job. I spent most of my time studying and picking up prescriptions. "You're a real piece of work," I said, "you know that?"

Chapter Eight

Pharmageddon

"Undercover detectives visited the clinic . . . to investigate complaints the doctor . . . was dispensing prescriptions to people without legitimate needs. . . . The office manager passed the officer 40 oxycodone pills without a prescription through the window at the front counter. . . . No charges have been filed."

—*The Tampa Tribune*

In our ever-increasing need for oxycodone I started looking for ways to minimize our acquisition time. I figured out that if a doctor shopper showed up to the initial pill mill appointment without an MRI, but could prove he had a previous script, most of the doctors would write him a prescription for thirty days. Some of them would continue refilling the scripts for the next two or three appointments. That's sixty to ninety days. So I started printing my own labels from Eckerd Drugs and CVS Pharmacy with new doctor shoppers' names for the maximum dosages of roxies and oxys on them; then I would stick the labels on empty pill bottles and send the doctor shoppers into the pill mills. Nine out of ten came back with scripts. That cut down our acquisition time from over a month to less than a week.

Through a friend of a friend of one of my cousins, I met a radiologist technician who worked in Tampa General Hospital's Radiology Department. He was kind of a drunk and extremely unreliable, but for a thousand dollars he would put my doctor shoppers' names on the MRIs of patients with significant back problems such as herniated discs or compression fractures of the vertebrae. This allowed us to get virtually anyone a permanent prescription.

On May 5, 2008, Kenna, a girl I've known since middle school, and I were smoking a joint on our way to the beach. She had one hand on the steering wheel of her Toyota Camry and the other pinching the roach as we passed a Pinellas County Sheriff's cruiser. *Sonofabitch!* The deputy looked right at her as we drove by, he flipped on his overhead emergency lights, and I thought, *Shit!* I had nine roxie 30s and a couple of Xanax in my pill vial. *Fuck! Fuck! Fuck!* Kenna pulled the Camry to the curb and flicked what remained of the joint out the window. I slowly unfastened the necklace with the intention of tossing it out the window, but I never had a clear shot. Instead, I slipped it underneath the passenger seat as the deputy approached the driver's side window.

Deputy Spatz was an average-looking patrolman; pudgy with dark features and short cropped hair. He immediately told us he smelled marijuana. "I'm gonna need to search your vehicle," said Spatz, and asked us to step out of the car.

We told him we had no idea where the smell might be coming from, but when he searched me he found a baggie of weed in my pocket. *Shit! I forgot about that.* If that wasn't bad enough, he also found the pill vial located underneath the passenger seat and proceeded to slap a pair of handcuffs on me.

I'll never forget when he tapped out the roxies on the hood of his cruiser and started counting them. "Two. Four. Six. Eight." When he got to nine, Deputy Spatz looked at me and said, "You're in a lotta trouble son." Then he shoved me in the back of the patrol vehicle and let Kenna go.

I was brought downtown and put in a bleak interview room. Flickering fluorescent lights and filthy walls. Four cheap chairs and a Formica table. Deputy Spatz and an undercover narcotics officer, a tall and lean biker-looking douchebag in his late forties with a motorcycle mustache and long bushy hair pulled back under a baseball cap, sat opposite me. "That's two felonies," said the narcotics officer, pointing at two vacuum-sealed evidence bags of pills, lying on the table. "You haven't been booked yet, so there's still time to help yourself. Here's what you're gonna do; you're going to bring me to your dealer, introduce me to him and vouch for me—"

"What're you talking about, those aren't even my pills!"

"Well," he growled and slid the bag toward me, "we've got you for 'em. Nine oxycodones, that's a three-year mandatory minimum sentence in state prison, plus the Xanaxes—you're looking at five years. That's *five years*. Or you can start cooperating." He wanted me to set someone up. I could've given him a dozen of my junkie sponsors or even my network of high school and college friends distributing painkillers across the country. I thought about it for a split second, but that would have been ridiculous. I couldn't do it. I wouldn't do it. Not to Lance. Not to my friends. Not even to the junkies. "Once we book you, you'll show up on the Pinellas County Arrest website, and it'll be too late."

"Nine roxies isn't even a gram."

Deputy Spatz interjected, "The combination of the oxycodone contained in the Xanaxes puts you over one gram. That's trafficking!" I couldn't help but smile at the bad cop, bad cop routine. "Something funny?"

"There's no oxycodone in Xanax, and even if there was, the minimum weight required for an oxycodone trafficking charge is four grams." The two officers glanced at one another and shifted uncomfortably in their chairs, embarrassed a teenager had seen through their ploy. The narcotics officer shook it off and told me I was still facing two felonies for possession. I could still end up with five years, he said. But I was finished listening to him. "Sir, I'm sorry, I can't help you."

After I was photographed and fingerprinted, I called Lance from this beat-up pay phone in the central holding pen. I explained the situation and Lance laughed, "Should I call your mom?"

"Don't fuck around, bro!" I growled into the phone. "I need you to bond me out—it's ten grand." By that night, Lance had paid my bond. He and Kenna picked me up in the Pinellas County Jail's parking lot. When I got into his truck he asked, "Bro, be honest . . . were you violated?"

The following day, I hired attorney Clementine Conde, a state criminal defense lawyer that Lance's mother recommended. Clementine was a younger version of Hillary Clinton: thick waisted and hard looking, lots of pants suits and cotton knits. Aggressive as a pitbull. We met in her office in downtown New Port Richey. She had already told me on the phone it was five grand per felony and a thousand for the misdemeanor. I slipped the money on the table and she asked me to tell her what happened. As she counted out the cash, I went over the search and arrest. When I got to the part about the deputy telling me I was looking at a three-year manda-tory minimum Clementine chuckled. "That's definitely Spatz," she said. "He's notorious for let's say . . . embellishing the truth." She slid his arrest affidavit in front of me and pointed to the narrative. "He said you admitted the drugs were yours."

"That's bullshit," I mumbled, as I read over the affidavit: "Pills were located in the red medical alert container. Post Miranda the defendant admitted the pills were his, and that he did not have a prescription." I looked at Clementine wide-eyed in bewilderment. "I never said that. They're not my pills."

She ignored the denial and told me she could probably get me two years. If I went to trial and lost, the state attorney would make sure I did three to five in the Florida Department of Corrections. "They don't have air conditioning in state prison," she said. "I hear it sucks."

"It wasn't my car and they weren't found on me. They're not my pills."

She grinned skeptically. "Can you prove that?"

I knew Thomas had a prescription for Roxicodone and Xanax, along with a dozen other scripts. "Definitely."

That night I asked Thomas if he would write an affidavit stat-ing he had accidently left his pill vial in Kenna's Toyota. He start-ed writing without hesitation. The next day, I asked Kenna if she would write a supporting affidavit. She didn't have a problem with it either. Almost a week later they signed the affidavits at Clemen-tine's office as her secretary made a copy of Thomas's prescriptions.

Clementine looked over the affidavits and the scripts and said, "This might just do it." Then she forwarded everything to the pros-ecutor's office.

A week went by, then two, and Clementine called my cell. She told me the state attorney's office wasn't going to drop the charges. "They're offering three years," she said, and the temperature spiked as my pores immediately started producing marble-sized drops of sweat. *Three years!* "But I wouldn't worry about it," said Clementine. "They can't go to trial with Spatz's testimony. It's a bluff."

After another anxiety-ridden week, Clementine called and told me she had gotten them down to one year, "plus some probation." *One year!* My stomach started to percolate like a kettle. "But I'm still working on 'em," she said. "They don't have anything."

A week before the trial she called and told me the state attorney had buckled. "They'll drop the possession of the oxycodone and the Xanax," she said. "But not the marijuana charge."

I got nine months probation. At the first meeting with my probation officer he asked me to take a piss test—which I passed. We then talked about my classes at Pasco-Hernando Community College and how often I smoked weed. "Is it gonna be a problem?"

"Nah, I smoke every once in awhile, but I'm not a pothead."

He made a note in my file and asked, "Are you going to be able to pay your probation fees? It's forty-five dollars a month."

"Not a problem." I mailed him a $405 cashier's check—nine months of fees—the following day. The guy loved me. The way he saw it, I was just some college kid that smoked pot every once in a while—why give me a hard time? Other than for a couple urinalysis tests, I never saw him.

After my close call, Lance and I decided we needed our own oxycodone scripts. My guy at Tampa General Hospital's radiology department had temporarily sobered up and found God at an AA meeting, so he was out. "Pretty Boy" Landon had injured his knee while wrestling in Tennessee. Nothing major, I think he tore his meniscus. But Landon had recently undergone surgery to have it corrected and had a legitimate MRI, so we took him to Doctors R Us. The problem was, Landon's knee injury was so minor that all the doctor would prescribe was Opana, not the pain reliever we were looking for.

At Landon's next appointment he asked the doctor for something stronger. "I was hoping for some oxycodone."

"I'm sorry Mr. Barabas," said the doctor, "I rarely prescribe anything that strong for a knee injury. Now if you had a back injury, that would be a different story."

On the way home, Landon told me and Lance what the doctor had said. Lance suggested we use acetone—nail polish remover—to "wash" the prescription, and re-write it for 240 Roxicodone. "We've got the script," said Lance. "Chris and Dan (two guys Landon knew from high school) wash 'em all the time."

It was a common tactic used by junkies. They would dip a Q-tip in acetone and dab it on the doctor's inked scribble. The ink would separate and get absorbed into the Q-tip's cotton. You could then rewrite the script. The most important thing was that signature, the stamp, and that the Pharmaceutical number matched. The quantity is the last thing to worry about, as long as the new number didn't go past the max prescribed quantity. By now, we all knew what those numbers were. However, the script could easily be traced back to the patient, and police had caught on to the trick.

"No way," I scoffed, shaking my head. "Landon could end up getting busted."

"Shit!" Lance stomped around for a couple seconds, stopped, looked up at me and grinned. "Jimmy." We knew Jimmy had several prescriptions for oxycodone with multiple doctors. But nothing was wrong with him. No herniated or bulging discs. Nothing.

Maybe a day or two later, we hooked up with Jimmy and Lance asked him, "How'd you beat the MRI?"

"It wasn't that hard," he said. Jimmy coached us on what to do to get an MRI. He explained how to arch and slightly twist our backs to put pressure on our lower spine.

"That's what causes the disks to temporarily bulge," Jimmy told us. "It works every time."

The first hurdle was getting a referral for an MRI. My personal doctor wouldn't do it, saying, "Opiates are too addictive, Douglas. They're poison." We ended up going to Dr. Rivera, a heavy-set, slovenly guy. I really played it up, walking in slowly and slightly hunched over. I even asked for help to get on the table. When he asked what the problem seems to be, I told him I had been in a car accident. "They had to use the Jaws of Life to get me out, doc," I said, wincing from the pain. "I've never been the same." Rivera scribbled out a recommendation for two X-rays and an MRI.

We went to Rose Radiology, a high-tech diagnostic facility. Clean and impersonal. A female lab tech asked me to slip on a hospital gown, and led me into a sterile room where the MRI machine was housed. The machine itself was the size of a small van, bulky and tubular. It was white and smooth with a cylindrical opening. The flat plastic gurney connected to the MRI was cold and hard. As the lab tech slid the gurney into the enclosure she told me I had to lie perfectly still. "It's going to take roughly an hour."

I arched and twisted my back, just like Jimmy had instructed us to do, but after a while it became increasingly uncomfortable in the coffin-like space. Periodically, the machine would make this whirling sound and then it would start thumping and humming. My arched position soon became unbearable. I started to squirm inside the spherical recess and the lab tech called out over the speaker, "Mr. Dodd, I know you're in pain, but you've got to stop moving." I thought I was never going to get out of that thing.

A week later, I picked up my lab results, rushed to my Jeep, and flipped through the paperwork to find my results: disc bulges with bilateral mild to moderate neural narrowing of L-3, L-4, and L5-S1, in addition to space narrowing at L5-S1. "I've gotta problem, bro," I said to Lance over the phone. "Bulging discs, exactly like yours." I was stoked.

Within a couple of days I was sitting in a pain management clinic's waiting room along with twenty-five other patients squeezed into a space barely fit for twenty. Most were seated, but some were standing. The place was so packed that people were standing outside smoking, waiting to be called. There were people from all facets of life. I even remember seeing an elementary school friend's parents—another couple of junkies waiting for their thirty-day fix—and I thought about approaching them to maybe sign them up as doctor shoppers, but I couldn't bring myself to do it.

Over the next two hours, I watched the pill mill churn out two dozen patients at the initial consultation fee of $500 and monthly follow-up fee of $100. I calculated the average doctor sees around one hundred patients in a day, assuming each patient remained with the clinic for three years the average patient represented about $110 per consultation. That's eleven grand a day. A perpetually growing stream of physician-monitored, pharmaceutically-supplied addicts. Pharmageddon.

Eventually I was called into a standard doctor's consultation room to see Dr. Frederick Cornelius, a frail, Keith Richards-esque looking guy in an oversized white lab coat, which probably hid the track marks. Cornelius stopped at the door, leaned into the hallway, and yelled to one of the nurses, "Bring me a big green," the street name of Purdue Pharma's OxyContin 80 mg pills, green in color. They were also known as "green goblins," "big dogs," and "green apples." I knew right then Cornelius was a stone cold junkie.

I told him about the car accident as he gave me a cursory examination that lasted all of thirty seconds. "So what're you looking for?" he asked.

"I need something for the pain. Not Tylenol. My uncle gave me something called Roxicodone once. It worked real good."

"Okay," he said, pulled out his prescription pad and started writing. "I'm giving you two hundred and forty thirty-milligram Roxicodones. And I want to see you in two weeks."

At my next appointment I told Cornelius the roxies were working, but they wore off too quickly. "I need something that'll last a little longer, Doc." He refilled the script and wrote me an additional script for sixty controlled-released morphine 60 mgs. Not exactly what I was looking for. At my next appointment I told Cornelius the morphine wasn't cutting it. "I want OxyContins."

"Well, why didn't you just say that," he chuckled, and scribbled out a script for 240 Roxicodone 30 mgs, 120 OxyContin 40 mgs, and sixty Trazadon 50 mgs—so I could sleep better. I didn't need them at the time, but figured I could get a couple bucks for them.

Back in the parking lot, I hopped in my Jeep and noticed my elementary school friend's parents sitting in the sedan next to me. They were frantically crushing up an oxycodone on their dashboard and snorting the powdery residue. My friend's mother glanced over at me, recognizing her child's playmate. She placed her head in the palms of her hands and turned away.

Cornelius had cut us the scripts so quickly we sent Landon to see him. The doctor wrote him a script for 120 Roxicodone 30 mgs, but told him the only way he could prescribe anything stronger was if Landon had a back problem—accompanied by a supporting MRI. We then sent Landon to Rose Radiology, where he arched and twisted his back and ended up with an MRI identical to mine and Lance's. Cornelius then prescribed him 240 roxie 30s and 120 oxy 40s.

Lance then sent his older brother Larry "the Lineman" to Rose Radiology to get an MRI, and repeated the process with a dozen other guys.

We were legit!

Around the same time, Lance and Tiffany got into a huge fight—over something juvenile, I'm sure—and broke up. It didn't take either of them long to hook up with other people. Lance started seeing this girl Lora and Tiffany started dating some guy named Roman Diveroli.

A couple weeks later, Tiffany, Roman, his sister Stella, and his friend Stewart were at Sand Soccer, a tournament held on the white sandy beaches of Clearwater. Big logo-branded aluminum and canvas pavilions lined several soccer fields of sand, surrounded by beach-goers, tourists, and fans. There were palm trees and concession stands, and the crowds were drinking and screaming.

At some point Stella—who was a big fan of pharmaceuticals—swiped Stewart's prescription bottles of Roxicodone, OxyContin, and Xanax. Stella then grabbed Tiffany and said, "Come on, let's check out the games."

The girls spent most of the morning prancing around the tournament in their skimpy bikinis, teasing the sweaty "soccer boys," and sipping watermelon vodka out of Tiffany's Big Gulp to wash down a couple roxies. Tiffany never thought to ask where Stella had gotten them. The girls both got more than a little drunk and high. They were barely standing, giggling uncontrollably when they returned to their towels.

Sometime around noon the temperature peaked and Stella asked to borrow Tiffany's car "to make an ice run." That's when she stashed the pills in Tiffany's trunk. Not long after Stella returned from her "ice run," Stewart realized his drugs were missing. Because the girls were both so fucked up on opiates and alcohol, he immediately accused them of taking the pills. "Where's my shit?!"

"We don't have 'em," they shot back. The whole scene quickly deteriorated into a screaming match on the beach.

The way I heard it, a couple Clearwater Beach police officers noticed the teens shoving and yelling at one another and asked, "What's the problem here?"

Stewart—who was in serious need of some oxycodone—pointed to Tiffany and Stella and growled, "Those two bitches stole my prescriptions."

"That's bullshit," slurred Tiffany, peering at the officer through her glassy eyes, while continuing to sip out of her Big Gulp. "You can search me." Then she pointed toward her Honda Accord sitting in the parking lot. "Search my car. I don't have 'em."

As far as she was concerned she had nothing to worry about, but once the officers started digging through her car things went bad in a hurry. In the trunk, buried underneath several beach towels, they found approximately three hundred oxycodone—a fifteen-year mandatory minimum—and forty Xanax tablets.

"Those aren't mine!" snapped Tiffany, when the officer emerged from the back of her trunk holding the pill bottles. He asked whose they were and Tiffany instantly realized Stella had stolen the pills. She glanced at her boyfriend's sister hoping she would confess.

The officer glanced at Stella expectantly. "They're not mine," she said.

The officers' eyes darted between the two girls and Stella said, "It's her car."

Tiffany fired little lightning bolts of hatred at her and growled, "Bitch!"

They were both arrested for trafficking oxycodone and possession of Xanax. The cops handcuffed them and threw them in the back of separate Clearwater police cruisers. Within minutes of the arrest, a mutual friend of Lance and Tiffany's called and relayed the situation to Lance. Despite their tumultuous relationship, Lance and Tiffany were still hooked on each other. Lance called his mother and she contacted Tiffany's parents. By the time Tiffany was photographed and fingerprinted Ms. Barabas had a bail bondsmen waiting to spring her son's ex-girlfriend. That night she contacted Clementine Conde—my top-notch criminal defense attorney—and scheduled an appointment for Tiffany and her parents the following day.

Tiffany wasn't all that worried. It was just some pills. She had seen me and Lance with thousands of them. But when Clementine met with Tiffany and her parents, she explained the seriousness of Florida's mandatory minimum sentences. "Your little girl is facing fifteen years in a Florida state prison." She leaned back in her chair and looked over Tiffany, from her curly brown hair to her tight little ass. "You'll be very popular with the lifers."

"Oh my God," mumbled Tiffany, and the blood drained from her face. Her mother burst out in tears.

Clementine told them she would do everything she could for their daughter. "But it doesn't look good."

At the end of the day, Stewart didn't feel it was Tiffany that took the pills. For $25,000 Clementine convinced Stewart to write an affidavit stating that he had mistakenly left his prescription bottles in the trunk of Tiffany's car. She then convinced the state attorney to drop the trafficking charges against Tiffany (Stella's charges were also dropped) and got Tiffany's arrest record expunged. Clementine Conde was a beast of a criminal defense attorney!

Chapter Nine

Prescription Painkillers

"Possession of four grams of either drug—the equivalent of seven hydrocodone pills or 31 oxycodone pills—without a valid prescription carries a mandatory state prison sentence of three years. Larger amounts carry 15- and 25-year sentences."

—*South Florida Sun Sentinel*

I can't tell you how awesome it was to have my own script. Not a week after I got it, I was driving down Ridge Road and a Pinellas County Sheriff's cruiser pulled up behind my Jeep. After following me for a couple miles the deputy hit the lights and I pulled to the curb. I half expected to see Deputy Spatz exit the patrol car, but this guy was way younger and way fatter. We'll call him "Chris Farley."

"You know why I pulled you over?" asked Deputy Farley, leaning casually on my car. I didn't. "Improper lane change." But I hadn't even changed lanes while on Ridge Road. He asked for proof of insurance and ran my license and tag. When he asked me to step out of the vehicle and two additional cruisers pulled up to the scene, I knew this had nothing to do with an "improper lane change."

The deputy told me to turn around and he snapped a pair of handcuffs around my wrists. "Mr. Dodd," he said, as two of his fellow officers gathered around me, "here's where we're at. I can write you a ticket for the improper lane change, or you can give us permission to search your vehicle."

"For what?"

"Oxycodone." *Shit.* That's when I noticed Deputy Spatz sitting in one of the cruisers with a toothy grin smeared across his face. "I've got some oxys," I admitted. The deputies glanced at one another, their eyes lighting up, and the corners of their lips curling. "And two hundred roxies."

"Where're they at?" growled Deputy Farley.

"In the glove box." They began smiling and nodding, as giddy as a couple high school girls on their way to prom. Then Farley stepped toward my truck and I added, "Right next to a copy of the prescription sheet."

"You've got a . . . got a . . . prescription?" asked the deputy with a sigh.

"Well, yeah." I arched my brow in mock confusion. "How else would I have gotten them?"

They searched my truck while I sat at the edge of Ridge Road, still handcuffed. They found my scripts in the center console, then looked underneath the seat, the floor mats, and the cargo area, but couldn't find anything incriminating. They even brought in a drug dog, which had a fit because the interior of my Cherokee always smelled like weed. But the K-9 didn't find anything either. Ten minutes later they uncuffed my wrists and tossed me the keys to the Jeep. "You got lucky this time," mumbled Deputy Farley on his way back to his cruiser.

I got lucky the next time they pulled me over, too. And the time after that. And the one after that. It got to the point where I was getting pulled over two or three times a month. Once, Lance and I were picking up several of his doctor shoppers' prescriptions—hundreds and hundreds of oxycodone pills tucked in white pharmaceutical bottles—and several bottles ended up in the back of my Jeep. Over nine hundred Roxicodone and nearly five hundred OxyContin.

It was after eight o'clock. Lance took off before me. I was roaring down Moon Lake Road in the pouring rain when I came up behind Lance's truck. Out of immaturity or pure stupidity I shot by him going sixty—maybe seventy—while simultaneously shooting by a Pinellas County Sheriff's cruiser parked on the side of the road. I have no idea if it was Deputy Spatz sitting in the vehicle, but I like to think it was. Maybe the deputy recognized my Jeep, maybe he didn't.

Seconds later my cell phone rang. "Bro, you're fucked!" yelled Lance. "There's a sheriff's deputy coming up behind me." The patrol vehicle roared passed Lance's truck. "Fuck! He just passed me." I had a twenty-five-year mandatory minimum sentence sitting in my back seat and a sheriff's deputy closing in on me. Plus, I was still on probation! "Get rid of the pills!" screamed Lance, but there wasn't enough time.

I immediately dropped my cell on the passenger seat and it bounced to the floor. I frantically scanned the side of the road for a place to pull over and hide. Spotting an opportunity, I swerved the Cherokee into a strip mall parking lot, pulling in between a van and a pickup truck. I shut off my Jeep and hunched over the center console. I could still hear Lance yelling, "Get rid of the pills!" from the passenger side floorboard as the cruiser sailed past.

I picked up my cell and laughed. "Lost 'im."

"Fuck! You still got the pills?"

"Yep."

"Lucky motherfucker."

I was pulled over the following morning on my way to school and on the way back. Can you believe that? But they didn't find anything.

Maybe a week after that, sometime in October or November, I was leaving Walgreens Pharmacy with one of my doctor shoppers' prescriptions. I had a plastic bag of around seven hundred oxycodone stuffed underneath my seat that I'd neglected to drop off at Lance's that morning. I had just turned on to Ulmerton Road when a Pinellas County Deputy pulled in behind me and flashed his lights. *Fuck! Fuck! Fuck!* For a millisecond I thought about making a run for it, but there was no way my Grand Cherokee was going to lose a 350-plus horsepower Chevy Malibu Police Interceptor, so I slowly pulled off the road and came to a stop. *This couldn't get any worse,* I thought. Then Deputy Spatz stepped out of the patrol vehicle.

Spatz leaned into my window and grinned. "You didn't make a complete stop back there Mr. Dodd."

"Come on, we both know I stopped," I replied, irritated at the fact I was about to spend the next twenty minutes sitting on the curb in handcuffs and an additional twenty-five years sweating my ass off in a Florida state prison for trafficking oxycodone. "I handed him my license and insurance. "If you wanna search the truck, just search it—you don't have to keep coming up with these bullshit traffic violations."

"Huh," he grunted, while glancing around the interior of my Jeep. "You got anything in here?"

"Do I ever?!" I snapped back, as if this was a huge waste of my time, and not the beginning of a long prison term.

His eyes darted to mine as he narrowed his gaze—Clint Eastwood style—and growled, "I'm gonna be keeping an eye on you, Dodd." Then he dropped my license and insurance card into my lap, stood abruptly, and said, "Get outta here," as he stomped off.

Yeah, I got lucky a lot.

By this point we were buying and distributing twenty thousand oxycodones throughout the country every month. Sometimes more. We were hooked on our product and making bad decisions. Lance "the Little General" walked into a dealership and paid for a supercharged Ford F-150 Lightning with cash. I'll never forget the look on the manager's face as Lance peeled off something like twenty-five grand in fifty- and hundred-dollar notes, making nice little stacks of cash on his desk. "So, you fellas in a cash business?" asked the manager, smiling at the two of us. "Ya'll, male strippers or something?"

"Yeah," snickered Lance, "somethin' like that." On our way back to his place I had to talk Lance out of getting custom plates that read, "OXY-80S" on them. That's how reckless he was—OXY-80S!

"What about just ROXIES?" he whined. "That could mean anything."

"Do you want to go to prison?" I snarled.

I was being pulled over for "traffic violations" and having my vehicle searched on a regular basis and this nutjob was flaunting cash and pills every chance he got.

At night, Lance would get drunk and high, sit on his balcony with his AR-15 assault rifle and target people on the street with his laser sight. Pedestrians would be ambling along the sidewalks of Channelside, minding their own business, when suddenly a red dot would appear on their chest. Most of the time they would never know it, but every once in a while some couple would be having a romantic stroll along the channel, holding hands and staring into one another's eyes, and from out of nowhere a red dot would appear on one of their foreheads. They would scream or look up at the surrounding buildings and point. That's the kind of stuff Lance did, despite knowing he had $40,000 in cash and a thousand pills sitting in his dresser. It was tantamount to driving around in a stolen car with a broken taillight and a body in the trunk—pure stupidity.

Around the same time, I stopped by Lance's loft to drop off several thousand oxycodones and walked in on him and Jack Henry, a mutual friend from high school, using an automatic money counter to tally up several hundred thousand dollars' worth of drug proceeds. Gutted teddy bear carcasses, piles of cotton, and stacks of cash were strewn across the kitchen table. Lance's .308 Remington sniper rifle was sitting on a bipod at their feet and a Glock .45 was lying on the table—it was a scene straight out of *Scarface*.

"What the fuck are you doing!" I screamed.

Jack wasn't a part of our organization and shouldn't have known about any of this, let alone helped count the cash, and Lance knew it. "You're paranoid!" snapped Lance. "He's all right."

I threw the bag of roxies and oxys on the table. "I'm telling you," I growled, as I walked out the door, "you're gonna get us busted."

A week or so later I booked a flight to upstate New York to see my buddy Andy. I wanted to bounce the idea of shipping him five hundred to a thousand oxycodone per month to test the market. New

York prices weren't as good as Tennessee's, but I trusted Andy. He was still running his grow operation in the woods near our old high school, so the opiates were a good fit.

I packed my Roxicodone and OxyContin prescription bottles full of painkillers and threw them into my overnight bag. Then I stuffed $25,000 in cash into the crotch of my boxer briefs—I was planning to ask my dad to hold the money for me—and headed to Tampa International Airport.

I had gone through TIA's security checkpoint a dozen times in the past, but this was the first time I really paid attention. The security personnel were randomly pulling commuters out of line and searching them, patting people down and digging through their bags. Everyone had to pass through a metal detector and a new aluminum and Plexiglas phone booth–looking thing that blew air around you then analyzed the air's chemical content for drug and explosive residue.

As I placed my overnight bag on the X-ray machine's conveyor belt, I recalled that virtually all money contains trace elements of cocaine due to residue on banks' money counters. And I had $25,000 of drug money in my underwear. *Fuck!* Plus, Alejandro Diaz's Florida driver's license—my fake ID—in my front pocket. *Fuck!* My heart started pounding in my chest like a brick in a clothes dryer. I thought about turning around as my carry-on slipped into the mouth of the X-ray machine, but there were several security officers behind me and I knew I would never make it out of the room. I stepped into the booth and the stream of air enveloped my body. The machine beeped several times as I stood there perspiring. After what seemed like eternity, the security officer glanced at me from behind her station and nodded me through.

I slipped a couple of roxies into my mouth as I boarded the plane and twenty minutes later I was thirty-five thousand feet above Florida, headed north toward New York. My seat was next to a forty-something hot teacher type with black curls and brown eyes—a MILF that reminded me of Amanda's mom, the aging ex-stripper. We spent the first hour of the flight tossing semiflirtatious glances back and forth, eye fucking each other miles off the ground. She eventually leaned into me and asked, "How old are you?"

"Nineteen," I replied, fighting the urge to glance down her blouse.

"Nineteen, huh?" she whispered to herself, and quickly looked away, trying to hide what I imagine was an inappropriate smile.

She was quiet for a while; then turned toward me and asked if I had a girlfriend. I didn't. Neither of us could stop grinning at the question. When I mentioned I was going to college and currently lived with my grandmother she turned red. We both laughed at the situation; a woman in her early forties flirting with a nineteen-year-old college student. Or was it a nineteen-year-old college student trying to pick up a woman in her early forties? Either way, it didn't stop either of us.

"How about you?" I asked, and she mentioned recently divorcing her high school sweetheart. Her current boyfriend was twenty-six years old. "He's a lot more fun than my ex-husband."

Around the same time she alluded to the possibility of meeting for lunch or maybe dinner after work when we both got back to Florida, I asked, "Where do you work?"

"I'm an agent with the DEA," she said. "I'm currently working out of the Tampa PD building—downtown Tampa." She started talking about the drug task force she was assigned to, and I felt like the plane had gone into a nosedive. Adrenaline flooded into my bloodstream and I became acutely aware of the cash stuffed in my underwear and the oxycodone in my carry-on bag. "The job's not nearly as exciting as it sounds."

"I'm sure," I muttered, and the conversation cooled considerably. I kept up the polite smiles and eye contact, but my fear of the DEA had killed off the attraction. Just before we disembarked, she slipped me a Drug Enforcement Administration business card with her cell number scribbled on the back and told me to give her a call. I never did.

I met up with Andy the next morning. We agreed on a price, and I handed him the pills. "I can move two or three thousand of these a month," he said. "Shit, probably more."

"There's no way I can send you that many." I told him I had an agreement to supply Lance with fifteen thousand to twenty thousand per month. "And half the time I can't even do that." I ended up sending Andy a thousand here and fifteen hundred there. I don't think it ever amounted to more than a couple thousand a month.

The day before my return flight I had lunch with my father. We went to a breakfast-anytime place, the kind of place you can get eggs and a steak all day, and the waitresses smack and pop their gum while they take your order. We spent the time talking about school, my new truck, and several other toys I had recently bought. When the check came I pulled out a wad of cash—like an idiot—and said, "I've got this."

"Yeah," mumbled my dad, as I peeled off several twenties and slipped them to the waitress, "I can see that."

"What?" I said with a grin. I had spent the last couple days taking my stepsisters to movies and to the mall. I'd spent some money on them, nothing really, and my dad was starting to give me strange looks.

"I'm worried."

"It's not as bad as it looks."

I stuffed the cash back in my pocket and was about to ask him to hold the $25,000 I had stashed in my jacket's pocket, when he said, "Doug, I'm not one hundred percent sure of what you're into, but I'm sure it's drugs of some kind, and that Andy is involved." Andy had already sold off most of the painkillers I had given him; he had stopped by to see me at my dad's house half a dozen times to drop off money and talk about coming to Florida to get his own scripts. My father ran a hand over his bald head and took a deep breath. "You're getting older now. You're smart, you're in college, and you've got a lot of things going for you. You need to start making better decisions. Whatever you've got going, get out of it before you end up in—"

"Dad, I know what I'm doing. I appreciate what you're saying, and I plan on getting out." I can only imagine what he would have done if I had slapped the $25,000 on the table and asked him to hold onto it for me. Instead, I flew back to Florida with the cash stuffed in my underwear again, more anxious than ever. Thank God for Xanax!

It wasn't long after that I sat down with Lance at his loft and said, "We've gotta start making better decisions."

"How so?" he asked. "We're doing good, bro."

"Yeah, but eventually everyone gets caught. We need to start investing in something else . . . something legal." We ended up buying a Florida resale license from LUCI e-cigarettes. They had just hit the market and we were sure e-cigarettes were the next big thing. Essentially, they're tobacco-free electronic cigarettes that look, taste, and feel like the real thing. We bought the license because LUCIs were a healthy alternative to smoking and the business model wasn't all that different from pills: we purchased a minimum of 250 per month at a price of $24.95 each, then resold them for roughly $100 per device.

Lance printed some business cards and we started calling around to local businesses and asking if we could set up a display stand and some brochures in their establishment. I convinced the owners of a couple of Metro PCS Stores in New Port Richey to let us put up a display, as well as several kiosks at the USA Flea Market and a few other miscellaneous businesses. We weren't making more than a couple thousand dollars a month off the LUCIs, but Lance started funneling $30,000 to $40,000 of our oxycodone proceeds through the business account every month. As a result, we started looking pretty good on paper.

Richard bought three vans and opened a shuttle service to drive groups to the airport or home from bars. After a couple months, I think it actually started turning a profit.

We were trying to clean up the money—our first foray into money laundering.

The constant searches of my Jeep got me thinking about a new vehicle. I wanted a Toyota Tacoma. Not a Hummer H3 or a special-edition Ford Mustang, but something nondescript. Unlike Lance, I had no intention of walking into a dealership with cash.

There were two good reasons for avoiding cash, according to Uncle Tony. One, it raises suspicion; and two, the authorities can seize any vehicle used in a narcotics transaction unless it's got a lien on it. I wanted that protection for my new truck so I talked to the loan officer at Wachovia Bank, where I had my savings and checking accounts, as well as my safe-deposit box. I filled out a loan application and she checked my credit. "You've got a seven hundred and seventy Beacon score," she said. I had multiple credit cards and more than enough money in my savings account to buy the truck, but because I was only nineteen years old I had only claimed one year's worth of taxes, and that wasn't enough. "Here's what we'll do," said the loan officer, "we'll transfer some of your savings into CDs to secure the loan, and all you'll need to do is get a cosigner."

My grandmother agreed to cosign for me, but the loan officer said she didn't have a sufficient income. My cousin had bad credit and my uncle was still on federal probation. I was seriously considering taking some cash out of my safe-deposit box, walking into a dealership "Little General" style, and tossing twenty-five grand at them. That's when my grandmother suggested I ask my mother. "I'm sure she'll do it," she said. "Call her. She's your mother."

I explained my dilemma to my mother and she said, "So now that you need something you call?"

"Mom, I've got the money in the bank . . . it's a secured loan. I just need a signature."

"I don't know, something's not right." She told me she had the feeling that she would end up paying for my truck somehow, like the whole thing was a scam. As if I were trying to screw her over the way she had screwed me over my entire life. I told her she could call the loan officer if she had any questions. "I don't know Dougie. I think I should call a lawyer."

"A lawyer?! Forget it!" I snapped and hung up on her. My dad ended up cosigning for the loan.

I spent the next few days trying to track down a Tacoma. I looked online and called several ads. About that same time, I was driving Landon home one day and saw a blue Tacoma sitting at Stadium Toyota, a dealership in Tampa. I whipped into the lot, hopped out, and took a look at the truck. It was a royal blue, with an extended cab and an off-road package. Perfect!

Landon was checking himself out in the driver's side mirror and I was reading the sticker when a salesman walked up to us. He was a slightly overweight, middle-aged guy in rumpled clothes. I asked him if I could take it for a test-drive. He looked me up and down, from my tennis shoes to my T-shirt, and scoffed, "You know it's twenty-six thousand, right?"

Like I couldn't afford it. "Yeah."

The salesman begrudgingly got the keys, drove me around half a mile into a residential neighborhood behind the dealership, and swapped seats with me. Mr. Chunky then asked me to make a U-turn and he directed me back to the dealership. He never told me one thing about the vehicle. When we pulled into the lot I asked, "That was it?"

"Look," he sighed, "if you can get financed we'll take it for a ride all over Tampa; until then, yeah, that was it."

I already had financing, but I wasn't about to buy anything from this asshole. "Whatever," I snapped, and got out of the truck. "I could buy this with cash if I wanted to."

He grinned skeptically. Like I was just some punk kid out for a joyride. I jumped back into my Jeep with Landon and we drove off, pissed.

Land O' Lakes Swamp Challenge Wrestling Tournament. I went undefeated.

With a friend after high school wrestling practice.

Four-wheeling with Landon.

Graduating and receiving my diploma from Hudson High School.

Spring break at Daytona Beach. From left to right: Richard, me, Lance, and Landon.

Lance and I getting ready to go to Tampa.

From left to right: Ethan, Richard, Landon, me, and Lance at Clearwater Beach.

Just messing around.

Hanging out with Lance.

Okeechobee Mud Fest 2008. Okeechobee, Florida. A huge get-together for any-body that has a mud truck. People come from all over and camp out for a week. We rented a RV and brought all of our toys out for the weekend.

Maya and I head out on the town in a stretched limousine.

From left to right: Richard Sullivan, Landon Barabas, and me at Coleman Federal Complex in Florida.

From front to back: me, Seth, Richard, Landon, and Boston Mike after a workout at Coleman.

Simpler days. Me at ten years old, with my dog.

The funny thing is, that night I found the same upgraded version of the truck on Craigslist—except it was a silver four-door with leather. So my Uncle Tony and I drove out to this doctor's house, took his Tacoma out for a quick test-drive, and bought it.

I was so excited, the following day I brought my new truck to Stadium Toyota dealership for a full detail. While I waited in line I saw the same salesman pushing quarters into a vending machine. He glanced at me and nodded, not quite sure where he had seen me before. He grabbed his Coke and the lightbulb snapped on. He turned, jabbed his chubby little finger in the air at me, and said, "The Tacoma, right?"

"Right," I replied and motioned to my new truck sitting in the service area's parking lot with my chin. "I bought one yesterday . . . cash." That wasn't one hundred percent true, but screw him! His eyes darted between me and the truck. I like to think he was questioning his half-assed test-drive and condescending attitude. "Yeah," I grunted. "You fucked up."

He snorted, popped the top on his soda, and walked off.

The scripts weren't always a blessing. At one point I made the mistake of selling 240 Roxicodone to a "friend" of my cousin Tony Jr.'s, which was something I just didn't do. One, my uncle told me not to deal with anyone I didn't know, and two, everything I got was already promised to Lance. Regardless, Tony Jr. kept calling and calling, pleading, "Come on, cuz, I need the money. He'll pay fifteen dollars per pill." *Fuck it*, I thought, *I've got plenty of roxies.*

We were sitting in my new truck outside Bourbon Street Bar, waiting for my cousin's guy, and I kept asking, "You sure this guy's okay?"

"Yeah," said Tony Jr. from the back seat, "he's a friend of Carlos's wife . . . he's good." *Great*, I thought, *now it's a friend of a friend.*

The guy got there around midnight and hopped into the vehicle's front passenger seat. He was a wannabe gangster—a "wangster." He looked antsy, glancing around nervously. I handed him my prescription bottle and he counted out 240 pills. Then, using his palm, he funneled the painkillers back into the bottle and handed me a thick wad of greenbacks. In the darkness of the truck I started counting out the $3,600. Suddenly the wangster popped the door and quickly started to exit the vehicle. I immediately reached out and snagged the tail of his plaid shirt with my right hand. "Whoa," I said, "you've got my prescription bottle, bro."

That bottle had my name and information on it. The last thing I needed was this guy getting busted—or even worse, overdosing—with my pill bottle clutched in his cold, dead hand. No thanks. But instead of dropping back into the seat the wangster started frantically struggling to escape my grasp. I had him by two fingers, but he was squirming away. "Let me go!" screamed the guy as he struggled to pull free of my grip. "Let me go!"

I yelled at my cousin sitting in the back seat, "He's got my bottle, grab 'im!" As I tossed the cash and lunged at the wangster with my other hand, the money went everywhere, raining throughout the cabin.

Tony Jr. reached over the seat and grabbed a handful of his shirt. "What's going on?" he yelled, as the guy squirmed and pulled. Then suddenly he tore right out of his shirt and took off. I bolted out of the Toyota and hit the pavement running. The wangster was maybe ten yards ahead of me, but I was closing the gap quickly. I was jacked up on adrenaline and confused as hell as to why he was running, but I was determined to get that bottle.

When he rounded the corner of the building he slowed and I didn't. I clipped his leg in a PIT maneuver, knocking his feet out from under him and sending him to the asphalt with a thud. I whirled around and headed back toward him, but before I could get to him, he was back on his feet. At six feet and two hundred-plus pounds he towered over me. I wasn't about to go toe-to-toe with him, but I would not let him leave with that bottle.

I glanced toward the parking lot, expecting my cousin to come racing around the strip mall any minute, and the wangster looked toward the alley—his only escape. "Give me the bottle!" I barked. "All I want is the bottle!"

"Fuck you!" he growled and rushed at me. I dropped down and grabbed him in a double-leg takedown, scooping his legs out from underneath him and sending him flailing through the air. His arms swung wildly as he flew backward and hit the pavement. Hard. That should've knocked the wind out of him, but he just jumped right back to his feet and started swinging at me with the bottle in his hand. I yanked his legs out from underneath him a second time and he slammed back onto the pavement with a grimace. He looked up at me in shock. We had a David and Goliath thing happening and I knew he would eventually reach the conclusion this wasn't going to end well for him. He jumped up again and I whipped his legs out from underneath him for the third time. When he hit the ground the pill bottle popped out of his hand, rattling as it rolled to a stop about ten feet away. The wangster immediately flipped over and scurried toward the bottle. He snatched it up and ran toward the rear of the strip mall with me trailing behind him.

He tore around the corner and down the alley toward a new Dodge Challenger parked near several large dumpsters. The passenger door opened and the engine was running, but I didn't slow down. He slammed himself into the Challenger and I dove in after him. The wangster and the driver, who was nothing but a screaming silhouette to me, shifted around haphazardly in the cabin. The three of us were bouncing around, and somehow in the confusion I grabbed the wangster's wrist and wrenched the bottle partly out of his hand. He shoved me toward the open door while the driver hit the gas and I was thrown backward out of the vehicle. Luckily, I had a firm grip on the bottle and the wangster had a strong hold on the lid. The bottle snapped open and little blue roxies exploded into the night air. I slammed onto the pavement along with around a hundred of the painkillers, but I didn't care. I had my bottle.

Tony Jr. came jogging up behind me and said, "What happened?" as the Challenger roared down the alley. "What was that about?"

I stood up, scratched and scuffed, hunched over trying to catch my breath. I looked at Tony Jr. who hadn't even broken a sweat. "You're fucking useless," I panted. "You know that?"

I was afraid that the wangster would loop around and grab the money, so we quickly picked up the pills we could find and huffed it back to the Tacoma. Fortunately, the cash was still lying throughout the cabin. I scooped it up and started counting out the fifties and hundreds. After twenty or thirty bills I noticed the weight and feel of the paper weren't quite right. Something about the consistency was off, too. I flipped on the interior light and looked at the coloring. There were no colored fibers. Nor was there a security strip. "Fuck! It's counterfeit money. Motherfucker!" I whipped around, looked at my cousin, and I asked, "So where does this guy live?"

Tony Jr. shrugged. "I don't know, he's a friend of Carlos's wife."

I was pissed off at Tony Jr.—and myself—for dealing with a friend of a friend.

We shot across New Port Richey to Carlos's house to talk to his wife. It turned out she didn't know where the wangster lived or even his last name. He was just some customer she had met at her bartending job who asked if she knew anyone that sold oxycodones.

Tony Jr. felt like he had let me down—which he had. He suddenly flipped out on her, accusing her of setting us up and demanding the money for the pills. The next thing I know Carlos comes through the front door with a Samurai sword. He put it to Tony Jr.'s neck and told him, "If you don't get the fuck outta here, I'm gonna gut you like a fish!"

When my Uncle Tony found out about the guy bolting with the pills he laughed about it. "Serves you right," he said. "Rule number five: never deal with anyone you don't know."

By this point I was certain my uncle was making up the rules as he went along. "Oh yeah," I said. "What's rule number three?"

"Never talk about business on the phone."

"Number ten?"

"Don't use guns and don't deal with people that do."

"Seven?"

"Don't ever keep product or cash at your house."

"Eight?"

"Cease all contact with anyone under a state or federal criminal investigation." He rattled them off so quickly I realized he actually had them memorized. When I asked if I could get a copy of the "rules" he grinned. "Rule number twenty: never write anything down."

Between Alaska, Florida, and Tennessee we were making a lot of cash. Jimmy was providing a significant amount of the pills, and as a result, I ended up hanging out with him more and more. We had a lot in common. We were both hard-working, even-tempered, no-nonsense kind of guys, motivated by the money. Eventually, we decided to start a landscaping business called, "A Cut above the Rest." We both threw around $20,000 into it and bought two zero-turn riding mowers, edgers, blowers, chainsaws, a generator, and other equipment. We picked up an enclosed trailer and tricked it out with graphic decals. Jimmy already had several contracts, so we ran an ad on Craigslist for employees.

In the middle of putting the whole thing together, we were sitting in his kitchen, snorting a couple oxy 80s, and my cell rang. "Yo, yo, yo, what's up dog?" yelled Lance out of my cell. He was manic and jacked up on God knows what. "I need whatever you got, blueberries, green apples, oranges—"

"Bro!" I snapped. "What're you talking about? Don't call me with that shit!" and I hung up on him.

Jimmy looked at me and shook his head in disgust. "What's with your boy?" he asked. Jimmy told me Lance called him at least once a week and tried to have open conversations regarding oxycodone deals. No matter how many times Jimmy had told him not to talk on the phone Lance couldn't seem to stop himself. "He's gonna get busted bro, and when he does, he's gonna take you down with 'im."

"Nah. Not Lance." We had been best friends since we were in middle school. "He loves me like a brother."

"When people get arrested they change. In the end everyone talks," said Jimmy, and his face took on a hard façade—cold and emotionless. "Lance can't handle the volume of business running through his hands. It's too much responsibility for him." He told me Lance's mouth would get him in trouble someday. Lance was constantly flaunting his cash and bragging about what he was doing. What *we* were doing. He did everything shy of introducing himself as a drug dealer. "You need to think about cutting him off and dealing directly with these guys in Alaska."

I reared my head back, slid off the stool I was sitting on, and stepped away from Jimmy. "I'm not gonna do that."

Jimmy took a deep breath and sighed. "You need to get away from this kid," he said. Then he leaned over and snorted a line of oxycodone off the counter. He sat up and wiped a bit of the powder from his nostrils. "Between you and me, I'm just waiting for them to ask me about him."

"Who?"

"The DEA." I'd heard rumors that Jimmy had gotten a light sentence by cooperating with the DEA in his case, but I had never believed them. Nor had I ever asked. I immediately became conscious that one of Jimmy's many surveillance cameras was pointed at us. My pulse picked up and a quiver of panic rippled through me. "How do you think I've been able to operate all these years without getting busted?"

"I'd . . . I'd never thought about it." For years people around Jimmy had been getting picked off by the DEA, but he had always managed to avoid an indictment. "You wouldn't say anything about us?"

"Look, I keep a low profile and they leave me alone. Sometimes I throw 'em a bone, but every once in a while they ask me to set someone up. I wouldn't be shocked if Lance was one of those guys."

Jimmy told me he liked me, but as far as he was concerned Lance was fair game. "The way he talks it'd be easy to crack his head wide open." Jimmy told me if I wanted to deal oxycodone long-term, I needed to think about working with the DEA as a confidential informant (CI). But I didn't want to deal oxycodone "long-term." I wanted a chunk of money and I was out. "Eventually, you'll show up on their radar too, and it'll be over."

I did the best I could to act like I was entertaining the idea. Then I bolted. Just before I got in my truck, Jimmy said, "Doug, this was just between you and me, right?"

"Right."

That night I couldn't sleep thinking about all the transactions Lance was making with Jimmy and the $20,000 in equipment I had sitting in his backyard. The next morning I showed up at Jimmy's house around 7:30 a.m. with an enclosed trailer, and started loading up my half of the stuff. Jimmy walked out of the house just as I was finishing up. "Oh, come on, Doug!" he said, throwing his hands in the air. "I knew I shouldn't have told you."

"I'm not judging you bro, I just think we should go our separate ways," I said, as I closed the back of the trailer. He tried to convince me that Lance and I had nothing to worry about, that he wasn't going to say anything. I wasn't so sure.

"Bro," he said, "do yourself a favor and don't mention this to anyone . . . especially Lance. I'd hate to have to put you in their sights. But if this gets out, I will."

Later that day, I asked Lance to meet me at the Florida Aquarium. It's a large facility located in downtown Tampa, right across the street from Lance's loft. "We need to talk," I said and motioned for him to follow me into the aquarium. Tiger sharks and stingrays swam by us in their panoramic glass tank. I relayed what Jimmy had told me to Lance.

"I don't believe it," he whispered, as a group of school kids on a field trip walked by. "He's an informant?"

"You've gotta stop talking on the phone, bro."

"Fuck . . . a fucking CI." But as shocked as Lance was, he never stopped openly talking on the phone.

That night, Lance told Jimmy they wouldn't be doing business together anymore. Jimmy called me a couple times, leaving messages, but I never returned any of them.

Less than a year after the DEA suspended Cardinal Health's controlled substance license, the company's CEO settled the charges by paying a $34 million fine. No one at Cardinal went to prison, of course, and their license was restored. By September 2008, the floodgates were opened again and opiates poured back into Florida pharmacies.

Chapter Ten

Opiate Addiction

"Matthew Gaddis died Jan. 27, 2009, after overdosing on pain-killers. He was 25. 'He really couldn't come to terms with the loss [of his older brother],' Brian Gaddis, 33, one of the two surviving brothers, said Wednesday. . . . 'He just sought any means possible to numb the pain.'"

—*Tampa Bay Times*

On the last Saturday night in October, Lance and I were in Ybor City for Guavaween, a Latin-tinged Halloween celebration and one of the largest festivals in Tampa. We watched the Mama Guava Stumble Parade's floats make their way down 7th Avenue while costumed figures threw candy and beads to the spectators. We listened to live bands and gawked at the drunk girls dressed up like hookers, strippers, sexy nuns, and nurses. The streets were filled with intoxicated vampires and superheroes.

By ten o'clock, Lance and I were drinking Coronas, watching people stumble around drunk and puke in the street. "I've gotta take a piss," I told Lance, and headed toward the port-a-potties.

Roughly a block off the strip, I ran into one of my ex–doctor shoppers in the crowd, a guy that had let me pay for his MRI, his initial pill mill appointment, and his scripts—roughly $2,500. Then he turned around and started selling his scripts to someone else. A mutual friend told me he ended up getting hooked on the product. He missed some doctor's appointments and ran out of pills. Eventually he lost his job, his car, and his apartment.

"Doug," he said, patting me on the back and giving me a big smile like we were old buddies. Like he hadn't fucked me over. "You got any oxys on you?"

"You've gotta be kidding . . . The way I see it you owe me twenty-five hundred bucks."

"Come on man," he said, and scrunched up his face as if I was being petty. "You're not still upset about that?" Then he went into this bullshit explanation about how it wasn't his fault, how he had planned to pay me back. Just like a junkie. But before he could reimburse me—plus interest, he added—he needed a couple of oxys. "To take the edge off, you know?" I did know, but I wasn't about to give him any. "Come on man!" he snapped. "You think I don't know about you and your buddies? You guys are rolling in oxys!"

People were starting to pay attention. "I don't know what you're talking about," I said. When I walked away I could feel his eyes boring into the back of my skull.

I walked to the port-a-potty area. A dozen blue dominos stacked side by side just off the strip. There were some costumed pedestrians loitering, but the area was mostly deserted. I stepped into one of the rectangular plastic crappers and managed to piss into the makeshift toilet, filled with thick blue disinfectant, without touching anything. I quickly buttoned and zipped up my pants and turned to exit. That's when I heard and felt something slam into the back of the shitter. The entire room violently shifted, and I was knocked into the interior wall behind the toilet as the rectangular room toppled over. I slammed onto the door, which was now the floor, as the entire contents of the makeshift toilet gushed on top of me. My stomach contracted and heaved as the blue disinfectant slush of feces, urine, and toilet paper exploded everywhere. Dark blue syrup covered every inch of me. The stench was overwhelming, and I immediately puked my guts out, compounding the mess.

When I realized the door was facing the ground and the structure was wedged between two other port-a-potties—making it impossible to roll over and open—I had a slight claustrophobic meltdown. *Fuck! Fuck! Fuck! This can't be my life.* My days were filled with dodging local law enforcement and arguing with pill heads. At night I was getting ripped off and attacked by junkies. Between the sheriffs, police, DEA, CIs, and the opiates I was so sick to my stomach I could hardly eat anymore.

I fumbled for my cell in the darkness, slick with sludge—and dialed Lance's cell. "What's up big daddy," he said, high and a little drunk. "Where you at?" I explained that I thought, although I wasn't one hundred percent sure, my ex–doctor shopper had pushed over the port-a-potty. With me in it! Once Lance stopped laughing. He asked, "Which one are you in?"

"The one on its fucking side!"

That started him laughing all over again. He eventually reached the face-down port-a-potty, lying in a puddle of neon-blue waste. I heard him giggling outside, saying to himself, "This is disgusting," as he pushed it upright. When I stepped out, Lance burst into laughter again. I was dripping with blue slime. "Ohmigod, you look like a Smurf," he said. "No, no, like a . . . like a member of Blue Man Group!"

He drove me, slipping and sliding in the bed of his truck, back to his place. I had never been so angry in my life. I stripped down to my boxers and put the clothes in a trash bag and threw them in a nearby dumpster. I scrubbed myself for like an hour with antibacterial soap while Lance was laughing his ass off, sitting on the pool deck and smoking a blunt. When I was done I dove into the swimming pool, hoping the chlorine would eradicate any germs that might be left, then I got out and scrubbed my entire body again. The whole time I thought about what I would do to that guy if I ever ran into him again, how badly I wanted to reconstruct his whole face. Of course, Lance didn't ease my thoughts about the situation. "If it was me," he said, "I'd kill 'im." To this day, I've never seen him. Last I heard, he got arrested for grand theft.

Maybe a week after Guavaween, around six o'clock, Lance and I were at his loft, counting out roughly twenty-five hundred oxycodones on his dining room table and watching the local news. He was jabbering about some argument he'd had with Richard or Landon, when I heard an anchor say, ". . . drug enforcement advocates and state representatives are teaming up to push for a statewide prescription drug database."

Both Lance and I stopped and turned our full attention to the plasma screen. A database would limit patients' ability to obtain prescriptions from multiple doctors; doctor shopping would be a thing of the past. The news played file footage of a spokesman for the Centers for Disease Control and Prevention. "Doctors are prescribing oxycodone at an alarming rate in pain clinics across

Florida." The anchor said that painkiller overdoses had killed near-ly fifteen thousand Americans in 2008. "It's an epidemic that has at-tacked America more suddenly than any drug has before."

The camera jumped to a Washington, DC, press conference packed with reporters. "The toll our nation's prescription drug abuse epidemic has taken in communities nationwide is devastat-ing," said Obama drug czar Gil Kerlikowske, standing behind a po-dium, an American flag standing in the background, "and Florida is ground zero."

The screen flipped back to the news studio. The anchor looked into the camera and said, "Opponents are concerned a statewide database would be an invasion of privacy and will only make it more difficult for patients that truly need the popular medication."

"Abso-fucking-lutely!" yelled Lance, as he poured a hundred Roxicodones into a funnel perched on top of an empty vitamin D bottle. "It's only gonna make it harder for regular patients to get oxys," he barked at the television. Then he turned to me and snick-ered, "It's not like it's gonna stop us," as he filled up another brown plastic bottle. He was right. The bulk of our doctor shoppers weren't going to more than one doctor. "What they need to do is decrimi-nalize drugs and tax 'em . . . like Amsterdam." Massive addiction, opiate dens, and overdoses. Yeah, that's the answer.

Not everyone paid. Sometimes people avoid you or make excuses why they can't pay. Hell, sometimes they just hang up the phone or tell you to "fuck off!"

In Tennessee, "Pretty Boy" Landon had been having this problem; he fronted a fellow student and dealer, Mark, with one to two thousand painkillers a month. For the first few months, Mark was solid. But then he started using more and more, and coming up short week after week. Sometime around early November Mark showed up at Landon's apartment and asked him to front a hundred pills. "Fuck that," snapped Landon, "you're into me for four thousand dollars, dude."

"Come on, man," replied Mark fidgeting and scratching. "I'm good for it." Landon had been listening to his excuses for the last few months. "I'll have it in two weeks, man."

Landon was so hopelessly addicted himself he took pity on Mark and fronted him ten roxie 30s. "If you don't have the money in two weeks, Justin and I are gonna come to your house and beat the cash out of you. I'm not fucking around anymore."

Roughly a week later Mark stopped answering Landon's calls and moved. Landon was pissed! It took him several weeks to find out where Mark was living—a wood frame bungalow in a historic area near Cumberland University.

On December 3, Landon stopped by the house and banged on the front door. When Mark opened it Landon yanked him out onto the porch. "You forget to tell me you moved, motherfucker?!" he yelled, while pushing Mark up against the exterior of the bungalow. "Where's my fucking money?!"

Mark was, without a doubt, eye-bulgingly terrified. "I got the money!" he sputtered out. "I got it! Jesus, I got it!" Landon relaxed his grip while Mark explained the money was inside the house. "I was gonna call you." he said, running his hand over his rumpled T-shirt, as he walked into the house to retrieve the cash. "Give me a sec."

Less than a minute later the front door squeaked open, Landon turned to see Mark pointing a flat-black semiautomatic pistol at his forehead. Apparently Mark had spent some of the cash on a Glock 9 mm. "I ain't got shit for you!" growled Mark squeezing the grip so tightly the weapon was shaking. Landon slowly backed off the porch toward his truck. "You couldn't just let it go could you, fuckboy?"

"I'm coming back for that money," said Landon, as he climbed into his vehicle.

"No, you're not. I've got something for ya."

Later that day an anonymous source contacted the local law enforcement's narcotic squad. According to a DEA affidavit: "Detective Kenny Powers of the Lebanon Police Department informed DEA agents that he had received information that Landon Barabas had been receiving packages from Tampa, Florida that possibly contained narcotics." Detective Powers then contacted the Cumberland University post office and asked them to notify him the next time Landon Barabas received an overnight package.

About that same time, Landon called his kid brother in a panic. "Lance, you've gotta overnight me some pills today." Despite the fact that Landon was distributing close to ten thousand pills per month in Tennessee, he was so strung out on opiates that he somehow managed to run out of oxycodone for himself. "I'm down to a couple berries. If I don't get something soon, I'm gonna get sick." Those roxies wouldn't be enough for his needs.

"Seriously?"

"Do I sound like I'm fucking around?!" Lance FedExed four hundred painkillers to Landon's Cumberland University post office box.

The next morning—December 4—Landon pulled into the post office parking lot. He shot into the building and signed for the package. No problem. But when he turned to leave, Landon noticed an undercover sedan with two law enforcement types inside, slowly cruising through the parking lot. Landon stopped, glanced around the lot, and checked the interior of every vehicle he could. As the sedan drove away, he decided they weren't there for him.

He exited the post office, tore open the package, and grabbed a vitamin bottle. Landon's entire body ached for the opiates, and he was perspiring, despite the frigid temperature outside. As he unscrewed the vitamin bottle's lid, four black sedans converged on him. They screeched to a stop, and half a dozen Lebanon narcotics officers swarmed out of the vehicles with their weapons drawn. "Down on the ground!" they screamed. "Down on the ground!"

Landon dropped the pills and hit the pavement, adrenaline shooting through him as the agents pushed him face down into the puddle of Roxicodone and cuffed his hands behind his back. Landon was so strung out he shot his tongue out like a gecko and slurped up several pills before the officers could stop him.

They found over $22,000 in cash, dozens of empty vitamin bottles, and a four-foot stack of *Muscle & Fitness* and *Men's Health* magazines in a search of Landon's room—but no painkillers.

The way I heard it, Landon was taken to the Lebanon Police Department and placed in a windowless interview room where four florescent light fixtures hung from the ceiling, only two of which had working bulbs. The walls were filthy and the tiled flooring was stained. They left Landon in the room for several hours, waiting for his blood opiate level to drop. By four o'clock he wrapped his arms around his torso, rocking himself in the cheap plastic chair, hoping to ward off the aches and tremors. Around six o'clock, he was thoroughly pill sick. That's when two tough-looking narcotics officers entered the room, dropped into a couple chairs, and handed him a bucket. Instinctively, Landon hunched over and puked chunks of his breakfast into the receptacle. "Look," they growled, as Landon dry heaved, "you need to help yourself out here." They had seized almost four hundred roxies and oxys; there was no denying that Landon was trafficking oxycodone. "The next few minutes of this conversation are going to determine the rest of your life," said one of the officers. "Understand?"

"Uh huh," whimpered Landon, face down in the bucket, perspiration rolling down his neck.

"Who's Lance Attaway?"

Landon looked up from the bucket and grunted, "Uh . . . " Now, Landon has always maintained that he told the agents "Attaway" was just some guy in Tampa, Florida, that occasionally supplied him with painkillers. Nothing more. He certainly did not give up his brother or any of his friends. However, DEA agent Bethel Poston's affidavit—and multiple other reports—contradict Landon's account: "Landon Barabas stated that his brother, Lance Barabas, sent him similar packages two or three times per month and that he [Landon] was selling the pills for a profit."

Back in Tampa, Lance gave his mother a wad of cash and put her on a plane. Once she was in Knoxville, he arranged to have one of his associates front the cash for Landon's criminal attorney. Ms. Barabas paid a bondsman $5,000 to put up the $50,000 bond, and she flew Landon back to Florida.

When Lance told me about the arrest I flipped out. "We should stop shipping to Tennessee or at least limit the amount of—"

"Are you fucking crazy?! I'm not gonna stop shipping. We need to be shipping more not less." All Lance could think of was pumping up the volume. The very real possibility of going to prison wasn't a part of his business model.

"You're gonna get us fucked."

The corners of Lance's lips pinched up for a split second and he chuckled. "I'd rather die a legend than live as a man."

I burst out laughing at his absurd reasoning and Lance got a big grin on his face. "Bro, where'd you come up with that?" I asked.

"I think it was *Braveheart*."

"That's the kind of thinking that's gonna get us all busted."

"Stop worrying! My mom's gonna take care of it." Pretty Boy had been arrested half a dozen times for trespassing, disorderly conduct, assault, burglary of a conveyance, and grand theft. And Ms. Barabas had always managed to get him off. "He'll be fine. It's not like Tennessee has a mandatory minimum."

The shipments were rerouted to Justin, along with several other distributors. And the oxycodone pipeline continued to flow into Tennessee.

It wasn't long after Landon's arrest that things started going wrong. I had watched people go within a few months from taking a couple roxies at a party to selling off everything they owned just to fund their addiction. I'd seen Ashley Cutter, a girl I knew in high school, get high on a "death cocktail" of Xanax and oxycodone, and die when she slammed her car head-on into another vehicle. I watched Matthew Gaddis, another friend addicted to painkillers—at this point, desperately trying to get clean—overdose on oxycodone while he had a pocket full of Suboxone, a detox medication.

My cousin Pete went into a methadone coma and had to have his stomach pumped at the emergency room. Around the time this was happening, my cousin Julian, another oxycodone addict trying to quit, came by my grandmother's house to ask me to front him some pills. "Doug, I just need a couple oxys," he pled, "I'm trying to get off 'em, I swear."

Why he thought I would give him the oxycodones, I don't know. I had just talked to him about getting off the shit, I wasn't about to feed his or any other family member's habit. "It's not gonna happen," I told him. "Why don't you just go to a rehab?"

"I can't afford it." A minute later, we were standing outside, Julian's eyes rolled back in his head, his knees buckled, and he took a nosedive into the lawn. He had taken thirty Somas, a muscle relaxer, in an effort to wean himself off the opiates and overdosed. I was so freaked out I stuck him in Town and Country Drug Rehab in Tampa the following day.

Later that week, I came home from class, walked through the front door with my book bag slung over my shoulder, and my grandmother was standing in the living room wiping tears out of her eyes. "Eric died."

"What?" I couldn't grasp that my cousin was dead.

"He's dead." Eric's mother had found his cold, lifeless body lying beside his bed hours earlier. Dead of a death cocktail. I remember my bag slipped off my shoulder and hit the floor with a thud. I could hear the rattle of my bottle of Roxicodones. Shocked doesn't begin to describe how I felt. I was overwhelmed by white noise. Blank. Numb.

Eric was cremated a few days later. My father and most of my family attended his viewing at my Aunt Bridy's house. There was nothing left of Eric but an urn and some photos of a happy, healthy, fun-loving guy who died of a lethal combination of oxycodone and

Xanax, the same combination of pharmaceuticals I was crushing up and snorting on a daily basis.

As my family stood around sharing stories about Eric, I couldn't help but think how long it would be before they were doing the same for me. I was already waking up two or three times a week with cold sweats and aching from opiate withdrawals. I was popping a couple roxies to get myself out of bed in the morning and smoking crystal (lime-green hydroponic marijuana that looked like it was covered in crystals) to work up enough of an appetite to drink a strawberry-and-banana smoothie for breakfast. I was doing between seven and ten roxie 30s a day, plus a few 40 mg oxys—roughly $5,000-a-month worth of pills.

Oxycodone had gone from recreational to an all-consuming addiction. It was destroying everything in my life. My family and friends were getting arrested, overdosing, and dying. I made up my mind to cycle myself off the opiates as soon as possible. But it was much harder than I thought.

The aches and pains. The chills and shakes. Dry mouth. Insomnia. I started taking Suboxone and Subutex, another detox medication, to help with the cravings. The withdrawals were nothing compared to the shit I had to put up with from Lance and the guys. While I was desperately struggling to get sober they were increasing their doses, slamming and snorting more and more oxycodone every day. For the most part Lance was holding it together, but Landon had deteriorated into a straight junkie.

They fucked with me mercilessly for trying to get clean. "Dude, you don't have to quit, just cut back," Lance suggested when I told him I was quitting. But it was impossible. One or two oxys was never going to be enough. "You're not gonna be any fun anymore."

"I'll be plenty of fun, bro." The truth is I was already trying to distance myself from the parties and the clubs. The mere thought of a club like Parana or Sky made me want to pop a Xanax and snort an oxy. "Another couple hundred thousand and I'm gonna quit."

"I'll believe that when I see it."

For Christmas, I flew up to New York. I needed to be around a semifunctioning family, some semblance of normalcy. An opiate-free holiday with my father, stepmother Debbie, and three sisters. Weed-free brownies and non-spiked eggnog.

Christmas morning, after everyone had torn open their gifts and raided their stockings, my stepmother's best friend showed up with her seventeen-year-old daughter, Maya, a five-foot-three dirty blonde with forest-green eyes, porn-star breasts, and girl-next-door looks. I had met her while attending school in Richfield Springs. She was several grades behind me and we ran with different cliques. I was a little party animal, selling weed in the boys' room and she was a prudish preppy socialite who sang in a Christian rock band. We had never had any real interest in each other, but that morning when Maya walked in my dad's house, her face lit up.

My dad, younger sister, Maya, and I all went snowboarding on Labrador Mountain. There were six inches of powder on the slopes—perfect for snowboarding. We had a blast. Maya and I flirt-ed most of the day; there was a lot of grinning and giggling. By the time she left later that night, we had swapped numbers. We hung out over the next couple days, went to several graduation parties, and I even let her drag me to an event at her church.

For New Year's Eve my dad, Debbie, three sisters, and I drove to New York City to watch the ball drop in Times Square. It took about three hours to find somewhere to park in midtown. Then we had to hike up to the intersection of 7th Avenue and 43rd. We stood among a crowd of over a hundred thousand waiting for the ball to drop. The big screen counted down and the crowd counted with it, "Three! Two! One! Happy New Year! Happy New Year!" and everyone burst out singing, "Auld Lang Syne" ("Should old acquaintance be forgot . . . "). As cold as it was, it was worth the drive.

The night before I went back to Florida, I snuck Maya into the spare room I was staying in. By this point, the sexual tension between us was so thick you could taste it in the air. We had been incessantly dry-humping each other for the past week and kissing to the point of chapped lips. Now I finally had her alone with her shirt unbuttoned and I slipped a hand inside her jeans.

It went on for a minute or two, then I moved to pull her jeans off. Maya grabbed my hand and said, "I can't." My first thought was, *She's got a boyfriend. Or maybe a girlfriend. Who knows?* I was totally caught off guard when she said, "I'm a virgin."

"A virgin!" gasped Lance. We were at his loft and I was telling him about my trip. He was staring at a picture of Maya I had taken with my cell phone. "You're telling me there's a hot seventeen-year-old *virgin* living in the United States?"

"Yeah. Bro, she's so sweet and—"

"Bullshit! The seventeen-year-old virgin is extinct; like Tyrannosauruses and mammoths." Then "the Little General" said if I had told him I'd seen a yeti, Bigfoot, or an alien, he would have believed me. "But not a virgin."

"She's very religious. She's a Christian."

"Christian!" he spat. "Now you're just making shit up. Next you'll be telling me her older brother's Jesus and she drives a donkey." Lance slipped a 40 mg OxyContin tablet into his mouth and laughed. "I don't even know what a virgin looks like. I haven't seen one since I was fourteen, have you?"

I yanked my cell phone out of his hand and pointed to Maya's picture. "That's a virgin, asshole!"

"My God!" He grabbed the phone back and took a closer look. "You're delusional, dude. Next you'll tell me that you believe unicorns are real."

Chapter Eleven

The Drug Enforcement Administration

"The Drug Enforcement Administration . . . is cracking down on pill mills—rogue doctors and shady pharmacies that divert highly addictive pills such as oxycodone to drug dealers."

—*USA Today*

On February 27, 2009, I was dropping off an assortment of nearly 1,900 roxies and oxys at Victory Lofts. Right as I walked through the door Lance said, "Don't freak out, but you've gotta see this." He was sitting on his couch watching the news. There were roughly a dozen DEA agents and Pasco County sheriff's deputies on the screen, leading over a dozen handcuffed defendants—*people we knew*—into the federal building in downtown Tampa. Lance pointed at the flat screen and said, "That's Billy" as a middle-aged sleeved-out biker exited the van full of conspirators. Then I saw Jerald Gulio, whose younger brother went to school with me, and little Jessie Krumm, a guy I used to get stoned with.

The shot returned to the studio. The anchor turned to the camera and announced, "Today, federal agents of the Drug Enforcement Administration arrested nineteen suspects in Operation Oxy Express. According to court documents, Arde Olsen, age fifty-one, has been running an extensive ring of 'doctor shoppers.'" The scene broke to the field reporter in front of the federal building's entrance. "Federal authorities say the defendants were paying for MRIs, doctor visits, and prescriptions for oxycodone at area pharmacies. They would then distribute large quantities of the drug to dealers across Florida and throughout the country."

Some of those guys were friends of my uncle. Guys that lived down the street from us. Guys that I had seen on and off my entire life. Guys I'd seen dropping off doctor shoppers at some of the same pill mills and pharmacies I frequented. A ripple of fear ran through me as the lead DEA agent looked into the camera, into Lance's living room, and growled, "We're conducting operations like Oxy Express throughout Florida in an effort to quell the painkiller epidemic plaguing the southern states."

Lance looked at me and sighed. "Stop worrying," he said. "We're good." The King of Hudson organization that was busted in the operation was run by career criminals with decades of experience. If they got caught, so could we.

A week or two after the bust, I was sitting in the parking lot of M.D. & More, a health clinic, studying economics, and waiting for one of my doctor shoppers to come back from his appointment—pretty typical stuff. The lot was packed with patients' vehicles. I'm not sure why, but I glanced up from my textbook and noticed a couple guys sitting in a grey Ford sedan with dark-tinted windows parked catty-corner from me. Hard-looking law enforcement types with short-cropped haircuts and chiseled jaws. And they were staring directly at me. I slowly glanced around the lot and noticed another Ford sedan, white with two silhouettes inside, and a black Chevy van that I imagined was full of SWAT team members or DEA agents. My heart started thumping, hard and fast, like a Black & Decker jigsaw.

I had around ninety roxies in my brown plastic pharmacy bottle sitting in my glove box—a mandatory minimum of fifteen years—but I had a prescription for them.

Unfortunately, I had two of my doctor shoppers' Walgreens bags in the back seat, both containing 240 Roxicodone 30 mgs and 120 OxyContin 80 mgs—a total of 720 oxycodone tablets and a mandatory minimum of twenty-five years. No fucking way I could talk my way out of that. Then it hit me, and I hate to admit this, but I thought, *Landon was just arrested and he's probably cooperating with the feds.* For all I knew the DEA had been watching me for weeks and I had never even noticed. I'd certainly incriminated myself by this point and they were here to catch me in the act with a doctor shopper and a car full of pills. *Fuck!* Just then my doctor shopper walked out of the clinic. He actually grinned at me from across the parking lot and waved his scripts in the air like a flag. That's when the agents popped their doors and jumped out of the sedans, and the van's cargo door slid open and half a dozen agents in black Kevlar vests poured out—DEA stenciled across their chests in a bold, white font, their M-4 assault rifles and Glocks held ready.

"Outta the car! Outta the car!" several screamed as the entire group converged on my Toyota Tacoma. My doctor shopper froze, his eyes bulged slightly, and he slowly raised his hands while frantically swiveling his head from agent to agent. The air thinned and I couldn't catch my breath. This might sound crazy, but when the agents got roughly twenty feet away I suddenly remembered I hadn't mowed my grandmother's yard. I raised my hands to the ceiling and thought, *Who's gonna mow Grandma's yard?*

They kept yelling, "Outta the car! Outta the car!" as they approached. But when I reached for the door handle one of the agents stopped me. He placed his hand on the outside of the door as the entire group passed by my Tacoma and continued to scream at the passengers sitting in the Chevy Tahoe behind my truck, one space over. I took a deep cleansing breath as a wave of relief flowed through me. My blood pressure dropped and my heart slowed its beating. I glanced over my shoulder at the agents yanking on the Tahoe's locked doors. Two of them raised their assault rifles and used the butt of the weapons to smash the driver and passenger windows into a thousand pieces.

My doctor shopper slipped into my truck as several DEA agents dragged the two Tahoe occupants out of the smashed windows. As we drove off, the agents struggled with their suspects, yelling, "Stop resisting! Stop resisting!" and pummeling them into the pavement.

"Jesus!" gasped the doctor shopper watching the scene out of the rear window. "I thought that was for us."

"So did I."

After we picked up his pills I went home and mowed my grandmother's yard. Then I cleaned the gutters and washed both dogs. When Grandma came home I was pulling a load of clothes out of the drier. "My Lord!" she gasped, "what's going on, Douglas?"

"Nothing Gram, I'm just catching up on some chores."

She meandered around the house for a few minutes and came back into the living room where I was folding my clothes. "Well, something's wrong," she mumbled. "You never do the laundry."

Several months later Maya graduated Richfield High School. I filled a couple prescription bottles with roxies and oxys and caught a flight to New York. I dropped off the pills with my buddy Andy and watched Maya walk across the stage in her cap and gown.

She stayed with me at my father's and stepmother's house. We rolled around half naked most of the night, but Maya wasn't about to give it up. The next morning we were all eating breakfast and my dad gave me a *Did you sleep with her?* look. I growled under my breath, "Not even close."

I remember he grinned at me and whispered, "Sorry, buddy." Then he started laughing uncontrollably in front of everyone.

Once Maya left, he said, "She's giving you a hard time, huh?"

"You have no idea."

By the time I left, the virgin thing was wearing thin. I flew back with blue balls and $10,000 in cash from Andy, $5,000 shy of what he owed me. That was another regular problem.

Meanwhile, Lance wouldn't stop shipping. He hired Larry "the Lineman," his four-hundred-pound older brother to help him co-ordinate the shipments and launder the cash through the LUCI e-cigarette account. Lance was blowing money and throwing parties every weekend, even though Landon had just been arrested and the police were certainly investigating the source of the oxycodones.

Every single time I collected a bag full of pills from one of my doctor shoppers, or handed them a fistful of cash, I was certain the

DEA was going to pounce on me. If I arranged a swap of pills in the mall or a fast food restaurant, I would swear everyone with a cell or an MP3 player was watching me.

Once I picked up a doctor shopper from a pharmacy and a middle-aged man driving a Cadillac gave me a double take. It was nothing, but I spent the next hour driving around in circles checking for a tail.

In early June of 2009 Lance told me he wanted to go to the Bonnaroo Music and Art Festival in Tennessee. "Come on!" he begged. "We'll drive up with a shitload of pills and hook up with Justin and a bunch of his guys. It's gonna be a blast."

"I can't. I'm in the middle of too much right now." I was trying to get our LUCI kiosks into several Smoothie Kings and a few Subway sandwich shops, making calls and writing emails to multiple people at both franchises. Between the two of us I was the only one actually trying to make the e-cigarettes business work. Plus, I was still struggling to stay off the opiates.

I had grown tired of being dependent on the pills. The fun or joy of getting high had now become a routine of getting my fix in order to operate at a normal mental capacity. I knew I didn't want to continue taking the pain pills much longer so I was working hard at slowly cycling off them.

Four days at Bonnaroo—no fucking way could I have stayed clean, and Lance knew that.

"Bro—music, drugs, tits, and ass," he said. "Tell me you're not gonna pass that up?"

"Yeah. I am."

"Bro, fuck those robot-cigarettes!"

"Sorry."

"I knew it!" he snapped. "You're no fun at all anymore, bro."

Later that month, Lance and Richard drove up to Tennessee with five thousand oxycodones and met up with Justin and his friend Dustin. A thin crop-cut Tennessean with perpetual five o'clock shadow, Dustin was Justin's right-hand man for distribution. They were joined by a couple of guys who were selling for Dustin: Brett, a dark, shaggy-haired druggie, and Tyler, a tall, thin kid with curly hair. They rented an RV and headed to the festival in Manchester, a two-hour drive from Knoxville. Roughly seventy-five thousand people attended the four-day event. People were rolling on ecstasy and tripping on LSD while roaming from tent to tent, listening to Snoop Dogg rap "Gin and Juice," and the Beastie Boys do "No Sleep till Brooklyn."

Lance and the guys were selling roxies and oxys out of the back of the RV like it was legal. By day two they were out of pills and completely fried. Richard was so fucked-up on K2 (a type of synthetic marijuana) and ecstasy, Lance had to tie a string to his belt to keep old "Shit Dick" from wandering off. It was four days of debauchery and drug-induced insanity that I'm glad I missed.

By the time Bruce Springsteen came out and did "Born in the USA" and "Dancing in the Dark," they were out of weed and pills and ready to head back to Knoxville.

The morning after Bonnaroo, Lance stumbled out of Justin's condo, crawled into his Ford, and made his way down I-75, what law enforcement calls the "OxyContin Express," with a grocery bag full of cash.

Roughly a week later—June 23—Lance threw one of his *Blow*-style parties at Victory Lofts. There were silver trays of cocaine and goblets of roxies being passed around. The place was filled with college kids smoking weed, drinking out of Jagermeister kegerators, and dancing to Top 40 music.

Lance spread out one hundred grand on his king-sized bed and let a dozen drunken sorority girls snap photos of each other rolling around in the cash before posting them on Facebook. Coeds were getting fucked up on pills, striking *Charlie's Angels* poses in nothing but lingerie, and holding Lance's assault rifles and handguns.

Around ten o'clock, Lance and I were smoking a blunt on the balcony and listening to the music billowing out of the sliding glass doors. "Bro," said Lance, "you've gotta get a place here."

My associates were all living in posh houses and condos, but I had never moved out of my grandmother's spare room. "She's seventy-seven years old, bro. I can't leave her."

Five hundred miles away in Knoxville, Tennessee, Justin and a couple of buddies were about to call it a night, smoking a joint in the condo he and his girlfriend shared. The way I heard it, when Justin's buddies left, they took the blunt with them. They stepped into the hallway and took a couple tokes in front of several neighbors who were returning home for the evening. They continued downstairs to the lobby, smoking and laughing like everything was cool.

The neighbors immediately called the Knoxville Police Department, and five minutes later, at 10:30 p.m., two officers knocked on Justin's door. He opened the door and the officers instantly smelled the pungent odor of marijuana and saw drug paraphernalia in plain sight. Justin was glassy-eyed and his speech was slurred.

The officers asked him for permission to search the residence, but the oxy distributor refused. However, based on what the officers witnessed, it didn't take long to obtain a search warrant. They contacted Special Agent Bethel Poston, or "Bubba," a stocky, clean-cut DEA agent with a thick head of gelled hair. The Knoxville police officer asked if Bubba and several other agents would help assist them with the execution of the search warrant.

After the DEA arrived, Justin and his girlfriend were placed in handcuffs. They sat quietly at the dining room table as the agents and officers ripped through his closets and drawers. They found around $3,000 in cash, a garbage can full of empty painkiller prescription bottles, bags of Roxicodones and OxyContins, marijuana, an assortment of steroids, approximately twenty-four vials of injectable human growth hormone, and a blank prescription pad to a Miami pill mill. But what really upset the agents and officers was Justin's arsenal: a Smith & Wesson 9 mm handgun, a KelTec 9 mm, a Walther P22, a Sig Sauer P226, and an Intratec TEC-9 machine pistol—all with fully loaded magazines.

The Knoxville Police Department placed Justin and his girlfriend under arrest for armed trafficking.

The following morning, as we were lying on the beach recovering from the party at Lance's place, Justin was walking out of the Knoxville Police Department. He dialed Lance's cell and said, "We've gotta talk, man," and immediately recounted the arrest, though he played down the seriousness of the charges like it was no big deal. "I'm not that worried," he told Lance. "With a good lawyer I can beat it."

Keep in mind that the pills seized by the Knoxville Police Department were from Lance and me. In addition, Justin owed Lance close to $100,000, and now he needed money for an attorney. "We'll work it out," said Lance. "I'm coming up."

Maybe an hour later, Lance and I were shoveling down a couple of hot dogs we had bought from a beachside roach coach as Lance explained the situation. "It's not that big of a deal," he said. "I'll take care of it."

Rule number eight: Cease all contact with anyone under investigation. "I know you like Justin, bro," I remember telling him, "but it sounds like he's in a lot of trouble. The smart move here is to give 'im some cash and walk away."

"It's Justin. He's family," scoffed Lance. He said the "smart move" was to fly up there, make some moves, and get Justin an attorney. "You think everyone's gonna cooperate. Trust me, he's good."

By this point Justin had become our main distributor in Tennessee.

The three of us hung out and partied together when he came down but I never really cared for Justin. Lance, however, thought the world of the kid. They became friends very quickly. Every time Justin came down they were doing something big, such as getting VIP service in the clubs, going to concerts, skydiving.

That night Lance flew up to Tennessee. Justin only had $60,000 of the money he owed Lance; out of that, Lance gave him $50,000 for a criminal attorney. Everything seemed under control. When Lance flew back a couple days later, he told me it was "all taken care of."

Shortly thereafter, the State of Tennessee dropped Justin's charges. But due to the prescription pad, steroids, oxycodones, and the weapons, the feds immediately picked them up.

For most drug dealers, the involvement of the US attorney's office would have been devastating. Unlike state criminal courts, in the federal system, the accused has very little in the way of rights. As a result, the US attorney's offices boast a 97 percent conviction rate. And the sentences are draconian.

I expect that Justin's lawyer explained that he had little recourse in fighting the federal government. On July 10, 2009, Justin and his attorney attended a meeting at the federal building in downtown Knoxville. Justin spilled his guts out to a conference room full of DEA agents and Assistant US Attorney Lewen—a tall, lean, clean-cut conservative type sporting a 1950s haircut, a gray suit, and a serious expression.

In an affidavit, Special Agent Poston relayed the details that Justin shared: "Knox told agents that he had been receiving drug packages from [Lance] BARABAS and sending bulk drug proceeds back to BARABAS for approximately one year. He said that he had previously been supplying [Dustin] WALLACE with the drugs from [Lance] BARABAS and LANDON, and WALLACE and Tyler HENRY distributed the drugs to others unknown in Knoxville, Tennessee." Justin then explained how we would ship the packages and get the bulk of the money: "Members of the organization would fill otherwise legitimate pill bottles to store illegally obtain oxycodone. Knox collected the proceeds from the drug sales by WALLACE and HENRY and sent them to the BARABAS brothers in Tampa, Florida. Knox stated that the typical drug money package contained between $5,000 to $9,000 each."

Justin gave them everything. The pill mills. The scripts. The shipments. The money.

Everything.

The feds never did indict Justin. But as a result of the weapons and ammunition seized from Justin's condo, and the number of weapons Lance had registered in his name, Assistant US Attorney Lewen requested that the DEA fast-track or "rush" the investigation into the Barabas Criminal Enterprise. The operation was dubbed "Oxy Rush."

Shortly after that meeting, Lance and I were out on his boat, spearfishing, and Justin called Lance's cell, "I'm too hot. I think the DEA might be watching me."

"I understand," said Lance. "Cool off for a couple months and we'll pick up again." Justin then suggested Lance start dealing with Dustin Wallace directly, and ship the packages to Dustin's residence. "Sounds good," agreed Lance.

Roughly the same time Justin called, DEA agent Poston and Lauderdale County Drug Task Force officer Jason Butler sat down with an informer who called Dustin Wallace to set up a deal for OxyContin 80 mgs. "I need to meet up and get some Big Dogs. Ten of 'em."

"Uh huh," grunted Dustin. "I got you." They spoke briefly and arranged to meet at Admiral Farragut Park later that day.

Special Agent Poston taped a body wire to the informer and handed him $550 cash for the buy. At roughly 6:10 p.m., the guy met Dustin at the park. They sat at a table underneath a pavilion where the two swapped the cash and the oxys. A month later, on August 5, Poston and Officer Butler met with their man a second time. He was equipped with a wire, and $1,800 to purchase ninety Roxicodone 30 mg pills. At around 2:45 p.m., the informer purchased ninety roxies from Dustin at the residence of a man named William Kaman.

On September 9, as a result of the audio recordings made during the drug buys, Special Agent Poston convinced US District Judge Thomas Varlan to sign a court order allowing the DEA to intercept audio and electronic (text) communications of Dustin Wallace's telephone.

According to the DEA's report, they began the intercepts on September 10. At 1:34 p.m., they listened in on a call from Lauren F. as she tried to score OxyContin 80 mg pills. "You home?" she asked. "I need to come by and get some of them you know, eighties. Twenty of 'em." Dustin met her in his apartment complex's parking lot, where Lauren handed him a wad of cash for a bag of painkillers. All of this took place under DEA surveillance.

Around the same time, James LaPointe, an oxy customer of Justin and Dustin who owned a security company, called Dustin and told him he wanted to buy "ten to fifteen Xanax." They met about thirty minutes later in Dustin's parking lot. Agents filmed the entire transaction.

Over the next few weeks Dustin set up dozens of drug deals using his monitored cell phone. He met Pamela P. at a Shell station at 7:58 p.m. She bought a gang of roxie 30s. Twenty minutes later he hooked up with Jasmine R. at a Sonic to sell her a batch of roxies and oxys. After that, he connected with Jenessa C. at a Sears. Not long after that he met Kerri C. and Justin L. at his apartment.

Then Michael B., Joseph A., Jennifer B. The list goes on and on.

Every transaction was captured live and in color by DEA surveillance.

Unfortunately, while Dustin was making his deliveries, he was openly talking with Lance about "running low on 'blues'" and "needing more 'bigs.'" Sometimes it was the lower dose of oxy, or "forties." They talked about shipping via UPS and FedEx, and making cash deposits into Lance's Bank of America accounts. All of this was also recorded on audio and video.

As a result, on September 30, the DEA easily convinced Judge Thomas Varlan to issue audio and electronic intercept warrants for Lance Barabas's cell phone.

I later found out that the Tampa DEA also started following us and staking out our houses.

They set up surveillance of me at an empty Habitat for Humanity construction site catty-corner to my grandmother's house. The agents took multiple photos of me climbing in and out of my Toyota with a backpack full of textbooks and possibly prescription pill bottles. I was probably headed to class or a pill mill.

I have no doubt they took similar photos of Lance shipping tens of thousands of painkillers throughout the United States via FedEx, UPS, and DHL offices.

Because my Uncle Tony had done some time in federal prison for a drug conspiracy, and I occasionally stopped by to see him, the DEA spent a considerable amount of time staking out his welding shop. I'm certain they were convinced he was involved somehow. But he wasn't.

While the DEA was watching the "Barabas Criminal Organization" and their associates conspire to distribute oxycodone throughout the Unites States, Maya flew down to Florida. She had been offered a full scholarship to Full Sail University's School of Music in Orange County. She spent a day wandering around the campus, then shot across the state to New Port Richey.

My grandmother stayed at her "friend's" place most of the week, so Maya and I had the house to ourselves. Not that it mattered. My seventy-seven-year-old grandmother was seeing more action than I was. Maya and I spent most of that first night rolling around underneath the sheets of my bed, but nothing serious. So, I decided to focus on the tourist thing; we rode the roller coasters at Busch Gardens, slid down the waterslides of Adventure Island, went rafting in Okeechobee River, and got sunburned on the beach at Clearwater.

A couple nights before Maya left, my buddy Louie rented a limo for his girlfriend's birthday and took us and some of his girl's friends around town. Maya was only eighteen at the time, and didn't look enough like my buddy's twenty-two-year-old sister to use her Florida ID. So when the limo dropped us off at Reef, a club in Clearwater, Maya wasn't able to get in. While Louie, his girl, and her friends went dancing, we ate dinner at Carrabba's. At about eleven o'clock, the limo picked everyone up again and took us to the Hard Rock Casino. But Maya couldn't get in there either.

We ended up walking barefoot on Clearwater Beach at midnight. I remember Maya was irritated because a girl had been flirting with me in the limo. "She's probably a whore," griped Maya. "Is that the kind of girl you like?"

"No, she was disgusting." Actually, she was a very sexy brunette with amazingly long legs and exactly the type of girl I liked. "I'd never—"

Maya gave me a skeptical sideways glare. "If I move down here, I want us to be together," she said. "Doug, you can't be sleeping with girls like that if we're gonna be together."

"I'm not seeing anyone right now." But I wasn't committing to anything, either. I liked Maya; she was the type of girl I could see myself with. However, she thought Lance and I were legitimate LUCI e-cigarette retailers; not opiate wholesalers. Not conspirators in a multistate, multimillion-dollar drug-trafficking ring. That seemed like the type of thing that might be a problem for her.

Chapter Twelve

Outta Control

"As Clint Wilson closed his tattoo parlor at about 11:30 p.m. Tuesday night, someone shot him twice in the head."

—*St. Petersburg Times*

When Landon got back to Hudson, Ms. Barabas put him up in a rental house she owned. She tried to keep an eye on him—we all did. Maybe he had too much time on his hands or was stressed out about his pending charges, but Landon was out of control. He partied all the time, popping Xanax, snorting coke, and downing way too many oxycodones.

Lance and I were trying to taper him off and get him sobered up—at least I was—when he crossed the line. Landon had several friends from Cumberland University's wrestling team come down to party, and they wanted painkillers. Landon knew not to ask me for anything. One, I wasn't interested in feeding his addiction, and two, everything I had went to his brother. So Landon tried to ambush my buddy Thomas as he was getting in his truck outside the Beef O'Brady's restaurant in Hudson. They talked for a couple minutes and Landon asked, "You got any oxys?"

"Yeah." Thomas shrugged. "But everything I've got goes to Doug."

"I've got cash," replied Landon, and he flashed Thomas a wad of greenbacks. "Doug doesn't have to know."

"I don't think so, bro." I'll never know exactly what happened, but as soon as Thomas pulled out of the parking lot he called me and recounted the conversation. "Landon tried to fuck you outta my pills," he said point blank. My jaw went slack. "I thought you two were tight."

"So did I."

When I called Landon, he told me he had only asked for any extra pills Thomas might have. "I wouldn't try and snake you outta Thomas's shit, bro," he laughed nervously. "You know me, dude."

"I thought I did," I growled, then hung up. I ignored his calls for the next month, but eventually he caught me at Lance's loft and made a heartfelt apology filled with stuff like, "I love you like a brother, Dougie," and "I'd never betray your trust, bro," and "You mean the world to me, man." I still can't believe that I bought it. I told him I forgave him, but I damn sure didn't trust him anymore. You can't trust an addict.

Around the same time, "the Little General" was going to drive twenty-five hundred pills up to Knoxville. Just before he left, Lance told Landon not to fill his scripts, knowing his older brother wouldn't be able to resist taking some of them. It was only a four-day trip. But Landon couldn't stop himself. By the time Lance got back, Landon had filled his scripts and gobbled down a couple dozen pills. "You junkie fuck!" screamed Lance when he found out. "I needed those fucking pills!" Lance walked around in circles for a couple seconds, digging his fingers into his hair and grinding his teeth. Then he snapped, "We're done! I'm cutting you off."

Landon had devolved into a complete degenerate. He was so strung out you couldn't even have a conversation with him. His speech was perpetually slurred and he was constantly nodding out. Landon's entire world had shrunk down to smoking weed and snorting pills. He went from a potential All-American collegiate athlete to a full-blown drug addict.

His mother spent $12,000 to have him admitted to Windmor Health Center (a residential drug treatment facility) for four weeks. However, Landon somehow managed to sneak his prescriptions of roxies and oxys into the facility and finished the program with opiates flowing through his veins.

The following night he went out with a bunch of his junkie buddies. Lance called me up and said, "Pretty Boy's out getting fucked up. The rehab didn't take."

While all of this was happening, Lance pulled some sleazy shit of his own. When Landon got arrested back in December, Ms. Barabas needed cash to pay for Landon's Tennessee criminal attorney. Danny, Lance's Alaska connect, fronted Lance $25,000 to put toward Landon's attorney fees. That was the kind of guy he was. But instead of paying him back, Lance took the opportunity to fuck him over. He had a dozen excuses to justify it, of course. "Danny owes me seventeen grand for this" and "three grand for that." But it was all bullshit. The way I see it, Lance fucked him out of the money. As a result, Danny wouldn't do business with him anymore.

It didn't take long before Danny friended me on Facebook and asked if we could talk. He wanted to discuss a "business arrangement." I kept putting off the meeting because of my friendship with Lance, but after fucking over Danny, Lance's actions continued to worsen. He was so hooked on weed and opiates that we'd go to Hooters or Wing House and he would nod out at the bar. He was smoking an ounce of hydro a week, by himself! Sleeping until noon. Spending every dime he made—often before he officially had the money—and going broke trying to prove to everyone what a big shot he was. It wouldn't have bothered me so much if it weren't for the fact that I had to front him everything on consignment. Finally, I agreed to meet Danny.

He drove down from Tennessee and I met him behind a Wal-Mart in New Port Richey. No cameras and lots of visibility. I knew Danny and I liked him, but I'd had so many close calls lately I didn't trust him. "Spread eagle," I said as soon as he got out of his truck. "Put your hands on the roof of the car—"

"Seriously, dude?"

"Fuck, yeah, seriously," I replied. Then I pushed him up against the vehicle and patted him down. I took the batteries out of both our cells and tossed them on the hood of his car. "Okay, start talking."

He started with, "You know Lance fucked me over, right?"

"Yeah," I begrudgingly admitted. "I know, and I'm sorry Danny. I—"

"It's not your fault, dude." There was a long uncomfortable silence, where we both thought about what Lance had done. Then Danny sighed and said, "I know you guys are friends, but I need some pills."

"How many?" He wanted as many as I could get him. "I can do five hundred, right now, but I can't guarantee the same amount every month, and I'm not gonna ship 'em."

"I'll pick 'em up," he said.

I sold Danny a combination of five hundred roxies and oxys and fronted him another 280 oxys. A little over a week later he was back with the cash. He paid for another five hundred oxycodone and I fronted him five hundred more. Danny was the kind of guy that I could see dealing with long term. He was quiet, reserved, and smart. It's all about longevity, which was something Lance couldn't understand.

The way I figured it, I could slowly start shifting my oxycodone supply from Lance to Danny without Lance finding out. Not that I cared if he did; he knew he was screwing up and that I was unhappy, but he wasn't making much of an effort to better his actions. He was becoming a serious liability.

In addition to the new agreement with Danny, my cousin wanted more pills all the time, and Ethan—my 6'8" Hawaiian-looking buddy from high school who was going to Louisiana for college—had already approached me about shipping him painkillers to sell at LSU.

Getting rid of the pills wouldn't be hard, and getting rid of Lance would cut my stress level in half. I seriously started thinking about branching out.

We were all still hanging out together, but our relationships were deteriorating quickly. For the most part, I was off the opiates and down to one, maybe two, Soboxone a day for the cravings. Sometimes I didn't take it at all. But Lance and Landon were straight junkies. Landon was lying about stupid shit and not paying people.

Lance was bossing everyone around with his Glock tucked into his waistband. The entire operation was beginning to feel more dangerous. It seemed like all our mistakes, all our bad decisions, were catching up to us.

Ethan used to carry around a grey metal combination box. He kept all his cash and drugs in it. He would show up at a drug deal, or we would be at his house playing video games, and he'd pull it out like it was his fucking briefcase. Ethan would punch in the combination and conduct the transaction right out of the box. He would count out the cash, divide up the pills or pot, tuck what was left back into the box, and take off. I told him a dozen times, "Someday someone's going to come looking for that box, bro."

"I'm not worried about it."

Sure enough, a couple of months later Katelyn, Jennifer, Angelo, and I were at Ethan's house with a few of his other friends, shooting the shit and popping ecstasy. Around twelve o'clock Jennifer, Angelo, Katelyn, and I left. Thirty minutes later a couple ghetto white boys, wearing wife beaters and black ski masks, kicked in Ethan's front door. They were waving around a shotgun and a pistol, screaming, "Where's the fucking box?! Where's the fucking box!?"

They forced everyone to lay facedown on the carpet. People were crying and whimpering. They pulled Ethan up and dragged him back to his bedroom. "Where's the box at, motherfucker?!"

Ethan pulled out the box and punched in the combination. But he had transferred the bulk of the cash hours earlier, so the box only contained around $3,000 in cash and a couple bottles of pills. "Where's the rest of it?!" yelled one of the robbers.

"That's it," whimpered Ethan. "That's all I've got."

They pushed him to the floor and took off, firing their guns in the air in the middle of a residential neighborhood. That would have been the end of it, except Ethan recognized one of the robbers.

About a week later he tracked the guy to a nice, quiet gated community. The second he saw Ethan pull up to the curb, the guy bolted. Ethan chased him down the street with his chrome-plated

Smith & Wesson .357 and shot at him until he disappeared into some woods.

Ethan called me up, panting, and said, "I almost got that fool that robbed me!" and he told me the whole story. The gun. The chase. "Next time he's mine."

"You've gotta stop this, bro," I pled with him. "Chuck it off. It's not worth going to prison over. The money's gone." My harmless friends were turning into gun-toting nutcases. And it didn't seem like they were all talk anymore.

Shortly after that, Lance, Landon, their girlfriends, and I were at a tattoo shop named Cherry Bomb owned by our friend Clint Wilson. Lance was pitching Clint on doing a tattoo party at a buddy's fraternity, while we were all passing around a blunt. "I'll bet half the brother's get Phi Delta tats."

"Yeah," agreed Clint. "I like it."

We found out later that Clint had a pill habit and had drained the shop's business account dry. His business partner was threatening to kill him if Clint didn't repay the money—it was a lot—but he couldn't come up with the funds. Less than an hour after we left Cherry Bomb, Lance got a call from Bill, another tattoo artist who had been hanging with us earlier that night. "Clint's dead," he said. "Someone shot 'im right after we left."

According to the surveillance footage, eighteen minutes after we left, Clint closed up the shop and headed to the parking lot. Someone slipped up behind him, put the barrel of a gun to the back of Clint's head, and blew his brains out. Over some fucking pills!

Around the same time, William Kaman, one of Dustin's Tennessee distributors, got a surprise visit from a couple of Knox County

Sheriff's Office detectives. Apparently, Kaman had sold some stolen merchandise to a local pawnshop, triggering an investigation.
When Kaman opened the front door for the detectives, they immediately noticed a bag of oxycodone and several small stacks of cash
sitting on a coffee table; there were multiple weapons and a digital
scale—in plain fucking sight!

But they didn't arrest Kaman there. The detectives questioned
him regarding the stolen property and seized the painkillers and
cash. They then contacted the sheriff's narcotics division regarding
the prescription medication, currency, weapons, and other contra-
band.

Kaman immediately contacted Dustin and told him about
the cops and the seizure. Dustin put Kaman in touch with
James LaPointe. As stated in DEA agent Bethel Poston's affidavit, LaPointe owned Integrated Security with George Crawley,
a former Knoxville Police Department homicide detective who
had been convicted of marijuana trafficking in 1982. Special
Agent Poston detailed LaPointe's role: "LAPOINTE is a very fre-
quent customer of [Dustin] WALLACE who resells oxycodone
and marijuana in Knoxville, Tennessee. LAPOINTE supplies
WALLACE, KAMAN, and other members of this organization
with weapons and ammunition, which are then used to protect
their drugs and money in furtherance of their drug trafficking.
LAPOINTE is a security advisor to this organization and utilizes
his special skills, training, and inventory of electronic surveillance supplies and ammunition to help this organization operate
more productively."

Lance and I had never met or spoken to LaPointe, but Justin
supplied us with several wall safes, money counters, and Fix-a-Flat

canisters with hollow bottoms from LaPointe's security business. We never received any weapons or ammunition from him. In any case, we damn sure weren't "operating productively."

According to the DEA's affidavit, Kaman was so flipped out about the Knox County detectives questioning him he called LaPointe and said he thought someone had "rolled" on him. "Do you have anything in your shop that can test for bugs in my house?"

"Yeah," replied LaPointe.

"All right, I need to borrow that. I need to search my house for bugs, wiretaps, anything."

The following day LaPointe went to Kaman's residence with the anti-surveillance equipment and swept his house. He found nothing.

Lance called me about the seizure a week later. "What up bro? Listen, one of Dustin's guys was visited by some detectives; they seized some of our stuff—cash and pills. But he didn't get arrested." Lance rattled it off so quickly I didn't even catch the "cash and pills" part or I would have hung up. He told me that LaPointe had swept the guy's house and it was clean. Then he started jabbering away about Dustin owing him some cash and out of nowhere he said, "Don't worry about Dustin's guy, he doesn't know we're supplying the stuff—"

"What the fuck! I don't know what you're talking about. Don't call me with this kind of shit," I snapped and ended the call.

The stakes were getting higher and higher while Lance was getting sloppier and sloppier. It just wasn't worth it any more.

Around the same time I decided to fly some painkillers up to New York.

I packed my prescription bottle of Roxicodone 30 mg with 240 tablets and my OxyContin 40 mg bottle with 120 tablets, shoved them into my suitcase, stuffed another couple of my script bottles full of roxies and oxys into my carry-on bag, dropped two additional bottles into a UPS envelope, and two more bottles into a FedEx envelope—a total of 1,400 oxycodone pills.

My thought process was that at no time would I ever be in possession of more than my doctor-prescribed amount of painkillers. If security noticed the bottles, they would let me keep them. They were my scripts. If the baggage handler caught them, they would leave the bottles in my bags. They were my scripts. If FedEx or UPS detected the bottles, they might have contacted the DEA. But I had a script. No big deal.

On my way to Tampa International Airport I swung by Lance's loft to drop off a thousand roxies and 720 oxys—$31,700 worth of pills—and specifically told him, "Don't send them to Dustin until you get the money he owes me."

"Right," said Lance. "I got it bro. Don't worry." But I was worried. I had a huge quantity of pills out on consignment and Lance seemed more concerned with getting high than with collections.

I left my truck in long-term parking, threw my carry-on bag over my shoulder, and hauled my suitcase to the elevator as a commercial jet roared overhead. I calmly rode the elevator to the mezzanine level and dropped the overnight envelopes into the UPS and FedEx boxes, respectively, on my way to security. I sent my carry-on through the scanner, stepped through the sniffer, and held my breath. The TIA X-ray screener stopped the conveyor belt as the contents of my bag popped up on her screen. She glanced at me standing in the sniffer, gave my bag a double take, and passed it through.

No one asked me about the scripts.

The next morning the UPS parcel arrived at my dad's house. Twenty minutes later FedEx showed up. An hour after that, I slapped two Ziploc bags of roxies and oxys into Andy's hand. "If I get you three thousand pills a month, can you move 'em?"

"Fuck yeah, bro," he chuckled, excited. "You know I can." We talked about me flying up to New York twice a month, and Andy coming down to get a script of his own. That way we'd both be able to move between New York and Florida without fear of a trafficking charge. "I've got a real good feeling about this," he said.

"Yeah, well, let's start by you getting rid of these ones."

I spent several days in New York hanging out with Maya. Typical stuff. Dinner. Movies. Long walks holding hands. I remember we went four-wheeling up in the mountains and pulled over near this pond to talk. Maya had recently decided to take the music scholarship and move to Orlando; she was chattering on about seeing each other on the weekends and me possibly moving to Orlando. "Obviously," she said, glancing up at me, "we'll have to get married before we move in together."

I heard a needle screech in my mind and paused briefly before saying, "Maya, I . . . I'm not sure how to say this, but I'm not buying a Lamborghini without taking it for a test-drive."

She reared back and scrunched her face in irritation. "Daddy says, 'You don't buy the cow if you can get the milk for free.'"

I called Lance that night and asked him if Dustin had sent the cash. "You get my teddy bear?"

"Not yet, but don't worry about it."

"That's cool, just don't send anything till you get my bear."

"Yeah, bro about that . . . listen." Lance took a deep breath and said, "I sent it. He's good for it and—"

"Motherfucker!" A rush of heat flooded over my entire body and I instantly went into a rage. I had specifically told him not to send the pills without getting the money. "I'm gonna rip your fucking head off!"

"Calm down—"

"You piece of shit!"

"It's not that bad—"

"When I get down there I'm gonna fucking—"

"You're overreacting."

"You'd better have my fucking money you little shit!" I screamed into my cell and disconnected. I stomped around for the next hour ignoring Lance's repeated calls. He left several messages explaining that the cash would be there when I got back. But I knew it wouldn't.

A week later, I flew back to Tampa, shot over to Victory Lofts, and walked into Lance's place, fists clenched and pissed off. He was manic, laughing and smiling at the fact that I was so angry, though he stayed level-headed enough to keep large pieces of furniture between us. The couch. The dining room table. As I moved left he moved right. "Come on man, calm down. It'll be here tomorrow," he said with a slight nervous tremble in his voice. "I just talked to 'im."

"It had better be." It wasn't. Not the next day, either. It took a week before Dustin overnighted a teddy bear with my $31,700.

At some point during the Tampa DEA's surveillance of the "Barabas Associates," the agents realized that Richard's residence, his father's house, was listed for sale by a local real estate agency. This gave the officers an opportunity to get a glimpse of one of the conspirators' living arrangements. They couldn't pass it up. Assistant US Attorney Lewen—posing as a potential buyer—contacted the real estate agent and scheduled an appointment. He jumped in a plane to Tampa the following morning.

"The market's soft right now," said the agent as she and Lewen toured the three-bed, two-bath home, "but it's reasonably priced, just over one point two million."

"I'm sure," Lewen grunted as the the woman pointed out the waterfront property's balconies, which overlooked the Gulf of Mexico. He listened and nodded politely as she went on about the hardwood floors and the stainless-steel commercial grade appliances.

"It's a wonderful neighborhood," stated the real estate agent, but the assistant US attorney was only interested in finding evidence that Richard, not his father, was the true owner of the house, thereby subjecting it to seizure, along with the nearly $200,000-worth of vehicles that filled the property's four-car garage: a Chris Craft fishing boat, a Harley Davidson Road King, a Dodge Viper, and Richard's limited edition Chip Foose Ford Mustang 5.0.

It must have killed Lewen to not find even a single pill.

Chapter Thirteen

The Oxycodone Super Wal-Mart

"American Pain was the biggest single clinic in the country, a Super Wal-Mart of addiction.... During the nearly three years the Georges' four primary clinics operated, investigators estimate that they churned out roughly 20 million doses of oxycodone."

—*NBC News*

In early September 2009, for "Shit Dick's" birthday, Lance insisted that he, Richard, and I go to the Doll House, a gentlemen's club in Tampa. Catwalks, stripper poles, spotlights, fog machines, all surrounded by tasteful decor. A top-shelf strip club—with twenty or so gorgeous exotic dancers prancing around in nothing but stilettos, pasties, and G-strings, sweet-talking customers out of drinks and into private dances.

We were all drinking and Lance and Richard were snorting pills. Lance was buying lap dances and bottles of champagne while Richard was desperately trying to pick up a platinum blonde with amazing curves—a miniaturized version of Anna Nicole Smith. He might have actually pulled it off had Lance not told her to be "extra nice" to Richard. "This might be his last birthday; he's developed a resistance to the AZT. His T cells are low, and the antiretroviral therapy just isn't working."

She reared back, scrunched up her nose and upper lip, like she'd smelled something rotten. "But," she gasped, "he looks so healthy."

"It's the drugs," said Lance. "He's a dead man. The guy's a walking petri dish. Toxic."

Richard didn't quite understand why the dancer kept wiping down her hands with antibacterial tissues. They were pink and raw by the time we headed to the Seminole Hard Rock Hotel & Casino. "I think that chick was germaphobic, or obsessive-compulsive, or something," said Richard as we pulled out of the strip club's parking lot.

"Yeah, it was definitely her," laughed Lance. "I'm sure you'll have better luck at the club."

We hit the Hard Rock's nightclub, Floyd's, this trendy brass-rail watering hole with velvet curtains and go-go girls dancing on pedestals. The place was packed with upscale patrons looking for a good time or a quick hookup. Lots of Giorgio Armani and Gucci. We pounded shots at the bar, which overlooked Floyd's kickass dance floor, checking out the laser light show and disc jockey.

After about an hour, I went to the restroom. On my way back to the bar, someone called out, "Dougie!" over the music. I whipped around and saw Amanda's mom Tania, the ex-stripper that Randy, Landon, and Richard had tag-teamed. Maybe it was the dark lighting, maybe I'd had too much to drink, but Tania looked sexy as hell. "Hey Ms. Brooks, how's it going?"

She reached out and hooked me by the waist of my jeans. "Dance with me baby boy," she yelled over Evanescence singing "Bring Me to Life." She grinned and flirted with me for a couple songs and I certainly didn't stop her. "Who're you here with?" she asked. "Girlfriend?"

"No ma'am, I'm with Lance and Richard," I replied. Her eyes locked onto mine at the recognition of Richard's name. She smiled and looked down. Maybe it was embarrassment or maybe it was pride. She was still a beautiful woman in her late thirties with young guys digging her.

She leaned in and whispered, "You have any oxys?" I told her my scripts were in my Tacoma and motioned toward the door. "Come on, I'll hook you up."

A couple minutes later she snorted a roxie 30 off my dashboard and her eyes glazed over. She got a euphoric look of desire, lust combined with hunger. I suddenly got worried about where this was headed. "Ms. Brooks," I stammered nervously, "maybe we should head back now."

She stared at me for a couple seconds and said, "You're so cute." I could smell the alcohol on her breath. "You look like my daughter's boyfriend."

My eyes lingered over her voluptuous body, her weathering beauty, and her inappropriate clothes, then dropped my gaze to the floor of my truck, embarrassed. "We should definitely head back—"

That's when she lunged forward, pushed her lips to mine, and slid her tongue into my mouth. She tasted like honey and Jack Daniels. As I slid my hand around Tania's neck and pulled her to me I felt a twinge of guilt about Maya. We weren't totally committed, but we did talk and text constantly. However, the lack of sex had me ready to pop like a shaken soda can. Tania slid her hand on my crotch and whispered, "I want it, Dougie." Something snapped inside me and I'd never wanted anything more. I climbed into the passenger seat, pulled the release, and dropped the seat back. We dry humped for a couple minutes and she started unsnapping and unzipping our clothes. I suggested we go up to the hotel room Lance had rented for Richard's birthday. "No. I wanna do it in here," she giggled. "Like a couple college students."

I looked up at her and admitted, "I'm *in* college."

"I know. I think that's so adorable," she giggled. "You could be my son. My little boy." God only knows what was up with that. She was a psych case study waiting to happen. Dr. Phil would have had a field day with her.

We banged and bumped around inside the cabin, struggling to strip out of our clothes. I slammed my knee into the dash pulling off my jeans and Tania smacked her elbow into the window when she yanked off her top. We bumped heads a couple times and started laughing uncontrollably. I dug a condom out of the center console and tore it open.

I felt like I was inside a pinball machine, an inch to the right and I banged my knees into the door handle or the dashboard, an inch to the left and I hit the center console. One elbow was squeezed up against the door and my right arm was wrapped up in the seat belt. Every time I tried to move I slammed into something. Several minutes into the bumpy car sex Tania dropped to her knees and finished me off. It was absolutely unbelievable.

On our way back to the club Tania said, "Please don't tell anyone about this, Amanda would be pissed."

"Yes, ma'am." I can only imagine how pissed her daughter must have been that her mother had nailed half a dozen of her boyfriends and a couple of dozen guys in her potential dating pool. "I won't say anything."

When I saw Richard at the bar he asked, "Where've you been?" That's when I remembered Tania's history and I thanked God I had worn a condom.

Later I went home and fell asleep. Around 2:00 a.m., I was lying in bed twisted up in my sheets and covered in sweat, struggling to escape something in my dreams. They were a distorted jumble of images combined with feelings of helplessness and desperation. Suddenly there were flashing blue and white lights. They were so vivid I was jolted awake by their blinding brightness. I jumped to my feet, darted to the window, and drew open the blinds. But there were no police or sheriff's cruisers, just a lone sedan idling at the end of the street with a couple silhouetted figures in the front seats. Probably DEA—that's how real the dream was.

I had roughly $100,000 in cash and a small stash of pills hidden in an enclosed trailer parked in the backyard. *Shit! Never keep your cash and drugs together.* I needed to move everything to my cousin Julian's house immediately. Unfortunately, the following day the urgency of the dream had diminished and I put off moving the cash and pills—a major mistake on my part.

A week or so later, in early October, Lance and I were at the gun range—an outdoor field set up with dirt embankments and multiple ranges. We were popping holes in cardboard targets when Lance got a call on one of his prepaid cells from the manager of a UPS Store. That morning Lance had dropped off three packages, containing a total of eight thousand oxycodones, to be shipped to South Carolina and two locations in Tennessee. The UPS manager was calling about a problem with the parcels. "We made a mistake with the postage," he stammered. Lance could envision the beads of sweat rolling down the manager's forehead as he nervously tried to lay the trap. "I'm going to need you to stop back by the store and pay the difference."

"Uh huh," grunted Lance as he cocked his head, holding the cell between his ear and shoulder, while lining up the X-ring between his AR-15's sights. I wasn't even listening to the conversation until I heard Lance say, "Just put the cop on the phone." That got my attention.

My heart started rattling around inside my ribcage, like a blender with a bad ball bearing. I turned to Lance and hissed, "What the fuck, bro?!"

The manager stuttered out something about there not being any cops there, but a second later an authoritative voice came on the line and said, "This is Officer Maxwell with the Tampa Narcotics Task Force. With whom am I speaking?"

"This is the sixth package you fuckers have seized," bellowed Lance into the cell; then he squeezed the trigger and put one in the center ring. "*Six*, asshole!"

I immediately reached over, grabbed the phone, and terminated the call. "Are you fucking crazy?" I growled. "Fuck! Fuck! Fuck! Was that a cop?!"

Lance nodded and squeezed off two more rounds. "Fuck 'em," he said. "You wanna worry about something? Worry about where we're gonna come up with the eight thousand pills we just lost."

He was right. We were weeks away from collecting that many, and most of those were already spoken for. I had been told by an

Alabama pillbilly I'd met at one of my doctor's appointments that a
bunch of pill mills in South Florida were churning out scripts to virtually anyone with a stubbed toe or paper cut. The whole operation
was run by twin brothers, Chris and Jeff George. The Georges' pain
clinics were quickly becoming the preferred destination of junkies
across the country, and they had just opened a twenty-thousand-
square-foot American Pain pill mill in Lake Worth, the largest pain
clinic in the country, dubbed the "Oxy Super Wal-Mart."

Lance popped a couple more holes in the target, and I asked,
"What about Super Wal-Mart?"

That night we drove down to Lake Worth—about two hours
away—and rented a room at a Motel 6. Thin walls and stained
quilts. The next morning, we shot over to Lake Worth Labor Center, a run-down two-story commercial building near an interstate
off-ramp. There were around forty middle-aged transient-looking
males standing outside the entrance. Greasy-haired, unkempt guys
hoping to make sixty bucks for a day's work.

"They're perfect," said Lance, as we approached a group of
around a dozen unshaven laborers. He gave them a thirty-second
elevator pitch on our plan to have them get scripts from the doctors
at Super Wal-Mart. None of the laborers seemed all that interested
until Lance told them we would buy the pills for roughly $1,000 de-
pending on the amount and dosage.

They didn't all jump at the chance. Some walked away. Others
asked if getting the prescriptions was illegal. "No," replied Lance.
"But selling them to us is. If it were one hundred percent legal we
wouldn't be paying you a thousand dollars to do it." Knowing exactly what part of the process was illegal seemed to reassure several
of them.

Lance gave his pitch to another couple dozen laborers and after an hour had convinced seven guys to climb in the back of our trucks.

Keep in mind these guys didn't have MRIs; we had planned on handing them empty pill bottles with fake labels and sending them into the clinic. It was risky. Seven patients with no MRIs and empty bottles might raise some red flags. But when Lance called American Pain to start scheduling the appointments, the office manager told him, "If you've lost your MRI or you've never had one, it's no big deal." They had a mobile MRI truck parked behind a strip club, and it had a one-hour turn-around time. One hour!

Regardless of the quick turn-around, we were never going to get all seven of the laborers' MRIs by the end of the day. Plus, seven patients showing up with MRIs dated the same day might look suspicious.

As each laborer exited the MRI van, Lance handed them twenty dollars in singles and told them to wait for us in the club. While I sat in my Tacoma with my laptop and portable printer, printing labels, Lance paid for the MRIs—roughly $1,200 a pop.

Around two o'clock, Lance and I gathered all seven laborers around a table in the windowless club. With several dancers working the stripper poles on the stage directly behind us, we coached the laborers on what to say to the doctors, passed out four MRIs and three empty Roxicodone and OxyContin bottles, piled everyone back into our trucks, and dropped them off behind American Pain.

The place was a monstrous warehouse, built cheap and designed for production like a Ford assembly line. Even the waiting room was huge. Vinyl floors and endless rows of plastic chairs. As large as it was, the place was filled to capacity with patients. Some may have been in genuine pain, but most looked like addicts, nodding off in their chairs while reading *People* magazine.

The majority of our laborers loitered around the front of the clinic, chain-smoking cigarettes and waiting their turn. With a staff of eight full-time doctors and ten support staff, Super Wal-Mart was able to churn out an average of three patients per minute. Over the next two hours, all seven laborers were processed through the pill mill's machinery. They filled out medical questionnaires, were given cursory examinations, and promptly written prescriptions for 240 Roxicodone 30 mgs and 120 OxyContin 80 mgs, which was the maximum amount and dosage allowed by Florida law. The doctors stopped just short of patting them on the back and saying, "Tell a friend," as they exited the examination room.

As they came out of the office, Lance and I loaded the laborers into our trucks and drove to a local drug store. We would literally go into the pharmacy and stand next to them as the pharmacists handed over the bags of oxycodones. By the end of the first day we had collected 2,520 pills. We were stoked!

That night, Lance and I shipped the bulk of the pills to Dustin in Tennessee via UPS.

On our way back to the motel Lance suggested we swing by the strip club near Super Wal-Mart. It was the kind of dive where the girls would slip their hand in your pants during a lap dance for an extra $40 and meet you in the parking lot for an extra $300. "I don't think so Lance."

"Why?" he asked. "Because of the *virgin*? All we're gonna do is check out some tits and ass." But I knew Lance wasn't going into that club to look. He had a pocket full of cash, a prescription bottle full of oxycodone, and there was no doubt Lance would pull a couple of dancers out of the place by the end of the night. "Come on, bro! It's right up here," he said, excitedly pointing out the windshield at the club. Then he started bouncing up and down in the passenger seat, chanting, "Strippers! Strippers! Strippers!"

My pulse started increasing as the club approached, and at the last second I spun the steering wheel to the right and swerved into the parking lot.

We spent most of the night watching a couple dozen whitetrash strippers—Pamela Anderson wannabes—strutting up and down the stage, seductively working the poles and twerking as the crowd gawked and cheered. I had definitely made the right decision.

Around ten o'clock we started putting twenties into the garters of every exotic dancer that slinked across the catwalk or shook their store-bought tits in our faces. Around eleven we started buying them drinks, and by one we were slipping them roxies and getting offers to "hook up after closing."

We zeroed in on Kerry and Kylie, two bottle blondes with great assess that were eager to meet us after their shifts. They introduced themselves as "twins" from Orlando, and based on their petite frames and fair complexions you would have believed it. When I later asked how old they were, Kerry said she had recently turned twenty-one and was "finally able to drink legally," while Kylie boasted she was twenty-six years old and working on her master's degree. Lance and I glanced at each other and grinned at the discrepancy.

When they showed up at the motel Kerry asked me to crush up a couple oxy 80s as she and Kylie slipped out of their clothes and into the shower. These chicks weren't fucking around. Five minutes later, they exited the bathroom, glistening wet, and dropped to their knees on the orange shag carpet next to the glass coffee table. Sad to say, it was the sexiest thing I'd ever seen: two naked strippers on their hands and knees in a cheap hotel snorting oxycodone through a rolled-up Benjamin Franklin. The euphoric look on their faces. The deep heavy breathing. The look of arousal in their eyes. It was a beautiful sight. When Kerry snorted the last of the powder, she looked up at me with her ass in the air, her breasts resting on the table, and asked, "You wanna fuck?"

She started by peeling off my clothes, tugging and pulling at the buttons and zippers. Then we found our way onto the mattress. I gently kissed her lips and breasts; she giggled and pushed me south. I was so drunk I buried my face between her thighs but then I started thinking, *If 25 percent of women in the United States are carrying the human papilloma virus, then 100 percent of strippers have to be infected.* And oral transmission of HPV is one of the leading causes of mouth and throat cancer. *Fuck!* I reared up immediately. *I'm gonna have to make another appointment at the Spring Hill Health Care Center.*

While I was busy contracting oropharyngeal cancer, Lance and Kylie were in the other double bed pounding away at one another like a couple of rabid dogs. Gnawing and biting. There was a lot of deep breathing and panting going on over there, and every once in a while I could hear Lance hiss, "No, don't do that," or "Seriously, cut it out." Kylie kept giggling, "Come on, you'll like it," and "Give it a chance." *What the hell's going on over there?* I thought. *Leave it to Lance to argue during sex.*

The following morning, once the girls had left, Lance and I were at the local Waffle House and I had to ask, "What were you two arguing about?"

Lance froze, bug-eyed, with a spoon full of grits halfway to his mouth. "That bitch kept trying to stick her finger in me!" I burst out laughing and blew orange juice through my nose. "It's not funny, bro," growled Lance. "She wouldn't take no for an answer."

"Well," I shrugged, coughing and choking on the citrus, "eventually she did."

"No, bro . . . she didn't." Our eyes locked and Lance said, "Tell anyone and I'll kill you."

An hour later we hit the labor center. Lance made his pitch to another dozen or so laborers, and nine of them agreed to obtain scripts in exchange for $1,000. Everything played out similarly to the previous day until Lance's second trip to CVS. Two of the three seemed a little nervous, glancing around the store and fidgeting. Lance hadn't paid them yet, so he wasn't concerned. As soon as the pharmacist handed them the oxycodones, they bolted. Lance immediately took off after them as they raced through the store toward the automatic doors. "You motherfuckers!" yelled Lance, as he closed on the two.

The door sensor triggered the glass doors to slide open, but the laborers were moving too fast. The guy in front slammed headfirst into the door and crumpled to the floor, but the second made it out of the store with Lance on his heels.

The pill thief raced into some traffic stopped at a light, slid like T.J. Hooker across the hoods of several vehicles, and disappeared behind a strip mall. On Lance's way back to the CVS he caught sight of the first laborer running across the pharmacy's parking lot. Again, Lance took off in pursuit. I'm not sure what Lance thought he was going to do if he had caught either guy—legally they weren't Lance's pills. Regardless, the laborer lost Lance after running into a residential neighborhood.

When Lance got back to the truck the third laborer was sitting in the back of his truck. "You still want these?" he asked, holding up his CVS bag.

"More than ever."

We ended up with roughly 2,880 oxycodones by the end of the day. Even so, Lance wouldn't shut up about the two guys that had ripped him off. "I see those two fuckers at the labor place tomorrow," he said, laying in bed that night, "I'm gonna kill 'em." But the next morning neither laborer was there. Not that Lance would've done anything. He was all thunder, no lightning.

We dragged eight more laborers to Super Wal-Mart the next day and ended up with another 2,880 pills. "Eighty-two hundred pills in three days—at half the price," said Lance, on our drive back to Tampa. "We should be doing this once a month."

Then he called his brother Larry. According to the DEA's records, on October 8, 2009, at approximately 5:55 p.m., a cellular call was intercepted between Lance and Larry. "Bro, we've gotta round up as many guys as we can and hit Super Wal-Mart, it's wide open."

"I'm on it," replied Larry.

I think Lance went back to the Super Wal-Mart a couple of times, but I never did. Several months later, the DEA simultaneously raided all the George brothers' clinics throughout Florida during Operation Oxy Alley. Agents seized between $5 million and $6 million during the raid. However, the government has stated that roughly $25 million remains unaccounted for. The Department of Justice then indicted the George twins along with thirty-two other individuals, including thirteen doctors, on racketeering charges. Federal prosecutors called them the largest, most sophisticated painkiller-trafficking organization in the country.

Two days after we got back from Lake Worth I woke up with a sore throat. More of a tickle, really. *Possibly oropharyngeal cancer,* I thought. A few hours later, I was sitting in a Spring Hills Health Care Center examination room when the doctor walked in. She stopped abruptly when she saw me and made this judgmental clicking sound with her tongue and cheek. "It's not what you think," I whimpered while rubbing my throat. "I wore a condom."

She glanced at my chart and asked, "Then why do you want to be tested for HPV?"

"Well . . ." I cleared my throat a couple times and gently massaged both sides of my Adam's apple. "I've kinda got a sore throat and . . ." I was so embarrassed, I couldn't even maintain eye contact with her. "She was a stripper. Seemed like a nice girl, but, well, you know . . ."

She instinctively smiled, then quickly suppressed it. She got a tongue depressor out of a clear plastic vial, turned to me, and said, "Open up and say, 'ahh.'" Then she stuck the popsicle stick down my throat and looked around. She pushed on my neck and even looked in my nose and ears. "When did this happen?" she asked while scribbling in my chart.

"Uh, it was . . ." I replied between repeated coughing and swallowing. I was certain I could feel the HPV virus mutating into cancerous cells, I could taste them in my throat. I coughed and swallowed again. "Coupla days ago."

"A couple of *days?*" she said, and shook her head while she looked down at me rubbing my throat. "Mr. Dodd, do you know what hypochondria is?"

"Oh my God," I whimpered, "it's cancer, isn't it?!"

The following day, October 12, Knoxville Police Department officer Steven Taylor pulled over James Hunter and Mary Wilson on I-40 for a traffic violation. Maybe Hunter was speeding. In all probability, Special Agent Bethel Poston requested Hunter's Acura be stopped. Regardless, Hunter seemed slightly uneasy when the officer approached the vehicle. Officer Taylor asked if he could search the Acura, to which Hunter replied, "Not without probable cause or a warrant."

"Not a problem," said the officer. He then requested a KPD K-9 Unit and within minutes two additional officers showed up with a German shepherd named Braith. The dog was immediately alerted to the odor of drugs, giving the officers probable cause, and the vehicle was searched. They found a prescription bottle, a drug ledger, a plastic bag with approximately nineteen blue valium tablets, two ounces of ecstasy, and a vacuum-sealed package containing several stacks of cash totaling just over $21,700.

Hunter and Wilson were promptly arrested for drug trafficking. The vehicle was towed to the KPD service garage, where Special Agent Poston and several other DEA agents were waiting to take possession of the evidence.

When Lance found out about the arrests he asked me to meet him in front of the Florida Aquarium, just across the street from his loft. It was close to midnight. The trolley was shuttling tourists and drunk club kids between downtown Tampa and Ybor City.

Lance glanced around nervously; he looked uneasy. "No big deal," he said, "but another one of Dustin's guys got arrested." It was the first time I had ever heard the name Hunter. I found out that he had been Dustin's main supplier for ecstasy and hydroponic marijuana, and Dustin had been his source for oxycodone.

"Who arrested him?"

"Well," Lance sucked in a lungful of night air, shifted around uncomfortably, and let it out. "Might've possibly been the DEA. But we don't know that for sure yet." The last thing I wanted to hear was "DEA" and Lance knew it. But I didn't say anything. I just stood there staring at him. There was nothing to say. By this point I knew better than to ask him to stop shipping. My only real option was to distance myself from him as quickly as possible, and I was already doing that. "The guy has no idea who Dustin's supplier is." His eyes haphazardly darted around the plaza, analyzing each pedestrian who walked past. "So we're cool."

I remember wondering, *What's he looking at—or for?* I glanced around and saw a couple guys standing on the sidewalk and several more people waiting for the trolley. I'm ashamed to say this, but for a split second, I thought Lance may have been wearing a wire. It was the first time I doubted his loyalty to me. I almost reached out and touched his upper chest where the microphone would be. Instead, I told him, "It's coming unraveled, Lance."

"No it's not," he snickered. "You're wrong." But it already had. He just didn't know it. None of us did.

Chapter Fourteen

Oxy Rush

"This case represents a significant effort by federal law enforcement to address the substantial dangers associated with the distribution and use of oxycodone."

—United States Attorney James R. Dedrick,
Department of Justice press release

On October 20, 2009, a Knoxville Federal Grand Jury filed a five-count sealed indictment for Lance, Landon, and Larry Barabas, myself, Richard Sullivan, Dustin Wallace, William Kaman, and James LaPointe, along with seven other Tennessee co-conspirators. Count One charged us with conspiracy to distribute and possess with the intent to distribute oxycodone, methylenedioxymethamphetamine, also known as MDMA or ecstasy, and marijuana.

Count Two charged Dustin Wallace and William Kaman with aiding and abetting each other with distribution of a quantity of oxycodone within one thousand feet of a school. Count Three charged Dustin Wallace with distribution of a quantity of oxycodone within one thousand feet of a playground. Count Four charged William

Kaman with possession of a firearm in furtherance of a drug-trafficking crime. Count Five charged Lance Barabas; Landon Barabas; Larry Barabas; Douglas Dodd; Richard Sullivan; and Dustin Wallace with conspiring to commit money laundering.

But we were all clueless to our impending doom.

Later that day, Lance called Dustin in Knoxville and asked for an address where he could FedEx a package. We later found out that the DEA was listening.

"How many?" asked Dustin.

"Four hundred berries and two hundred and forty forties," said Lance. "It'll be there tomorrow."

"Cool," grunted Dustin. "I'll text you an address."

Minutes later the DEA intercepted the following text message, "833 Lovell Rd. Num 47, Knoxville, TN 37932."

Special Agent Poston contacted FedEx in Knoxville and asked for the package to be held at the Tennessee distribution center. Two days later they contacted Poston to let him know it arrived, and the agent immediately obtained a search warrant to open the parcel.

At 2:00 p.m. Poston and Officer Butler opened the package and found three vitamin bottles containing 640 oxycodone tablets and multiple latent fingerprints.

Around the same time, the parcel disappeared off the FedEx tracking page.

Lance contacted FedEx customer service and after being transferred around for twenty minutes, was told by an employee over the phone, "We're working on locating the package. We'll let you know when we find it."

Over the next couple of hours, Lance and Dustin discussed the likelihood that the package had been seized by law enforcement.

"It wouldn't be the first time," laughed Lance. "But it's nothing to worry about. We're good."

The next morning, on October 23, FedEx contacted Lance and told him they had located the parcel. "We can deliver it tomorrow or you can have someone pick it up," said FedEx's customer service rep.

Lance called Dustin and instructed him to head over to FedEx. "You think it's a setup?" asked Dustin. "Like your brother?"

"No, someone snitched on Landon." Lance then explained that he'd had several packages seized by law enforcement. "If they'd caught the package, it would've been before it left Tampa. Trust me, bro, I know what I'm doing."

An hour later Dustin stopped into the Murdock Road FedEx as the DEA videotaped him from the parking lot. Once Dustin was inside, Special Agent Poston filmed him asking the clerk for the parcel from the other side of a two-way mirror behind the counter. As the clerk "searched" the storage area, Dustin stared into his re-flection—oblivious of the agent holding the camera, staring right back. He fidgeted and nervously ran his hands through his hair until the clerk came back empty-handed. "I can't find it," said the FedEx employee. "Sorry."

Dustin huffed and puffed, called Lance to discuss the issue, and gave his information to the clerk. "The second you find it, call me." He exited the store and suspiciously glanced around the park-ing lot, expecting a DEA SWAT team. But there was nothing except asphalt and empty vehicles.

Dustin never heard back about that package.

That night, Lance met me in the Pasco-Hernando Communi-ty College parking lot; he wanted another thousand pills. "Dustin needs 'em in Knoxville."

"What happened to the other six hundred and forty?"

Knowing I would flip out if he told me the truth, Lance chose to alter the events surrounding the missing pills. "They said the delivery truck was in an accident or something. There are packages all over the road. Some of them got run over by cars. There's stuff all over the place," he said, keeping a straight face. "They're working on it, bro. And—"

"That makes no fucking sense. If packages got torn open, then there's pills all over the road." I paced around the parking lot rubbing my hands through my hair, taking deep breaths. "You've gotta stop shipping all these small packages, it's stupid—"

"Stop worrying!" he snapped, hollow-eyed and sluggish. I had never seen him this thin, this strung out. "If I don't get 'em from you I'll get 'em from someone else."

That night I gave Lance four hundred Roxicodone 30s and 180 OxyContin 80s, and he got an additional 420 oxycodone tablets from one of his other connects—a total of a thousand tablets.

On October 26, Lance overnighted a second package containing a thousand oxycodone pills via UPS. This time, he shipped the parcel to LaPointe's security company, Integrated Security, in downtown Knoxville. Then he slid a couple roxies into his mouth and headed to the University of South Florida. He was transferring there from Hillsborough Community College and was in the middle of suffering through "hell week" as a Phi Delta Theta pledge.

On October 27, around four o'clock in the morning, dozens of DEA agents and local police officers in Florida and Tennessee assembled near their respective targets in Operation Oxy Rush. They briefly discussed tactics, looked at photographs of the subjects, and coordinated the multistate raids.

In the predawn gloom, at 5:30 a.m., the DEA began executing their arrest warrants. Lance and roughly thirty soaking-wet wannabe frat boys were doing calisthenics in their boxers on the front lawn of the fraternity house. Floodlights lit the group of pledges doing jumping jacks while being hosed down by a dozen Phi Delta brothers, who yelled insults at them. Twenty DEA agents wearing Kevlar vests and masks, waving M-4 assault rifles, swarmed in screaming, "Down on the ground! Down on the ground!"

As the stunned students dropped to the lawn, the senior brother spun around and snapped, "Whoa, whoa, this is private property! You can't—" The lead agent slammed the butt of his assault rifle into the senior's stomach and barked, "Down on the ground!" as the student hit the grass. The entire group was in the middle of being zip-tied facedown in the lawn, when one of the agents growled, "Who's Barabas?"

As he was loaded into a Suburban, in his sopping-wet boxers, Lance looked at the fraternity house and thought, *That's too bad, I was a shoo-in.* He was supplying half the brothers with painkillers.

When the DEA searched Lance's loft they found his .308 Remington sniper rifle, AR-15 Bushmaster, Sig Sauer assault rifle, Glock .45, and a pink Smith & Wesson 9 mm, along with extra magazines and boxes of ammunition. They even grabbed Lance's money counter.

Thirty miles away in Hudson, a second group of agents surrounded Larry's house. When the lead agents banged on his front door, Larry's pregnant wife made the mistake of opening it, and she and "the Lineman" were quickly forced to the carpet and cuffed.

Simultaneously, agents arrested "Pretty Boy" Landon as he pulled into the driveway at his family's place after a long night at the Hard Rock Casino. As Landon exited his vehicle, a dozen DEA agents rushed in with their weapons drawn. "Federal arrest warrant! Down on the ground!" they yelled. "Down on the ground!"

With a night's-worth of alcohol and illegal drugs coursing through his veins, Landon's response time was slow. They pushed him down onto the cement while his mother shrieked, "What's going on?! What's happening?!" Like she didn't have a clue.

One officer dug a knee into Landon's back as another cuffed his wrists. They threw Landon in the back of a Pasco County Sheriff's patrol vehicle and left Ms. Barabas sobbing. It went down just like a good old-fashioned kidnapping. Only these guys had badges and credentials.

They grabbed Richard at his house. The way I heard it, he was hip-deep in some cougar when the DEA agents rushed into his room, yanked him off the chick, and cuffed them both. "Shit Dick" was taken away naked as a porn-mag centerfold.

Meanwhile in Knoxville, Tennessee, DEA agents and task force officers served federal search and arrest warrants. They hit Dustin Wallace's apartment and seized marijuana stuffed into several Vitamin B-Complex pill bottles, hashish wrapped in tinfoil, a taser and cartridges, shipping labels, his prepaid cell phone, and an assortment of tablets. Dustin was immediately arrested.

Agents entered William Kaman's residence and subsequently arrested him after finding numerous pill bottles and two prescriptions. At the same time, across Knoxville, police gathered at the house of Dustin's friend Brett Webb. After repeatedly banging on the front door and screaming, "Police, we have a search warrant!" agents bashed their way in. Webb was placed in custody, and a search of the house revealed marijuana, a Kel-Tec .380 and two loaded magazines, and a Phoenix Arm Raven .25.

While those raids were occurring, officers with the Knoxville Police Department pounded on James LaPointe's front door. They breached the door and swarmed into the residence screaming, "Police, down on the ground!" LaPointe and two women in the house all dropped to the floor. They arrested LaPointe. A search of the residence revealed a small quantity of marijuana and one blue Roxicodone 30 mg pill.

Not long after Knoxville police took LaPointe into custody, DEA agents executed a search warrant at his security company. According to the DEA's investigation report, during the search, UPS attempted to deliver a parcel from Lance Attaway to Daniel Miller, Dustin's alias. The package contained assorted candy and three plastic Rexall brand vitamin bottles filled with one thousand oxycodone tablets.

One of the final task force targets was another of Dustin's associates, Matthew Golden. While sitting at his kitchen table, watching the officers tear his place apart, Golden stated, "I was just doing this to make some money for rent and college." Within hours of being brought into custody, he was spilling his guts.

Back in Hudson, Florida, several Pasco County Sheriff's Deputies and half a dozen DEA agents surrounded my grandmother's house and started banging on the front door around 6:15 a.m. I was jolted awake. The pounding was so violent and loud, I thought someone was trying to kick in the door. So I grabbed my North American .22 revolver, crept down the hallway, and looked out the living room window. There were six DEA agents wearing full Kevlar body armor and black ski masks. "Who is it?" I yelled through the door.

"DEA—open up!"

I darted back to my room and stashed the gun. While they banged on the front door and screamed, "Federal arrest warrant! Open up!" I remember stopping in my room, for just a second, taking a couple deep breaths, and thinking, *I can't believe this is happening. This can't be happening.* I started to go numb. I was contemplating whether swallowing a handful of oxys would help the situation. "Open up! Federal arrest warrant!" Then the thought of withdrawing inside of a jail cell crossed my mind. Fuck that!

By the time I twisted the dead bolt and opened the front door I was in a complete daze. The lead agent reached in and grabbed me by the wrist. He pulled me out of the house and passed me to the second agent, who snapped a pair of handcuffs on me. "Is there anyone else in the house?"

"Just my grandmother. But she's sleeping," I replied, as the remaining agents swarmed into the house with their weapons raised high. They carefully cleared one room after another. When my grandmother stepped into the hallway, the agents explained they had an arrest warrant for me. "Oh dear," she said. "Not Douglas?"

They sat me down at the dining room table and one of the agents—I'll call him Special Agent Titus Walley—a tall, lean, clean-cut law enforcement type explained, "You've been indicted in the Eastern District of Tennessee for conspiracy to distribute oxycodone along with several other members of the Barabas Organization." The dozen or so deputies and agents stomped through my grandmother's house and bagged my prepaid cell phones; my address book with all the names and numbers of my doctor shoppers and wholesalers; my Sig Sauer, Smith & Wesson, and North American; my empty prescription bottles; a money counter; and a safe-deposit box key. But the most damning evidence against me was the approximately one thousand oxycodone tablets and the duffel bag stuffed with $90,000 in cash they had found in the enclosed trailer behind my grandmother's house.

Minutes later one of the sheriff's deputies handed Walley my deposit box key. Walley held it up to my face and asked, "What does this go to?"

When I told him, "I've got a box at Wachovia Bank," he got a big grin on his face. I should've known something was wrong. He called the manager of the New Port Richey Wachovia and arranged for him to meet us at the bank. Around 8:30 a.m., as a detective with the Pasco County Sheriff's Office was digging around in my truck, Special Agent Walley walked me out to a new Range Rover. "You like my new undercover vehicle?" he asked sarcastically and popped open the rear passenger door of the glossy white sport utility. "I confiscated it from a drug dealer last week."

I was climbing into the rear of the vehicle when the Pasco County Detective exited my truck, holding a single blue Roxicodone 30 mg pill between his thumb and index finger, which I'm sure they felt gave them the right to seize the vehicle. "Titus!" he called out. "Look what I found in the console." There was absolutely no way he had found that roxie in my truck. No fucking way.

Walley turned around and chuckled, "Looks like I'll be driving your Tacoma next week."

"Oh, hell no!" I gasped. "That's bullshit!" Walley laughed, pushed me into the back of the Range Rover and slammed the door.

On the way to the bank, Walley told me I needed to be a "team player" and sign over the truck. "We're going to take it anyway."

"It's not gonna happen," I said. "I've got a lien on it, you're not getting my truck."

Once we were inside the bank, Special Agent Walley, two other agents, and I emptied out my safe-deposit box, filled with $6,000 in cash. Walley told me if I signed over my checking and savings accounts of their combined $10,000 balance, he would let me keep the $12,000 I had in CDs. "Or," said the agent, "I'll come back with a warrant and seize it all."

I closed out both accounts and handed it over to the agents. The DEA seized over $100,000 in cash from me and between $30,000 to $50,000 worth of roxies and oxys.

Within hours, the five of us were standing in the jury box area of this huge federal courtroom inside the Federal Building in downtown Tampa. Tall ceilings and expensive furnishings, dark wood paneling and computers on every table. Our temporary court-appointed attorneys were trying to convince US Magistrate Judge Thomas McCoun III we deserved bond. The government prosecutor disagreed.

"Your Honor," said Eduardo Toro-Font, the assistant US attorney for the government, "the United States would move for the detention of all the defendants. . . . These individuals had access to roughly $1.25 million of drug proceeds." He then told the judge that, based on the amount of pills and the fact that the majority of us were facing twenty years we were all flight risks and dangerous to society. "In the case of Lance Barabas, Your Honor, I can tell the Court that he was found to be in possession of firearms, . . . tested positive for marijuana and opiates, . . . [and] is one of the leaders and organizers of the group." Toro-Font then turned his attention to the rest of us. "In terms of Larry Barabas . . . he uses oxycodone and OxyContin and marijuana. . . . Landon Barabas [is] out on bond on drug charges out of Tennessee." In addition to his Tennessee charges "Pretty Boy" was fresh out of rehab and had tested positive for benzodiazepine, weed, opiates, and coke.

The assistant US attorney told the judge that I was caught with several assault rifles, pills, and over $20,000 in cash. That's when I realized the DEA agents hadn't turned in all the money they had seized. "So in general terms, Your Honor, those are my arguments for detention."

Ms. Barabas got on the stand and pled with the judge to grant her boys bond. However, Judge McCoun wasn't all that moved, recounting Landon's positive urinalysis test for multiple substances.

"He just did a twenty-one day program at Windmor," she replied.

"He didn't get much out of it apparently," snickered the judge.

She glanced at Pretty Boy and hissed, "Apparently not."

Ms. Barabas and Richard's dad were able to put up their houses to secure Larry and Richard's bond, but the rest of us were screwed.

Around four o'clock, we were transported to Pinellas County Jail and placed in a large bullpen with around seventy-five other people waiting to be processed. It was a big concrete-block room filled with plastic chairs. Everything was bolted to the floor. Lance and Landon were starting to go through the cold sweats and muscle aches of opiate withdrawal. Lance curled up in a chair, wrapped his arms around his knees, and started rocking. Within twenty minutes he was shaking and mumbling incoherently, but there was nothing to be done.

I was furious. All I could think about was all the things I had done wrong up to that point and how sloppy I had been. How stupid I was not to have cut ties earlier. My own overwhelming selfishness and greed ultimately caught up with me. I looked around the room, checking out all the deadbeats and derelicts. My peers. That's when I saw my cousin Tony Jr. sitting in a chair catty-corner from me. "Oh my God," I said. "What're you doing here?"

"Probation violation," he griped. He had failed a urinalysis and had to turn himself in. He glanced at Lance and Landon sitting across the room and asked, "What about you guys?"

I went over the situation. The drugs. The conspiracy. The money laundering. Tony Jr.'s eyes nearly bulged out of his head. "The federal prosecutor said I'm looking at twenty years."

He immediately glanced at Lance and Landon. "You think you can trust your buddies?"

I peered at the two of them huddled together, Lance curled up in the fetal position rocking like a mental patient, and Landon massaging his neck and shoulders, trying to rub out the withdrawal pains. Both were sweating and breathing heavily. Two years earlier I would have trusted them with my life, but now . . . "I just don't know anymore."

"You need to call my dad, cuz."

We were eventually called into the processing area, fingerprinted, and photographed. The deputies stripped us down and asked us to bend over, spread our checks, and cough. I can't imagine a small-caliber pistol or a cell phone has ever dropped out of an inmate's ass during a strip search. Regardless, they made us do it.

Several deputies then guided a group of about twenty of us to various wings of the facility. We were chained together in our jumpsuits like one long string of bright-orange beads. Lance and Landon were placed in one pod, and I was led to another, a two-tier cellblock with about a hundred inmates—mostly black guys—living in four-man cubes with bunk beds. There were tiled showers and a couple of televisions. The walls were freshly painted and surprisingly clean. There were some rough-looking guys. Lots of shaved heads, dreads, and gold teeth. But no one bothered me.

That first night was the worst. I lay in my bunk and prayed that this was all a bad dream. My entire life had been ripped apart just as I was getting it together. I had successfully completed my freshman year at college with a 2.9 GPA and I was off the opiates. I had managed to save over a quarter of a million dollars and now, in the blink of an eye, it was all gone. Everything had been flipped sideways. What the DEA hadn't stolen was out on consignment and virtually uncollectable from a cell. I'd never felt so crushed. So alone.

The next morning, over corn flakes and a carton of skim milk, I met some of the other inmates. Everyone was griping about "dirty fucking federal agents" and "snitch motherfuckers." But one guy in particular will always stand out to me: Andre Jefferson. He was a black guy who had served two federal bids and was awaiting sentencing on his third. "Don't listen to these fake-ass niggas," he told me when we were out of earshot of the others. "There's only two kinds of inmates in the fed—those that cooperated and those that wish they had. You don't have no homeboys no more." He told me the US attorney's office was sentencing defendants to so much time that the only choice you had was to cooperate. Most inmates cooperate, he said, "But one hundred percent of 'em lie about it."

"What about trial?"

"Trial," he scoffed. "Shit, only innocent people go to trial . . . and half of them are found guilty." He explained that the federal system worked on a point system and there was only one way to drop your points—cooperate. "The government ain't got no honor and the inmates ain't got no loyalty in this game. I've seen brother turn on brother and father turn on son. Don't trust your co-dees."

I didn't want to believe that about my co-defendants, but I knew he was telling me the truth. He'd been around.

Less than a week later, I turned twenty-one in Pinellas County Jail. Around noon I was called to the visitation room. It was a closet-sized space with a camera, an outdated desktop monitor, and a telephone receiver. My mother and both of my grandmothers were crammed together, peering at me from the screen. Grandma was holding a telephone to her ear. I quickly sat down and looked into my grandmothers' faces—the women that had raised me. The women I considered my mothers. I grabbed the phone and heard Grandma's voice squawk out of the closed-circuit system, "There he is. Dougie, can you see us?"

A lump started forming immediately in my throat, but I managed to croak out, "Yes, ma'am." It was everything I could do not to tear up. "I can see you."

They were somewhere else in the building; I could see some people behind them in small booths staring into cameras while talking into telephones. Grandma and Meme passed the phone back and forth asking if I was okay and if there was anything they could do to help me, to which I replied no. They never asked if I was guilty of the charges. My grandmothers occasionally wiped tears out of their eyes, but my mother seemed unmoved, indifferent to the situation. Not that I expected anything else.

When she was passed the phone she couldn't help but make a crack. "Happy birthday, Dougie," she said, as cool as ice while her eyes perused my surroundings. I smiled, trying to hide the rage welling up inside me, and we both chuckled sadly. "Do you want me to call Clementine?"

"No." She was a state criminal defense attorney and couldn't help me. "I'm thinking about going with a federal public defender—"

"Your Uncle Tony said not to go with the public defender. You need to call him." She told me she would try and come see me once a week.

"They're gonna move us to Knoxville soon—"

"Knoxville? For how long?" she snapped. "How am I supposed to see you?" Then she started complaining about having to drive to Tennessee and missing work, as if the federal government was doing all this to inconvenience her and keep her from seeing her baby boy. Though the fact that we had both lived in Hudson and barely saw each other never seemed to bother her.

"Mom . . . Mom . . ." I said repeatedly, trying to interrupt her chattering diatribe. "Mom . . . Mom!"

"What?!"

"The federal prosecutor, he said I'm looking at twenty years." Her eyes locked onto mine and instantly filled with tears. She turned to my grandmothers and I heard her say, "Twenty years." The three of them looked at me in the monitor and started weeping. "My God," whispered Grandma, and Meme gasped, "I'll never make it that long."

Our time ran out a few minutes later and the monitor snapped to black. I remember sitting there, holding the phone for a minute and staring through the thick wired glass into the blacked-out ten-inch monitor and wondering if I would ever be able to hug one of my grandmothers again. My heart was shredded.

Some days after that, my mother visited again, this time with her friend Christine. We all sat in front of the monitors and cameras and talked on the phone. Everything was going fine. They were both very sweet. They said all the right things; they told me everything was going to be all right. That wasn't true, but it was comforting to hear. That's when I noticed my buddy Alejandro waving at me in the background. Alejandro, Landon's girlfriend Katie, and Randy were visiting Landon and they recognized my mother. I waved back to Alejandro, which irritated my mother. Then Katie and Randy appeared behind her, smiling and waving. I waved back and my mother snapped, "Hey, this is my time! If they want to see you, they can do it during their time."

Katie and Randy retreated back to their visitation booth, while I listened to my mother tell me, "I carried you in my womb for nine months, breastfed you, and changed your dirty diapers." Her face got pink and shiny with rage. "My time," she mumbled.

"Listen to yourself. What's wrong with you?" I was facing twenty years in federal prison and my friends were trying to say a quick goodbye. "This isn't about you," I said. "It's not *all* about you."

"My son," she muttered, like a schizophrenic off her meds, "you're my son." I told Christine I was sorry, but I couldn't do this right now. I got up and walked out on my mother telling me how "ungrateful" and "selfish" I was.

Chapter Fifteen

Con Air

"Purdue Pharma L.P., the maker of OxyContin, and three of its executives . . . pleaded guilty to a misdemeanor count of misbranding the drug. . . . U.S. District Judge James Jones [placed] each of the executives on probation for three years."

—*NBC News*

The severity of the situation didn't really sink in until the US marshals transported us to Tampa International Airport on our way to Tennessee. As the prison bus pulled onto the tarmac, we saw a fleet of marshals with shotguns leading several hundred cuffed and shackled inmates off a Boeing 737. Everyone was wearing white T-shirts, khakis, and orange canvas shoes. With assembly-line efficiency, the marshals called out names and numbers and corralled the convicts into buses.

One of the inmates in the back of our bus whispered, "Con Air," talking about the movie about transporting prisoners on a plane that starred Nicholas Cage, John Malkovich, and a bunch of other big-name actors. I took a look at four inmates wearing "spit mask" hoods and black-metal disciplinary boxes on their handcuffs—the boxes were designed to dig the steel cuffs into their wrists at the slightest movement—surrounded by six marshals. That's when it hit me. I looked at Lance and said, "We're fucked!" He just stared out the window as the marshals marched another group of several hundred inmates onto the plane.

We had a blubbery black kid on the bus who had been begging the marshals to let him take a piss since we'd left the jail an hour earlier. By the time we were taken off the bus, this kid was in agony. "Please man," he begged one of the marshals, while shifting his weight from one foot to another, "I've gotta go."

"You'll go when you're on the plane," growled the marshal. Eventually we were funneled into the Boeing in a neat single-file line. Inside the plane, Lance, Landon, and I were seated right behind the kid. He almost exploded into tears when one of the marshals on the plane told him, "You can piss when we're in the air."

He shot up and wailed, "I'll never make it that long!" The marshal raised the butt end of his shotgun menacingly and yelled, "Boy, sit down or I'm gonna crack your skull!"

The kid dropped into his seat and started to rock back and forth mumbling, "I'm not gonna make it. I'm not gonna make it." A couple minutes later the Boeing roared off the runway and into the air. The second we leveled off the marshals started taking inmates to the restroom, row by row. They started at the front of the plane, but we were near the back. The kid begged to use the restroom, but none of the marshals had one milligram of sympathy for him. "I'm gonna piss myself if you don't—"

"So piss yourself!" barked a marshal. Another one said, "You gotta go so fucking bad, go!" A minute later the kid started crying as urine cascaded down his pant legs and collected in a puddle at his feet. Lance gaped at me in horror as the kid's piss saturated the cheap carpeting, slowly making its way to our feet.

When the marshals got to his row one of them growled, "You're up."

"I'm okay."

The marshals shrugged with indifference and kept moving. Lance looked at me and whispered, "We're in a lot of trouble."

We landed at Oklahoma City's federal transfer center. "Con Air" taxied across the runway to the Federal Bureau of Prisons building, where we exited the plane and were funneled into the facility. However, the volume of prisoners was so great, the federal correctional officers immediately loaded twenty of us onto a bus headed to Grady County Jail—a real shithole. Chipped-painted concrete floors and rusty steel doors. We were given baloney sandwiches and foam mats, then stuck in a large holding cell.

The next morning we were given another baloney sandwich, bussed back to the holdover center, then flown with two hundred fellow inmates to Atlanta. There, the marshals escorted us onto another bus for a six-hour drive to Ocilla County Jail—also a shithole. They gave us yet another slice of baloney with two pieces of bread, and a room number. When Landon arrived at his cell, he was met by a jacked-up 250-pound black guy yelling, "Uh uh, no fucking way! I ain't taking no fucking cellies!" He stared at Landon. "You ain't staying here, white bread."

Landon stepped backward out of the cell, glanced at me and mouthed *What the fuck?* I shrugged. Up until now the other inmates had been docile, almost passive. Landon stepped back into the cell and pushed the button to the intercom. "Uh deputy . . . I'm gonna need another cell. This guy's not accepting cellies right now." The deputy came over the intercom and gave him another room number.

Luckily, Lance and I both got decent cellies at Ocilla.

Race was never an issue for me or my buddies, but it is a very big thing in prison. They call it "politics." You have designated areas where you eat based on race. You have a white area, a black area, and different Latino areas. In some prisons people get killed for trying to intrude on another race's table in the cafeteria. There in the county jail we were also worried about the gangs. They were jumping their own and beating them with dominoes in a sock or chasing them with homemade shanks made out of razors and sharpened toothbrushes.

They woke us up at four in the morning, tossed us—yes, you guessed it—a baloney sandwich, and bussed us to Blount County Jail in Tennessee. This place made the other prisons look like the Ritz. During processing, the deputies had us strip down and led us into a shower with slimy green mold infesting the grout lines between the tiles. One of the deputies handed us a Dixie cup of liquid potassium carbonate and told us, "It's for delousing. You put it on your pubes and hair. Do not pour it out!"

We all poured it down the drain and washed off in the ice-cold water. None of us had showered in days.

As we stepped out of the processing area the deputies separated us. We were all housed in separate pods, or groupings of cells. One, two, and three. I was given another baloney sandwich—I was quickly getting sick of baloney sandwiches—and a thin mat, then placed in a two-man cell already housing two black guys. A couple of coke dealers from Tennessee, they already occupied the bunk bed. That left only the floor, which had a thin coating of dust and hairballs. I'm allergic to dust, but after spending what seemed like days on multiple planes and busses, all the while handcuffed, shackled, and wrapped in waist chains, I dropped my mat on the filthy floor, next to the stainless steel toilet-sink combo, and passed out.

The next morning I woke up coughing and congested. My eyes were red and itchy. I stood up, looked around the room, and told my bunkies, "I can't live like this." They informed me that inmates were only let out of our cells for two hours at breakfast, two hours at lunch, and two hours at dinner. Most of that time is spent waiting in line to take a shower or use the phones. Cleaning supplies were only available once a week, and because of the demand it was almost impossible to get them.

I turned around, hit the intercom and a deputy's voice barked, "What do you want?!"

"I need some cleaning supplies," I snapped back. My cellies glanced at me and then at one another. "This place is filthy."

"What do you think this is, Burger King?!" roared the deputy. "You don't get it your way. Don't fucking buzz me again!"

My two bunkies burst into laughter. "Oh, we're gonna like you, white boy!" hollered one of them, rolling around in his bed cracking up. "You're all right."

Steel doors separated all the pods, but they weren't soundproof. This made it possible to pass messages between pods by yelling into the door. As a result, I quickly learned Landon was locked up with Brett Webb and Lance was locked up with several of our other co-defendants.

I spent the next few days scraping together some money for an attorney.

At the time of my arrest, I had roughly $125,000 in pills out on consignment—God knows what Lance had out there. Once our distributors heard we had been arrested they started throwing away their prepaid cells and blocking our calls. Some answered, but I was on a jailhouse pay phone that immediately notified the caller of my situation, and most hung up just after the recorded voice asked them to push the pound key and accept the call. The few people that stayed on the line were timid and cautious. "Hey Doug," they'd say. "I'm surprised you're calling me." That sounded suspiciously like code for: "You shouldn't be calling me" or "Why are you involving me?"

"Yeah, well, I'm in a jam and I need what you owe me."

"Right, right, I'll . . . I'll put it in the mail today." I'm not sure how any of these guys were going to mail me anything. None of them knew my grandmother's address or where I even lived. "Good luck, man." Sometimes they would just hang up when I asked for the money. Sometimes they would try to convince me they were really going to send me the cash—without ever asking where to send it. Drug dealers and junkies aren't exactly known for paying their outstanding debts.

It took me over a dozen calls to scrape together the $42,500 needed to hire a federal criminal defense attorney. He introduced himself as Douglas C. "Fighting" McNabb. He worked out of Austin, Texas, and Washington, DC.

On November 24, 2009, I was transported to the federal building in downtown Knoxville where I met my attorney in a small, cold conference room with a wire mesh divider. McNabb was tall with broad shoulders and gray hair. He told me I had three options. One, I could fight the charges and go to trial. "If you win, you might go home. If you're found guilty, you'll end up with twenty years." Two, accept a plea and not cooperate. Or, three, accept a plea and cooperate. "Cooperation is your only real option here. You've got over a dozen co-defendants who'll probably testify against you. If you take a plea without cooperation, the assistant US attorney will ask for twenty years. Or you can cooperate." *Twenty years!*

"Twenty years.? But I've never sold any pills in Tennessee."

McNabb then explained the definition of a chain conspiracy according to Black's Law Dictionary: a single conspiracy in which each person is responsible for a distinct act within the overall plan, such as an agreement to produce, import, and distribute narcotics, in which each person performs only one function. All participants are interested in the overall scheme and liable for all other participants' acts in furtherance of the scheme.

"Well, what about the search of my grandmother's house? They didn't have a search warrant and they never read me my Miranda rights. And I've never provided or distributed any marijuana or MDMA."

"Mr. Dodd, you need to understand something; so far they haven't charged you with the weapons seized at your residence. You start fighting and they will." Statute 924(c)—possession of a firearm in furtherance of a crime of violence or drug trafficking—carried a mandatory minimum sentence of five years. Five *additional* years. "I'll make a couple calls about the marijuana and the MDMA," said McNabb just before he left. "But with thirteen co-defendants, there's not a lot of room to negotiate."

I went back to my cell and sat on my mat on the dirty concrete floor next to the toilet. For the past several years I hid money and wiped items to remove fingerprints, avoided stockpiling pills and talking on the phone, all to keep myself from ending up sitting in a fucking prison cell for the next two decades.

That night I called my Uncle Tony. I needed advice. I needed to hear him tell me to be strong. To go to trial. To fight. He asked me how I was doing and what my lawyer had said. "This guy's no Clementine," I complained. "I gave him over forty-two grand and his only strategy is to cooperate." I told Uncle Tony the DEA didn't have one phone call of me discussing selling or buying anything. Not one controlled buy. Nothing that connected me to any conspiracy. "The DEA didn't have a search warrant and—"

"Dougie," he said, "listen to your lawyer."

I chuckled nervously. "You're not listening, he's telling me to cooperate. He wants me to rat out everyone I know."

"Listen to me, son." I remember he took a deep breath, let it out slowly, and said, "You can never cooperate too much. Do it quick and do as much as you can." I'll never forget standing in the Blount County Jail—with twenty-five inmates screaming and yelling in the background—stunned motionless in disbelief. It was the last thing I ever thought he would say. I've always thought of him as an old-school mobster. I immediately thought about Sammy "the Bull" Gravano rolling over on John Gotti. Shocked doesn't cover it. "You're not dealing with the state. Don't play with these people, they're ruthless. Cooperate."

"But they don't—"

"Don't get cute, dammit! Cooperate!" I was so stunned by what I was hearing I couldn't even respond. "Did you hear me?!" he barked.

"Yes sir. Cooperate."

Less than a month later, my federal defense attorney was back. He told me he had gotten Assistant US Attorney Lewen to drop the conspiracy to distribute marijuana and MDMA. "But they've got you on conspiracy to distribute one hundred and fifty thousand oxycodone pills, and that's not going away." McNabb glanced at a legal pad with notes about my Tennessee co-defendants and said, "They've got Justin Knox and Matthew Golden, they're both ready to cooperate against you." He then slid a copy of Golden's signed plea agreement—with our names in it—across the table, and said, "Brett Webb is due to sign his today."

He slid a copy of the Federal Sentencing Guideline Manual out of his briefcase, flipped it open to the narcotics section and said, "Based on your criminal history—category two—and the amount of oxycodone . . ." He pointed to the complicated levels and categories of the guidelines and started shaking his head. "Your base-level offense is thirty. Then we've got to add an additional two-level enhancement for the possession of the weapon and ammunition seized at your residence. Plus two more levels for the money laundering . . . minus three levels for pleading out . . . " That came to level 31 in criminal history category two; for a total of 121 to 151 months of incarceration. "You'll end up with ten years, twelve-and-a-half years max, for the conspiracy. Plus, an extra five if the prosecutor decides to push the gun charge."

"Jesus."

"If you cooperate," he said—pronouncing his words slowly, "there's no limit to how much the government can knock off. You might end up with five years."

I remember taking a long, deep breath and exhaling it slowly. It was the hardest decision I've ever had to make, but I said, "I'll cooperate."

When I got back to the pod I called Landon to the pod door and told him, based on the amount of painkillers they had caught me with I couldn't go to trial. Justin and Golden were already cooperating. "According to my lawyer, the DEA has a ton of incriminating calls made by Lance. He'd be an idiot to go to trial." I whispered into the door, "It's not like wrestling one on one. Our indictment says the United States of America versus. There is no way we win here."

"What're you saying?"

"I'm gonna cop out and cooperate. It's your call, do whatever you've gotta do. I just wanted you guys to know."

Lance was furious. He had recently read *Busted by the Feds*, an instructional guide to the federal sentencing system, and he was certain the most any of us could get was five years. Our wing of the jail was shaped like an octagon and I could see from my pod into Lance's pod. He was stomping around, waving his arms in the air, and banging on the glass like a child throwing a temper tantrum. It was the first time I was glad we were separated. Not that I thought we would get into a fight. I just didn't want to hear his mouth. He kept sending me notes that read, "There's no reason to cooperate, bro. They can't give us that kind of time," and "Let's go to trial! Fuck the feds!"

But his attitude changed dramatically after he spoke with his attorney. He told Lance that the government had recordings, photographs, video, and controlled buys. All of it damning. "If I cooperate," he said, after returning from his first attorney-client meeting, "he might be able to get me twenty years . . . maybe." Because Lance was hit with a leadership role, his charges were based on the highest quantity of drugs. The government started him at level 36, added four points for leadership, two points for a gun, and two points for money laundering. The Federal guidelines call for a life sentence at level 43, and Lance was sitting at level 44. Lance looked like someone had kicked the shit out of him. Landon said he slept for two days straight.

I signed my plea agreement on December 18, 2009. As a result of me being the first "Florida boy" to plead out, Assistant US Attorney Lewen agreed to file a 5K1.1 motion to request that the judge reduce my sentence. But he wouldn't say by how much. They never do.

Shortly after I entered my plea, Lance, Landon, Larry, Richard, and the bulk of our co-conspirators also accepted plea agreements. It was the domino effect and at the end of the day thirteen out of the fourteen individuals in my case took a plea deal and cooperated.

On February 9, 2010, we all pled guilty in front of US District Judge Leon Jordon.

A couple of days later, I was sitting at a table in my black-and-white-striped jumpsuit and shower slides, playing checkers with "Pluke," a six-foot-five-inch, 260-pound black guy with short dreads or "twists." He was talking shit because I had been beating him consistently for an hour straight. "This game is too slow" he complained or "I'm not used to playing by these rules." Eventually, he announced we're going to play "flying kings" checkers. He went over the rules and I started winning at "flying kings." Pluke got so agitated that he abruptly stood up and grunted, "I'm done playing."

So I started playing one of his homeboys in regular checkers. I beat him something like six games in a row, while Pluke stood at the edge of the table making comments. I tried to ignore him, but when he said, "This cracker thinks he got all the sense," I looked up at him and snapped, "I'm not even playing you, bro, why are talking shit?"

I went back to playing the game. I didn't consider it a big deal until Pluke sucker punched me in the side of the head. I was so stunned that, for a second, I didn't know what had happened. Then I realized he'd punched me and I jumped up. We started swinging at each other, bobbing and weaving. At some point, I lost one of my shower slides.

Pluke had me by over one hundred pounds and almost a foot. He knocked me around once or twice, and I landed a couple of shots. It was like punching a damn tree, and I quickly realized there was no way I could take him in a straight-up fistfight. So I dropped down and yanked his legs out from underneath him. Pluke hit the concrete with an *umph!* and I smashed him in the head twice as he struggled to get up. The punches didn't even faze him.

At the same time, Pluke's two cousins came running out of their cells with several other guys. They lined up behind Pluke and it was starting to look like I was going to get jumped by six guys. Then my cellie Rudy and his two brothers—who were damn near Pluke's size—and several other guys stepped in behind me.

All the while, the deputies were watching this whole thing from the central observation room and they weren't doing anything about it. They just stood inside the window, staring at us and waiting to see what happened.

Pluke yelled, "Let's go into the cell and close the door!" That would have been a potential death sentence for me. I was so jacked up on adrenaline I started to head for his room when Rudy said, "That's not gonna happen, Pluke."

Then Pluke and my cellie started arguing. At one point Pluke said something like, "Fuck this punk cracker bitch!" and I smashed him two or three times in the ribs and yanked his legs out from underneath him so quickly he didn't know what hit him. While Pluke scrambled to his feet I dove on him and we grappled around on the floor for a few minutes. He was so big and strong I couldn't get a hold on him. Luckily he was out of shape, and after a couple minutes he started breathing harder and harder. Eventually he gasped, "Okay! Okay!" But I didn't let go. If I had he would have killed me. He was huffing and puffing, deeper and deeper, and suddenly he said, "All right! All right! That's enough." Several guys pulled us apart and we stomped off to our rooms. Neither of us could call it a win. I'd give it to him though, considering the black mark under my left eye.

My cellie came in just before they locked us down for the night. He tossed me my shower slide, grinned, and said, "You got lucky."

"No shit." We both started laughing as the deputy bolted the door shut.

The next morning, Landon told me—through the pod door—that I had a lot of guts to take on Pluke. Looking back, I think it was more adrenaline than guts. The fact that I didn't back down followed me throughout my entire sentence; in every facility I went to after that someone would say, "Don't fuck with Dodd; that white boy will go."

Sometime the following week, the marshals bussed us from Blount County Jail in Tennessee back to Ocilla County Jail in Georgia. Lance, Landon, Larry, Dustin, Brett, and I were all housed in the same pod. That was cool. Richard and several of our other co-defendants were in another pod. Eighty percent of the jail's inmates were black, around 15 percent were Mexican, and less than 5 percent were white. Our minority status sucked. I tried not to pay it any mind but some days it would get to me. I was raised to treat people how you want to be treated; for that reason, I always try to treat people with respect. It didn't work that way at Ocilla. We were constant targets of racism and intimidation.

The deputies at Ocilla didn't give a shit. The place was wide open and extremely violent. We had all seen a lot of fights since being incarcerated. But nothing compared to the amount of violence in Ocilla. There were Crips and Bloods, and gang members attacked rival gang members with dominoes in socks or stabbed each other with shanks. Inmates were constantly walking around bloody and bruised.

After being locked up for months, eating shitty food, and virtually never seeing sunlight, the average inmate is ready to fight over anything. A disrespectful crack or someone looking at him the wrong way could be enough to set him off.

The worst thing I witnessed happened maybe a week after we got to Ocilla. There was a black guy named "Prophet" who was bringing in cigarettes through his cousin that worked in the laundry and selling them in the pod at a hefty price. Eventually, a couple of gang members also started to sell cigarettes—most likely brought in by one of the guards—and Prophet suddenly became competition. There were some threats and a few episodes of some serious stare-downs—what the black inmates call "mean mugging." Ultimately, the two gang members got together and decided to carve up the pod's cigarette business by getting rid of Prophet.

One day, Prophet was in his cell and his competitors stepped into his room and closed the door on him. Everyone in the pod could hear the attack. They beat and pounded on him as he screamed and begged for them to stop. For someone to help him.

But no one stepped toward the door. Lance and I just glanced at one another as we listened to them bash Prophet's face into the concrete, kicking and stomping him. We both wanted to help him, to stop the beating, but neither of us had the balls to even try. If we had taken one step toward that door the gang members would have beaten us senseless.

At one point you could hear one of the competitors inside the cell yelling at the other one to stop before he killed Prophet. "Don't kill 'im. Fuck! Stop! You gonna kill 'im!"

That's when one of the female deputies came in for a walk-through and heard the banging and screaming. She hit the alarm and a minute later the guards rushed in with batons and stun guns. They walked the attackers out in handcuffs, and the medical staff carried Prophet off on a stretcher. The side of his head was swollen like a cantaloupe and his eye socket was crushed, along with his nose and cheek. The inside of that cell looked like a slaughterhouse. There was blood spattered on the walls and puddles of it on the floor.

The ambush really upset Lance and me. An hour or so later, Lance came into my cell. He looked extremely serious. Lance's eyes were moist with tears and he said, "I want you to know I'd never let anyone close the door on you. You damn sure better not let anyone do it to me."

"I wouldn't," I replied with a lump in my throat. "Never."

Lance held up his hand and wiggled his little finger. "Pinkie swear."

"Seriously, bro?"

"Fuck yeah, seriously!" he growled. We locked digits and shook on it.

Around roughly the same time the probation department prepared Pre-Sentence Reports, PSRs, on each of us. These reports are used by judges to help them determine defendants' sentences. The report calculated what each defendant should get based on the Federal Sentencing Guidelines. Ninety-nine percent of the time judges follow the PSR's recommendation. Lance's PSR recommended a sentence of twenty-seven to thirty-four years plus three months. When he got it in the mail, Lance actually laughed. "That's gotta be a mistake, right? They can't actually give me thirty-four years, can they?"

I almost cried for him. I loved Lance like a brother, and he was looking at over thirty years for illegally selling prescription drugs. The same thing that large wholesalers get caught doing—on a massive scale—all the time. But you don't see any CEOs doing thirty years or even thirty days.

Lance looked at me in my dimly lit cell, and said, "Thank God they only know about Tennessee. Can you imagine what we'd be looking at if they knew about Alaska and South Carolina and Florida?"

And New York, I thought. *Another month and I'd have been shipping pills to Mississippi, too!*

I think it was that same night that I was talking to my dad on the phone about having my friends and family send letters to the judge, begging for leniency. Out of nowhere my father said, "Buddy, I hate to tell you this, but Maya wants you to call her." I had received several scathing letters from her asking how I could have done this to her and accusing me of ruining both our lives. I wrote apologetic letters back, but the tone in her letters hadn't improved much. She asked me to call her several times, but I had been dreading the conversation. "She's . . . she's upset. You're gonna have to call her."

"Yes, sir."

Maya picked up on the second ring and lit into me immediately. The first couple of minutes consisted of a lot of angry comments like: "How could you do this to me?!" and "I'm so pissed off at you!" and "You lied to me! You lied to me!"

"And I feel real bad about that, Maya," I said. "But I—"

"Why?!" she snapped. "Just tell me, why?"

"I just wanted to save up some money, so I'd . . . so we'd have something for the future. Together. For us. Together."

"Uh huh," she grunted, unconvinced, but I could feel her anger subsiding. She sighed a couple of times and growled sarcastically, "So what's your plan now?"

"Now, I'm hoping to convince the judge to give me as little time as possible." I was in the middle of writing a letter to the judge, asking for a sentence reduction known as a Product of Environment variance due to being raised in an environment saturated with drugs and drug activity. Mother, stepfather, aunts, uncles, cousins, and friends—everyone I knew was involved in some way. I had never known a time I wasn't engrossed in a culture of drugs. My lawyer had refused to address the issue, stating, he didn't think I would qualify. But I thought, *If I don't, who does?* "It can't hurt to try."

Maya swallowed hard and asked, "How . . . how much time?"

"I'm hoping five years, but—"

She immediately started sobbing. "Five years! Oh my God!" Based on the thirty-four years Lance was looking at, five years seemed like a slap on the wrist. A time out. A minor detention.

Not that I wanted to do the time.

Chapter Sixteen

Gangster Informant

"Nearly everyone charged [with a federal crime] is convicted. And they usually face the prospect of a lengthy prison term. . . . Becoming an informant is the only chance defendants have."

—*USA Today*

Roughly a week after we got to Ocilla, Assistant US Attorney Lewen, Assistant US Attorney Alexandra Hui, and Special Agent Poston drove down from Tennessee to question us. The deputies pulled us out of our cells, one by one, and led us to this nasty eggshell conference room with flimsy chairs and a chipped Formica table. When I stepped into the room, the two federal prosecutors and the DEA man looked irritated, wrinkled, and disheveled. I pulled up a rickety chair and Lewen dug a cell phone out of his coat pocket. He placed it in the middle of the table, and said, "I want you to get me as much drug money and dope as possible." They had probably gone through my cell phones and found several names of known drug dealers; Miles trafficked oxycodone, Hernandez had been arrested for selling weed, and Leon was a coke dealer.

They wanted me to set someone up. Someone with a lot of cash and drugs. "The more you can get me, the better it'll be for you." Special Agent Poston said with a sneer.

"I've been locked up over four months and everyone knows it. No one's answering my calls anymore." I looked around the table at their stone faces and shook my head like they were crazy. "It's too late for that."

Poston interjected, "There were a lot of names in those phones. We'll take weed, coke, meth, guns—"

"All I sold was pills. I'm sorry." I tried to tell them about Jimmy Cage, who had supplied us with an outrageous amount of oxycodone. He certainly would have done it to us. But they didn't want to hear about a DEA confidential informant who was "double-dipping."

"What about James LaPointe?" asked Lewen. "You ever meet him?" LaPointe was the only one of our fourteen co-defendants dumb enough to go to trial. However, I had never met him and I told them so. Out of all of us, Dustin was the only one that had dealt with LaPointe. "Then you're not much good to us are you?"

"I guess not." It never even occurred to me to lie about knowing him. They never suggested it.

According to Larry "the Lineman," when the deputies brought him in, Lewen asked immediately about LaPointe. "I've never met 'im," grunted four-hundred-pound Larry. "Sorry, I can't help you."

"Are you sure you've never met him?"

Larry chuckled while slightly shaking his enormous head. "I know what you're getting at, and I'm not going to do it. I know how you guys operate. You'll end up using my testimony to convict LaPointe and turn around and give me an extra five years for perjury. No thanks."

By the time they got Lance into the conference room the assistant US attorney must have been pretty frustrated. Lance sat down and Lewen went over LaPointe's pending trial. Then he asked if Lance had ever met LaPointe. "He's one of Dustin's dealers," said Lance. "But I've never met him."

"Well," sighed Lewen, "LaPointe's going to trial and Dustin is going to testify. I need someone to back up the fact that LaPointe was receiving oxys for distribution from Dustin."

Lance told the federal prosecutor he hadn't been at any of the meetings between Dustin and LaPointe, nor had he seen LaPointe accept any pills. "The only package I even mailed LaPointe was the one the DEA intercepted," said Lance. "And Dustin gave me the address. I never spoke with LaPointe."

"You need to think about that," said Lewen. "You're looking at thirty-four years."

"What do you want me to do, lie?"

"No!" snapped the assistant US attorney. "I want you to do thirty-four years. What do you want to do?"

Lance took several quick breaths, thought about his mother, his brothers, his friends, and the thirty-four-year sentence sitting in front of him. "But, I . . . I wasn't there. I wouldn't know what to say."

"Don't worry about that," said Lewen, as a creepy grin slowly spread across his face.

When Lance got back to the pod, he pulled me into his cell, and told me about the conversation. "What should I do?"

Lance thought of himself as a gangster—a stand-up guy. But he was just a scared kid. We all were. Cooperating was his only shot at tasting freedom before he was fifty. What choice did he have? "As your friend," I whispered, "I'm telling you, you need to do whatever you have to do to get that sentence off your back. If you don't, someone else will."

Roughly a month before the trial, Lance and Dustin were transferred to the Knoxville County Jail. According to Lance, it was a nicer facility; they had microwaves and the food was good. It wasn't overcrowded and it was clean. Basically, it's where they place government witnesses to keep them happy and talking. A week before LaPointe's trial, Lewen had the marshals bring Lance and Dustin to the federal building. They were placed in a conference room and given pizza, chicken, and Mountain Dew for two days while Lewen went over their testimony. He gave them examples of what he believed LaPointe's lawyer would ask, and how they should respond to the questions. He went over their testimony, and over and over again, until they knew it inside and out. Until their stories were perfect.

In the middle of July, the United States tried James LaPointe. Over the course of the first day, and part of the second day, Assistant US Attorney Lewen had Dustin Wallace walk the jury through LaPointe's involvement in the conspiracy to distribute oxycodone. He went over the FedEx and UPS shipments. The "blueberries" and "big dogs." The DEA wiretaps.

Lance took the witness stand just before noon on July 13, 2010. He broke down how his organization obtained prescriptions for OxyContin and oxycodone, using doctor shoppers and pill mills in Florida; and then shipped tens of thousands of the painkillers to multiple co-conspirators in Tennessee.

"If the supply is so plentiful down there," asked Lewen, "why not just sell them to south Floridians?"

"The prices up here are way higher," replied Lance. He explained that an oxy 80 in Ybor City sold for twenty to thirty dollars, but in Knoxville, the same pill went for sixty to eighty dollars.

"You made, on average, how much per month?"

"Anywhere from ten thousand to twenty thousand dollars." With LaPointe's gaze boring into Lance from the defense table "the Little General" explained how he and Dustin supplied numerous Tennessee distributors. "They would give him cash . . . he would send it back FedEx or UPS."

"How else?"

"Through bank accounts, like different bank accounts I had, and my brothers' and friends' bank accounts in Florida."

"Let's talk about the actual packages. When you were sending them to Dustin Wallace, were you sending them directly to Dustin?"

"No, I wasn't." Lance explained the various ways he packaged the pills and the numerous individuals he shipped the packages to.

Lewen went over the transcripts of multiple intercepted cellular conversations between Lance and Dustin. One of them regarded the one and only package Lance had attempted to ship to LaPointe. "Line 11 you say, 'it's going to a business.' Whose business?"

"James LaPointe's."

During Lance's cross examination, LaPointe's lawyer, Jonathan Harwell, hammered away at the validity and motivation of Lance's testimony, emphasizing the massive sentence he was facing. "That's around twenty-seven to thirty-three [sic] years? . . . Do you hope to get something a lot less than that?"

"Yes, I do."

"And you know that your chances of getting a lot less than that depend in part on . . . the government saying that you've been very helpful?"

"I am supposed to tell the truth," Lance replied weakly.

"This is your one shot, right?"

Harwell's strategy was to paint Lance as a liar and an opportunist and LaPointe as an innocent pillhead, arrested by cruel DEA agents and indicted by an overzealous federal prosecutor. Primarily, he did that by calling LaPointe's fiancé, Sheena Clemons, to testify on her future husband's behalf.

Sheena told the jury LaPointe suffered from "extreme pain due to his back, legs, and feet. I've seen him in the fetal position crying from the pain."

"Did there come a time when you learned that Mr. LaPointe used drugs that weren't prescribed by a doctor?"

"He told me he was purchasing oxycodone from Dustin" she admitted. "He was in pain." Sheena told the jury that LaPointe wasn't part of any conspiracy; he was just an addict who got sucked into the indictment because he had sold Dustin some security equipment and occasionally bought pills from him.

Harwell walked her through the morning of the arrest. "I awoke to my house alarm going off. . . . I was nude. I grabbed my robe. I went to come out of the bedroom and there were police, DEA," she said, irritated. "They pushed us kind of down to the ground and handcuffed us. They took Jimmy away. They handcuffed me and my sister."

The agents placed Sheena and her sister in the kitchen on the floor. "And how long did you and your sister remain in the kitchen?"

"Two hours, hour and a half. It was a long time," she growled, while glaring at the federal prosecutor. Her sister had begged the agents to let her use the restroom, but they refused. "She started to actually pee on herself. She got up, still handcuffed, and sat down on the trashcan that was beside her. The agents started to yell at her."

As compelling as Sheena's testimony was, on the third day of the trial, the good citizens of Tennessee found LaPointe guilty, and he was sentenced to sixty-three months in the Federal Bureau of Prisons. He had never received a single package.

A month and a half after the trial Lance was taken back to court for his sentencing in front of Senior US District Judge Leon Jordan. As a result of his testimony against LaPointe, Assistant US Attorney Lewen asked the judge to reduce Lance's sentence from the PSR's recommendation of 324 to 405 months. "I'm sure your Honor remembers the testimony of Mr. Barabas as he explained to the jury in, I think, a very concise, compelling way, how this organization was structured and how it ran." Assistant US Attorney Lewen took a long look at Lance sitting quietly with his tall, distinguished lawyer, Serbo Simeoni, and paused briefly. "Outside of the mandatory life cases and all the cases I've done that involved crack, cocaine, methamphetamine, that's the highest guideline range I've seen in my time as an AUSA."

The federal prosecutor went on to emphasize the serious nature of the crime and the need for just punishment. He told the Court that at that very moment there were vehicles traveling I-75 and I-40, crammed full of people trekking to and from Florida for pills, and that any sentence still needed to be severe enough to deter others from following in that path. Lewen asked the judge to give Lance enough "time to harness that enterprising spirit that he has and put it towards something legal, so that when he comes out he can be a productive legal member of society and not a criminal."

He came to his conclusion: "For those reasons, the United States would respectfully request that a sentence of two hundred and eleven months be imposed against Mr. Barabas." That's over seventeen years.

There were numerous people in the gallery to support Lance; most had sent in letters, and some insisted on speaking about the Lance they knew. His family pastor told the judge what a "charismatic little character" Lance was. His Uncle Chris spoke about how "highly motivated and incredibly intelligent" his nephew was; and he asked the Court to show leniency. His mother spoke about his ADHD; and his love for his brothers, his deceased father, and wrestling. She said he was a good boy. A good son. "But somewhere along the line, your Honor, my son entered into a world of the unknown."

Lance's attorney asked the Court to consider his client's youth, his lack of criminal history, and how a wrestling injury led to an addiction that put him on the wrong path. Lance told the judge that he had made several bad decisions. That he'd never been in trouble before. That he was sorry for what he had done.

The judge concurred with the federal prosecutor, noting that this was one of the highest sentencing guidelines he had seen in his twenty-plus years of experience. He was moved by Lance's pastor, his uncle, his mother. But mostly he was moved by Lance's attorney's story of addiction. "It's my duty to determine a sentence that is sufficient, but not greater than necessary. . . . I believe that he has shown by his cooperation with the Government and by the statements he has made here in court that he has changed his life for the better."

The Honorable Leon Jordan gave him fifteen years. He was twenty-two years old, and he had never been in trouble before. "Pretty Boy" Landon got seventy-two months, Larry "the Lineman" got eighty-four months, and "Shit Dick" got thirty-five months.

Less than a month later it was my turn for sentencing. With my Pre-Sentence Report recommending 121 months, I was potentially facing ten years in prison. On September 21, 2010, Assistant US Attorney Lewen requested that Judge Jordan lower the sentence from 121 months to 91 months for my cooperation. Standing in a courtroom full of my family and friends, my attorney, Douglas McNabb, worked to get it much lower than that: "We thank the government for their recommendation, but we believe that what Mr. Dodd did was extraordinary, that he provided extraordinary substantial assistance. As the government has indicated, he was the first to sign a plea agreement," said McNabb. "His actions caused the defense in a large multi-defendant case to collapse, that his actions brought down a large drug conspiracy." Most of that was a stretch, but it sounded good.

McNabb then asked the judge to consider my family history. "We also ask the Court to mitigate Mr. Dodd's sentence on the basis of his childhood. . . . At a very early age, Mr. Dodd was surrounded by drugs, by alcohol, and by abuse. He began drinking at age six, he smoked marijuana at age nine, and . . . he was physically abused by his mother as well as her two husbands and other boyfriends." At that point my mother abruptly stood up and stormed out of the courtroom. I looked back as the doors slammed behind her and thought, *That figures.* "We are asking for a fifty percent departure for the reasons I set out, which would take it to sixty months. We are also asking for a variance based upon Mr. Dodd's childhood, twelve months down to forty-eight months."

Lewen's face got so red and blotchy when McNabb asked for four years, I thought he might have a heart attack. "Your Honor!" he snapped, "I disagree with opposing counsel that the filing of [Mr. Dodd's] plea agreement caused the defense of thirteen other defendants to collapse." He continued: "We also object to the variance based off of the traumatic childhood that this defendant has endured. . . . It is simply not a valid or sufficient basis to grant a variance."

By the time it was my turn to address the court I was hands-shaking, knees-trembling terrified. There were so many things that I wanted to say to Judge Jordan, but it all came down to this. "Your Honor, I got on the wrong path," I said as my voice cracked. "I figured I could make some money by the time I graduated college, and I went about it the wrong way." I apologized to anyone that may have been impacted by the sale of our oxycodone, for my actions, and to the state of Tennessee. And I asked for the Court to "have mercy on me."

The judge agreed that my childhood was "best described as traumatic." He had reviewed my personal letter to him along with more than a dozen letters from my family and peers asking for a light sentence. "I'm amazed that you were able to accomplish what you did in your junior and senior year in high school, and proceed to work and go to college. That is very impressive. It shows you do have the intelligence to do what is right." He said that the Barabas brothers and I made the wrong choices by taking drugs and then moving on to selling them. "These prescription drugs are our number one problem in East Tennessee, and you were feeding the problem." Judge Jordan then looked down at me from the bench, pinched his brow together, and said, "The Court [feels] that the sentence of eighty months will afford adequate deterrence and will provide just punishment."

I sat there with my stomach burning as I did the calculation and wondered who was going to mow my grandmother's lawn and clean out the gutters while I rotted away in the Federal Bureau of Prisons for the next six years and eight months. The house needed painting too. *Damn, what have I done?!*

While I was sitting in the holding tank at the federal building, feeling bad for myself, my co-defendants were back in Ocilla County, getting in trouble. The way I heard it, Landon and a couple of guys wanted to play cards, so Landon borrowed a deck from his cellie, Duke, without asking first. Duke was a six-feet-plus black crack dealer with golds. About halfway through the game Duke noticed that his cards were missing. He got upset and frantically started looking for them, eventually calling to Landon, "Bunkie, you got my cards?"

"Yeah," said Landon, "I got 'em, Duke!" Landon genuinely didn't think he had done anything wrong. When Duke had first arrived Landon had loaned him some hygiene products and given him a bunch of food. They had been cellies for several weeks and shared lots of items. As far as Landon was concerned, he and Duke were tight. He was wrong.

Duke walked up beside Landon, sitting at the poker table, and snapped, "You trying me, huh? You testing me?" Landon glanced up at him, unsuspectingly, and Duke smashed him in the mouth. The blow knocked him off the bench. Landon crumpled onto the concrete in a daze. He rolled onto his side and spit some blood out of his mouth, along with his left incisor. The tooth made a little *ting-ting* sound as it bounced across the floor. Duke walked back into their cell like nothing had happened.

As Landon tried to regain his bearings, Lance and Larry rushed out of their cells, along with Dustin and Brett. They were joined by the only other white guys in the pod, John and Ken. Landon staggered to his feet and he was pissed. He looked at his brothers, jabbed his finger at his cell door, and said, "Don't let anyone in that fucking cell, no matter what you hear."

He stormed into the room and closed the door behind him. Landon was considerably smaller than his cellie, but everyone knew Duke didn't have a prayer. Duke made some half-assed attempt to apologize. Unfortunately, it was too late for that. Suddenly, everyone heard banging and pounding. Landon was barking and yelling at Duke while slamming him around. Several of the black guys in the pod started to crowd around. After a couple of minutes it became obvious that Duke was losing the fight. He started screaming and crying out for help. After another minute of listening to Landon beat the brakes off Duke, several of the black guys tried to rush the room. But Lance, Larry, and the rest of the white guys shoved them back. It quickly turned into a screaming and pushing match. From the guards' observation center, it must have looked like a race riot.

About the time the first punches started to be thrown by Lance and the guys, the public announcement speakers started screeching, "Lockdown! Lockdown!" The main pod door swung open, and a dozen deputies in riot gear swarmed in yelling, "Down on the ground! Down on the ground!"

Most of the inmates dropped to the floor immediately. Those that didn't were quickly pummeled with batons or tased. The guards rushed into the cell and pulled Landon off Duke. Then dragged Landon, Lance, Larry, and several of the other guys off to the Special Housing Unit (SHU). The hole. Solitary confinement.

Around three o'clock, the marshals dropped me and several other inmates off at Ocilla County. We were shuffling into the main building, and as we passed the windows of the SHU I saw Landon banging on one of the windows. He was laughing and waving at me. I immediately noticed his jack o' lantern smile and thought *What the fuck is going on?* Two units down, I saw Lance standing at the window staring at me. He nodded and gave me a half smile. He looked devastated. Depressed by his fifteen-year sentence, no doubt. But more than anything, he looked drained of hope and full of regret. We all were. That's the last time I saw Lance—standing at the window looking sad.

Roughly a month later, Lance was transported to the Federal Correctional Institution in Miami, Florida. Despite everything that has happened, I will always think of Lance Barabas as my best friend. A brother.

Chapter Seventeen

Coleman Federal Correctional Complex

"Eight male inmates were injured with at least one suffering a gunshot wound, when a 'large-scale fight' broke out . . . in the Coleman Federal Correctional Complex. Sunday's fight follows a fatal stabbing at the prison."

—*Tampa Bay Times*

In the middle of December, the marshals bussed me to Lovejoy—a privately run prison—in Lovejoy, Georgia. After that, they transported me to the Federal Detention Facility in Tallahassee, Florida, then they shipped me back to Georgia to the Atlanta holdover facility. It was smack-dab in the middle of the ghetto—a medieval castle wrapped in chain link and razor wire with almost a dozen guard towers manned by corrections officers (COs) with assault rifles. Everything was grey and depressing, strictly concrete and steel. I was stuck in a cell with a low-level coke dealer. We were locked down twenty-four hours a day on the weekends, twenty-three hours a day during the week, with one hour to swap out dirty clothes, take a shower, or use the phone. There was never enough time to do all three.

I spent the Christmas of 2010 in the Atlanta holdover facility, locked in a concrete box with a lunatic bank robber, freezing my ass off, surrounded by rats and roaches.

On December 29, I was awoken at three o'clock in the morning, chained and shackled, and loaded onto a transport bus with forty other inmates for the ride to Coleman Federal Correctional Complex in Coleman, Florida. The complex houses roughly eight thousand federal inmates in two US penitentiaries, a medium- and a low-security prison, and a women's camp. It's the largest complex in the Bureau of Prisons system—a city of corrections.

For the entire bus ride to Coleman there were guys chattering on and on about "Pen 1" being one of the most violent high-security penitentiaries in the nation. Gangs and riots. Murders and rapes. One guy—an Aryan Nation brother sporting swastikas, an SS double-lightning bolt on his neck and shaved head—said that a couple of years earlier the FBI arrested a bunch of COs for smuggling drugs, weapons, and cell phones into the prison. "The MXs and the Surenos were stabbing each other on the yard," laughed the Aryan, talking about the Mexican mafia and a prison gang, "with knives they bought from the fucking screws!"

The bus pulled into Pen 1 around 9:00 a.m., and my blood pressure immediately shot up. I could feel the tension in the air change. Everyone got quiet and serious—deathly serious. It was everything I expected a federal prison to be. An ultra-modern correctional facility with layer after layer of fences, twenty-foot-tall walls, cameras, and guard towers with COs holding shotguns. We let off around ten guys there. Hard, rough-looking, tatted-up thugs. Then the bus shot over to Pen 2 and several more guys got off. The whole time I was praying, *Please don't call my name. Please don't call my name.* Then we stopped at the medium- and finally the low-security facility, where I got off.

The Federal Bureau of Prisons was roughly 40 percent overcrowded and significantly underfunded at that time. And it's only gotten worse. I had spent over a year in the county jails, locked inside concrete boxes, fighting boredom and other inmates. I expected federal prison was going to be twice as bad.

If that wasn't enough, I had heard one of the first things the "shot callers" (the inmates that run the gangs) ask for is your "passport," or PSR. They typically give you a couple weeks to have it mailed in by your lawyer or family. But that's it. If you can't come up with your Pre-Sentence Report you're labeled a "snitch" or a "rat" and told to check into the SHU or told "you can't walk the rec yard." That means that other than eating alone in the cafeteria, you would never leave the unit.

If you're told to check into the SHU and you decide not to, and you actually tried and walk the yard, you would be beaten or stabbed. Possibly killed.

When the COs marched us out of the Receiving and Departing area and into Coleman's low-security prison compound, I expected to see guard towers, officers holding assault rifles, chain-link fences, and concertina wire. Tatted-up gang members and dangerous-looking thugs stomping around in a concrete and steel prison. I couldn't have been more wrong. The compound looked more like a college campus than a prison. There were manicured trees and shrubs, lush green lawns, and flowers. To the left of the administration building was the cafeteria, an area for vocational training, a library, and a chapel. To the right was the medical facility and a huge recreational area. Directly in front of us were three massive two-story buildings, each containing four units. Every unit housed between 150 to180 inmates in semi-open bays. Each bay was divided up into two- and three-man concrete cubes.

Once inside my assigned unit—unit A1—I was told by the CO, "You're in cell forty-four upper." I didn't mind being in the top bunk. I figured it was safer than being on the bottom and having to worry about someone mauling and suffocating you for whatever the reason might be.

My cellies were Arthur Vallant, a short white meth-head convicted of robbing a bank, and Dean Jones, a kid serving time for some type of interstate commerce conspiracy. They were very hospitable and helpful when I arrived—probably just happy to have another young, clean guy in the room who didn't snore. Around four o'clock we were told to stand up in our cubes and the COs counted us. Then the guards screamed, "Chow!" and we were released for dinner.

The cafeteria was a huge warehouse-size building that held roughly five hundred inmates. I was standing in line and saw Richard—he had arrived at Coleman over a month earlier. He came running up to me and hugged me. "You just get here?"

"Yeah." I told him I had just come in on the bus and asked, "Has anyone asked you for your PSR?"

Our eyes locked, and he knew what I was worried about. Richard got this big toothy grin on his face and he chuckled. "It's not that kinda prison, bro." He stood there in line with me and explained that Coleman Low was designated as a protective custody facility; 1,800 inmates, of which, roughly 600 had been charged with sex offenses.

"Like pedophiles?"

"Right. . . . Like when some thirty-five-year-old pervert thinks he's met a sexually curious thirteen-year-old online, drives across state lines to meet her at a 'bait house,' and she turns out to be a pissed off middle-aged FBI agent." Richard started laughing and said, "He gets his heart broken and ten years in Coleman Low." If they were sent to a prison without protective custody the other inmates would kill them.

I looked around the hall and noticed that there were a lot of older white males. Chunky and soft looking. No tattoos. "Son of a bitch."

"Most of them were caught downloading pictures of preteen girls or boys. They're harmless to adults." He told me that 90 percent of the 1,200 remaining inmates cooperated with the government. They set someone up, wore a wire, or testified against their co-defendants. No one at Coleman ever asked to see my PSR, because no one wanted to have to provide theirs. There were ex-gang members, "dropouts" that just couldn't deal with "the life" anymore, or had ratted out their homeboys, and couldn't walk the yards at the penitentiaries. There were plenty of fights, but nobody was getting gutted with blades or stomped to death like they were right across the street. Richard asked, "You been to the rec yard yet?"

"No. How is it?"

"It's prison, but it sure beats the hell outta being locked in your cell eighteen hours a day like we were in Blount County."

After dinner, we went out to the rec yard and I was absolutely shocked. There was a live band of inmates playing Disturbed's "Down with the Sickness" and Nirvana's "Come as You Are." Guys were walking around selling ice-cold sodas, homemade cheese-cakes, burritos, and churros.

The prison had over eight acres of baseball, football, and soc-cer fields, and shuffle-ball, racquetball, basketball and tennis courts. There was a full gym with elliptical, rowing, and stair-climber ma-chines. Pool, foosball, and ping-pong tables. At first sight, I was ab-solutely dizzy at the amount of stuff there was to do. But with nearly two thousand inmates confined to such a small area, they have to provide them with activities to keep them from going crazy or tear-ing up the place.

I'll never forget when Richard asked me if I wanted to get a snow cone. "I know you're fucking with me," I said. "They don't have snow cones, do they?"

He shrugged. "We only get 'em on holidays, but yeah, they've got snow cones."

Richard went with piña colada, but I stuck with classic cherry. We spent New Year's weekend playing in the volleyball tournament and sunbathing. Coleman was like a nightmare summer camp with mean-spirited camp counselors, only it lasted for years.

Roughly two months later Landon showed up. The whole time I was locked up with Landon in the county jail he was talking shit about Richard. "He only got thirty-five months and Larry got seven years—that's bullshit!" and "He did way more than Larry." And the entire time Richard and I had been locked up at Coleman he had been saying, "I could give a shit where they send Landon," and "He's serious trouble." But the second they saw each other they were all hugs. Smiling and patting each other on the back like best friends. Human nature, I'm sure.

We spent the next several months working out together and entering tournaments—basketball, handball, volleyball, and anything else competitive. I won the dodgeball tournament twice, and came in second in the obstacle course—it had a slip n' slide and everything. The guards video recorded it and aired it over the television so everyone would get a good laugh. Landon won the mega-man challenge: dips, squats, pull-ups, push-ups, and burpees. He absolutely blew the doors off it. The brothers nicknamed him "the White Knight."

Here is the thing: for every dollar the Bureau of Prisons dumps into recreation they withhold a dollar from medical. You absolutely do not want to get sick or hurt at Coleman. While I was there, roughly a dozen inmates died; one guy had been to the medical facility three days in a row complaining of chest pains. On day three, the medical staff told him to come back the following morning. He died about ten minutes after leaving medical. He didn't make it to the following morning's appointment.

The actual medical staff consists of one doctor that no one ever sees and several physician assistants, who aren't qualified to diagnose anything other than scraped elbows and the flu. I knew one guy who continually complained about multiple pains in his midsection and abdomen. They told him the problem was in his head and sent him to the psychology department. The inmate got so frustrated he diagnosed himself using several medical references in the library. Finally, after a year of getting the runaround by Coleman's medical staff, his mother called Senator Marco Rubio's office in Washington, DC. Rubio's people called some people, who called some other people, and the inmate was given an MRI. He was diagnosed with several hernias and Coleman ordered him to be taken out to a local hospital where they operated.

I had an eighty-year-old cellmate with diabetes, receiving a set dose of insulin daily, regardless of his blood sugar levels. On several occasions he woke up in the middle of the night, thrashing about the bed and screaming in his native language that the world was coming to an end; he was completely delusional as a result of his incredibly low blood sugar. The COs cuffed him to a chair while I plied him with sweets until his sugar level increased enough to keep him from going into a coma. It was all we could do for him until the medical staff arrived two hours later. There is no medical staff available at Coleman between 10:00 p.m. and 5:00 a.m., no 911, no ambulance. You tough it out or you die. My eighty-year-old cellie toughed it out several times.

No matter how many snow cones they gave me or how many volleyball games I played, I was still in prison. I missed my grandmothers, my dad, Maya, Lance, my dog—hell, I even started missing my mother a little.

My fellow inmates and I were packed into three-man cells designed for two men—a space so small, it's legally unfit for three seventy-five pound dogs. But there's no PETA for federal prisoners.

There were roughly 150 inmates crammed into my housing unit. You had zero privacy. Even in the restrooms and showers—where you would think you could get a couple minutes to yourself—inmates were constantly yelling to one another; discussing the previous night's basketball game while sitting on the toilet, or singing in the showers.

Initially, I had a succession of decent cellies, but after a year or so I ended up with a "religious extremist." He was a Nation of Islam militant racist black guy. For six months he tried to convince me that Caucasians, like albinos or midgets, came from a defective gene in African Americans. Essentially, the white race was a flawed species—soulless, blue-eyed devils that should be exterminated for the good of humanity. Not surprisingly, we had some issues.

However, I can't say I liked him any less than the white supremacist in the cell across the hall from mine. This guy was covered in swastikas and lightning bolt tattoos, and he insisted that Caucasians were the "master race."

"They're all fucking mud people," I remember him saying, during one of his more aggressive rants. His face was pink with blood, and the veins in his neck were bulging with anger. Spittle would occasionally leap out of his mouth as he growled, "They should all be marched off to the fucking gas chambers!"

"Okay" I said, bobbing my head, like I was actually following his logic. "So, I'm thinking you're not a Will Smith fan?"

I'll never forget his response; he immediately switched from a raving lunatic to someone speaking in a civil tone, and replied, "He was pretty good in that movie *I Am Legend*." That's when the absurdity of what he had said hit him, our eyes locked, and we both burst into laughter.

The pure insanity of the system I was trapped in was mentally draining. I've seen innocent men get their cases overturned—after spending over a decade in prison—and released without even an apology. I've met dozens of wrongfully convicted people serving time they didn't deserve. I've even read an inmate's denial from a District Court of Appeals that stated, essentially, that they were going to uphold the conviction even though they couldn't find any law had been broken. The system is fundamentally broken and the government doesn't care.

The Bureau of Prisons runs a residential drug addiction program (RDAP) as part of its effort to rehabilitate federal inmates. The program consists of roughly nine months of inmate behavior modification therapy, course material, and group therapy sessions. A lot of people can't take the mental head games and drop out; others are kicked out for a variety of causes such as not knowing the material or cleaning rooms for money. Those that do make it through the program are eligible to receive a year off their sentence.

In August 2011, Richard completed RDAP and was sent to a halfway house. Amazingly, Landon managed to make it through the program despite getting high on Suboxone strips and nodding out in the middle of group meetings and smoking K2 in the bathroom every chance he got. He was constantly tested for drugs, but neither Suboxone nor K2 shows up on standard drug test. The lucky bastard left for the halfway house in June 2013.

A few months after I got to Coleman, Maya moved to Florida. She stayed with her uncle, enrolled in music school, got a job at Wet 'n Wild as a lifeguard, and started coming to see me regularly. Our first couple visits were tense. She was still irritated that I had lied to her, angry that I had sold drugs, and furious that I had somehow managed to get myself incarcerated for nearly seven years. There were a lot of glares and snide comments, but she eventually came around. We emailed through the prison's TRULINCS system several times a day and spoke on the phone—fifteen minutes per call—two or three times a week. When she came to see me, we would sit in Coleman Low's visitation room and hold hands, eat microwaved

Biggie Burgers, and drink Cherry Cokes out of the vending machines.

Eventually, Maya started asking questions like, "Do you love me?" and "Where do you see us in the next few years?"

"I don't know. I don't even know when I'll be out of here, Maya." There were so many variables regarding my release date, I couldn't give her the answer I knew she wanted. Nor would I make a promise I didn't know I could keep. I had entered RDAP in mid-2013 but found out that I was not eligible for the twelve-month reduction due to my firearm sentencing enhancement. At the time, I was in the middle of appealing that decision. On top of that I didn't know how much halfway house I would be getting. "I could be outta here in a year, or it could be three years. I just don't know."

"I love you Doug. I don't care how long it takes." I remember she grinned up at me and said, "And I know you love me too."

And I did love her.

Eventually, I was notified that despite my appeal, I would not be getting the year off for completing RDAP. Regardless, I felt the program might do me some good, so I stayed in. Unlike Richard and Landon, I didn't sail through easily. Looking back, it was entirely my fault.

I consistently got the highest score on tests, and I knew the course material as well as the drug treatment specialists. I participated in community group sessions and individual therapy sessions. Unfortunately, one of the specialists took an immediate dislike to me. She was a woman in her early fifties who reminded me of my mother. She would show up to work in tears, slam her hand down on the table, and yell at the inmates. She seemed to get an unusual amount of pleasure out of watching inmates in the program grovel in fear at her suggestion they might not get the year off. That was the problem between us—I didn't grovel because I wasn't getting the year off.

She began verbally attacking me every chance she got—twisting everything I said or did. When she accused me of not knowing the course material, I shrugged and said, "I got a perfect score on the last test."

"But you're not applying it, Mr. Dodd!" she screeched. "It just means you're book smart."

If I answered questions during group therapy sessions, she would snap, "You lack humility, Mr. Dodd!" When another inmate told her I was thinking about writing a memoir she growled, "You're trying to glorify your drug addiction and criminal behavior." I hadn't even put pen to paper and she had damned me.

Eventually, I got tired of the head games. I signed out of the program in August 2013. I probably should've cowed to the counselor, but she reminded me so much of my mother, I just couldn't do it.

Around that time Maya showed up for one of our visits with puffy, bloodshot eyes. She had been arguing with her uncle's new girlfriend. "It's not going to work out with them," she said. "She doesn't want me there. I'm gonna have to find someplace else to stay—an efficiency or something."

A week later, she told me there were some girls at school looking for a roommate. The rent was cheap and the complex was close to campus. "Sounds perfect," I said. "Are you gonna take it?"

"I think so, I'm still looking."

Less then a month after that, we were in the visitation room, and Maya told me she had moved in with two fellow Wet 'n Wild lifeguards. *Male* Wet 'n Wild lifeguards. Male Wet 'n Wild lifeguards *in their late twenties!* "What happened to the girls from school?"

She gave me an exaggerated shrug and looked at the ground. "This was way cheaper. Plus, they're real nice guys."

"I'll bet!" Let's face it, it was in their best interest to be "real nice" to their hot eighteen-year-old virgin roommate. "This isn't good Maya. A couple weeks ago you were moving in with some teen coeds and now you tell me you've moved in with a couple career lifeguards? It doesn't add up."

"What, are you jealous?" she giggled and shot me a huge grin. "They're just a couple really sweet guys that wanna look out for me."

I wanted to believe that, but after a month, Maya's emails were becoming sporadic and my calls were going to voice mail more frequently. She started telling me about getting drunk at parties with her roommates where she would throw up in the bathroom and pass out. "Thank God my roommate was there," she told me during one visit. "All I remember is waking up in the morning, in my bed. I'd have never made it home without him."

That was absolutely not what I wanted to hear. Not even close. This chick had me telling her I loved her and daydreaming about what our life could be together. Now my guts were churning with acid and anxiety. I lay in my bunk trying to shake the image of Maya in bed with the bronzed Wet 'n Wild lifeguards. I tossed and turned night after night, but the image was burned into my mind.

The deal breaker came on a Friday night. I called Maya around 9:30 p.m.—just before we're locked down for the night—and she was in a car, on her way to a party, with one of her roommates. I could hear the other passengers talking and the radio blaring in the

background. I immediately got the impression she didn't want anyone in the vehicle to know who she was talking to; everything was
"uh huh" and "yeah" and "okay."

When our fifteen minutes were up I said, "I love you," and she
responded in a muffled whisper, "Uh huh, me too."

Oh, hell no. It's over! I slammed down the phone; immediately
took her off my visitation list, cancelled her TRULINCS email account, and stopped calling her. I knew it had been just a matter of
time before it went bad, and now it had. Over the next couple of
weeks, I received several letters from her pleading with me to call
her and apologizing—telling me she wanted to come see me. But I
ignored them.

My stepmother eventually told me Maya started dating one of
her lifeguard roommates, flunked out of school, and moved back to
New York—with the new boyfriend.

I was more hurt than angry. I didn't want to fall in love with
Maya. I didn't want to be in love with anyone. Especially while
in prison. But she kept pushing and pushing, and when I finally
started thinking this could be my girl she reeled around and gutted me.

I emailed Lance every couple of days. Prison didn't change
him much. About a year before I was released, I was sitting in
the cafeteria with a couple of guys eating spaghetti and sipping
Kool Aid when a guy straight off the bus sat down at our table.
He was sleeved out and shaven bald—your basic-looking Aryan
Brother. He told us he had been down four years on a conspir-
acy case for trafficking oxycodone. "I just got here from Miami
FCI Low."

"Miami?" I asked. "You know a guy name Lance Barabas?"

"Fuck yeah!" he laughed. "Lance is my homeboy. He's off the chain, bro." He spent the next several minutes telling us Lance was running a gambling ticket and two poker tables. He had the "hookup" for anything you wanted out of the kitchen. "He's into everything, bro—porn magazines, cigarettes, everything. He's a straight-up gangster. You know they charged him as a kingpin?"

"Yeah, I heard that."

"They were trying to give him life, but he fought 'em. He was gonna go to trial; told 'em, 'kiss my ass motherfuckers, you don't have shit!'" Based on the fictionalized version of our case that Lance had told this guy, I gathered no one was checking PSRs at Miami Low either. "He only pled out cause they threatened to charge his girl," he said, bobbing his bald head up and down. "Lance is a stand-up dude. He went hard out there."

"Yeah," I said, trying not to laugh. "That's what I heard."

My grandmothers came up every few months to see me. At the end of every visit, Meme would tell me, "This might be the last time I see you Dougie. I'll be dead soon." I would grin and say, "I know Meme, I know." Then I'd hug her and kiss her goodbye. She's still alive and doing fine.

Grandma pushed and prodded me to build some semblance of a relationship with my mother. Eventually, I buckled and my mother started coming to see me every month or two. We spent most of our visits bickering about her twenty-five-year-old former-heroin-addict boyfriend. She would constantly tell me—her son in federal prison—how hard her life was. It was still all about her!

When I mentioned I was thinking about writing a memoir, she snapped, "Why, so you can tell everyone what a horrible mother I am?!"

"Well," I growled back, "if it walks like a duck and quacks like a duck . . ."

I spent years anticipating my release. Preparing myself mentally and emotionally. I studied everything from spirituality to business and finance. I took outside courses on drug rehabilitation, personal training, even yoga. I felt I did all I could do to prepare myself for life beyond the prison gates.

As my release date ticked closer and closer I was a jumble of nervous tension. I damn near teared up when I gave some of my goodbyes.

The night before my release I couldn't sleep, not a wink. Excited at the prospect of getting out mixed with the fear of what freedom held. I couldn't keep my heart or my mind from racing.

I was released at ten o'clock in the morning, and I remember the chills I got walking through the courtyard and out the big steel bar exit doors. It was surreal.

My grandmother and her new husband, along with my long-time friend Jennifer, picked me up. I loaded the trunk with a box of my stuff—books and notepads filled with stories and thoughts I'd written over the years. Through the chain-link fence adjacent to the parking lot, I could see a group of guys in the recreation yard exercising, running and walking the track. I jogged hundreds of miles around that track over the years, listening to my Sony radio, trying to escape the insanity of incarceration.

When we exited the parking lot, Jennifer and I were in the

back seat. I'll never forget my grandmother glanced at me in the rearview mirror. "It's over sweetie," she said. I smiled and signed in relief. *It was finally over.*

Author's Afterword

In the years since my release, some got clean, found good jobs, and are enjoying their lives. Others haven't changed a bit. And a few even got worse.

Lance "the Little General" Barabas is the one friend still serving time. He's still acting like a maniac in Miami Federal Correctional Complex, counting down the days until his release in 2022. According to Lance's emails, he's "running the fucking place." His hope is to someday walk out of prison a free man and stroll down Miami Beach, which is walking-distance away from the prison, smoking a blunt and drinking a Corona with me, Landon, Larry, and Richard.

"Pretty Boy" Landon Barabas got out of prison and went right back to partying like a rock star. Between drunken stupors, a near violation of probation, and a DUI, Landon started his own business, works out, and stares at himself incessantly in the mirror. Some things don't change.

Within a year of Larry "the Lineman" Barabas's incarceration, his high school sweetheart wife started sleeping around, filed for divorce, took both the kids and all of Larry's stuff, and left. Typical! Upon his release from Talladega Federal Correctional Institution in 2016, Larry started working with Landon and is now a small business owner as well. He's enjoying his freedom with his new girlfriend and kids.

It's my understanding that since "Shit Dick" Richard Sullivan's release he spends most of his time hanging out at his dad's bar, working out at the gym, and chasing girls. Who can blame him? Richard is an entrepreneur at heart and he'll continue to put things into play until something works out. His newest project is a blueberry farm that he and his father built. They expect to start harvesting the blueberries very soon. I hear he's even toying with the idea of giving the porn industry another go.

Kristina Williamson got pregnant and engaged—in that order—and moved to California with some guy. Poor bastard.

Maya eventually ditched the lifeguard, got pregnant, and married an aging playboy who was fifteen years her senior, with a substantial bank account.

Tiffany Sutler, Lance's old girlfriend, and my cousin Tony Jr. are still struggling with their opiate addictions. They've both been in and out of multiple drug rehabs, but neither can seem to beat the habit. I feel their pain, it ain't easy. I believe in them though.

As far as I know, Jimmy Cage and Miles Calvin are both still out there double-dipping and cracking heads for the DEA.

After my release in October 2014 I stayed at a halfway house for three months, and then I was placed under house arrest. House arrest lasted for seven months. I couldn't go anywhere—work, the grocery story, the doctor's office—without approval. I had to put in a request a week ahead of time and hope it got approved. That time was a real struggle for me. I was humiliated at every job interview I went to because of my criminal background. Things would start off great until we got to the felony question, and then the employer would start to backpedal. The thought of being a felon passes through my mind on a daily basis. The stigma is terrible—I hate it.

As far as women go, I can't wait to meet the right one. I'm sure there is a beautiful, sane, trustworthy one out there somewhere.

I'm twenty-eight years old and still extremely motivated. On June 9th, 2016, I graduated a technical college for logistics and distribution management as well as successfully completing the GLA (Global Logistics Associate) certification through APICS, a professional association for supply chain management. (Yeah, I have a little experience in that department.) I hope to work for a big company or start my own business one day. In May of 2018 I will walk across the stage at Pasco Hernando State College—to finish what I started ten years earlier—and receive my associates degree in business and communications.

I'm also enthusiastic about public speaking regarding the negative impact drugs have had on my life. So far I've spoken with several small groups, and I'm looking forward to speaking at venues like high schools and treatment centers across the United States. One of the things I want to talk about is the fact that there's a prescription opioid epidemic in this country—anyone that watches the news knows that—and that yes, my friends and I took advantage of it. It was a mistake that will stay with us the rest of our lives.

In addition, I'd like to emphasize that I no longer condone the behavior described throughout the book. I put myself and many other people's lives in danger; and I was wrong for that.

Although prescription painkillers took me to all-time highs, they led to a downward spiral that brought my life to a deeper, darker place than I could've imagined. Opiates are extremely addictive and unless you have severe pain I would advise you stay away from them at all costs. In the end, they're just not worth it.

I remain mindful of everything I've been through. I have learned that time is the most precious thing we have and I don't plan on wasting another second. I have a long way to go, but I'm headed in the right direction. One foot in front of the other. One day at a time.

A Note on Source Material

The following motions, transcripts, interviews, law enforcement reports, and articles were used to help create the most accurate version of my story.

Articles

ABC 10 News KGTV. "SDSU Stabbing Leaves 3 In Critical Condition," 12/15/2007.

Amrhein, Saundra. "Ecstasy Traffic Is on the Rise in Hernando," *St. Petersburg Times*, 11/24/2000.

Associated Press. "Purdue Pharma, Execs to Pay $634.5 Million Fine in OxyContin Case," 05/10/2007.

Balloch, Jim. "Major Drug Ring Exposed," *Knoxville News Sentinel*, 11/03/2009.

Davis, Lisa A. "Pasco Judge Denies Break for Driver in DUI Manslaughter," *Tampa Bay Times*, 05/18/2011.

Francis, Thomas. "How Florida Brothers' 'Pill Mill' Operation Fueled Painkiller Abuse Epidemic," NBC News Investigation, 05/07/2012.

Heath, Brad. "How Snitches Buy Their Freedom," *USA Today*, 12/14/2012.

Kalfrin, Valerie. "Second Person Arrested In Oxycodone Investigation," *The Tampa Tribune*, 06/20/2007.

Klaus, Krista. "Show Won't Go On At Pasco High School After Fatal Crash," *Hernando Tribune*, 11/14/2008.

Lawson, Guy. "The Dukes of Oxy," *Rolling Stone*, 04/23/2015.

Lee, Steve. "Bigger's Not Always Better on the Mats," *Tampa Bay Times*, 12/05/2006.

Leger, Donna Leinwand. "FedEx Facing Charges Over Drugs," *USA Today*, 07/18/2014.

NBC News. "Judge Rules That Drug Company Misled the Public About Addiction Risk," 07/20/2007.

Pavuk, Amy. "Florida's Crackdown Makes Big Dent in 'Pill Mills,'" *Orlando Sentinel*, 04/06/2013.

Pilkington, Ed. "How America Got Hooked on Killer Prescription Drugs," *The Guardian*, 06/09/2011.

Satterfield, Jamie. "22-year-old Testifies in Knox Man's Oxycodone Trial," *Knoxville News Sentinel*, 07/14/2010.

Silvestrini, Elaine. "Drug Case Nets Siblings," *Tampa Bay Times*, 10/30/2009.

Sullivan, Eric. "New Port Richey Tattoo Parlor Owner Shot in Head," *St. Petersburg Times*, 04/22/2009.

Swirko, Cindy. "Florida's Minimum Mandatory Laws Produce Uneven Sentences," *Gainesville Sun*, 08/13/2010.

Tampa Bay Times, "Five Men From Pasco Face Federal Drug and Money Laundering Charges," 11/04/2009.

Waters, Steve. "Better Behaved Cobra Becomes Contender," *St. Petersburg Times*, 01/13/2005.

WVLT (Local News 8), "Fourteen People Indicted on Multiple Drug Charges," 11/02/2009.

Interviews

Interviews with Lance Barabas, January 2014–June 2014
Interviews with Landon Barabas, April 2014–May 2014
Interviews with Richard Sullivan, May 2014

Law Enforcement Reports and Legal Transcripts
(listed chronologically)

Pinellas County, Florida Complaint/Arrest Affidavit and Supplemental Report, Report No. 200801764, CPL. J. Spatz, 05/09/2008

Department of Justice Master Affidavit, Case No. 3:09-MJ-R065, S/A Bethel R. Poston, 10/22/2009

Department of Justice Affidavit, Case No. 3:09-MJ-2066, S/A Bethel R. Poston, 10/21/2009

Department of Justice Drug Property Collected/Purchased/or Seized, Case No. K-09-0007, 10/27/2009

Department of Justice Nondrug Property Seizers, Case No. KC-09-0007, 10/29/2009 Department of Justice SMART Summery Report, File No. G6-100011, 06/02/2010

DEA Report of Investigation, Knock-and-talk/Search warrant and arrest: Justin Knox and Lauren Vest, File No. redaction, Dated: 06/24/2009, Filed by: S/A Bethel Poston

DEA Report of Investigation, Controlled buy: Dustin Wallace, File No. redacted, Filed by: TFO Jason Butler, Dated: 08/07/2009

DEA Report of Investigation, Arrest, search, and seizer: Mary Wilson and James Hobbs, File No. redacted, Dated: 10/13/2009, Filed by: Bethel Poston

DEA Report of Investigation, Wire interception: Lance Barabas and Dustin Wallace, File No. redacted, Dated: 10/21/2009

DEA Report of Investigation, Surveillance: Dustin Wallace, File numbers: redacted, Dates: 07/09/09, 09/11/2009, 09/23/2009, 09/25/2009, 09/30/2009, 10/13/2009, Filed by: TFO Jason Butler and S/A Bethel Poston

Indictment, U.S.A. vs. Lance Barabas, Larry Barabas, Landon Barabas, Douglas Dodd, Richard Sullivan, Dustin Wallace, Brett Webb, William Kaman, Matthew Golden, James LaPointe, Thallen Washington, Mary Wilson, Hunter Hobbs, and Tyler Henry, Docket No. 3:09-CR-141, 10/20/2009

Transcript of "The Barabas Criminal Enterprises'" First Appearance, U.S. Magistrate Judge Thomas B. McCoun III, Case No. 3:09-CR-141, 10/27/2009

DEA Report of Investigation, Wire interception: Lance Barabas and Dustin Wallace/Dustin Wallace and James LaPointe, File No. redacted, Dated: 10/28/2009, Filed by: Bethel Poston

DEA Report of Investigation, Arrest: William Kaman, File No. redacted, Dated: 10/28/2009, Filed by: S/A Michel T. Lee

DEA Report of Investigation, Arrest, search and seizer: Dustin Wallace, File No. redacted, Dated: 10/28/2009, Filed by: S/A Dave Lewis

DEA Report of Investigation, Arrest, search, and seizer: Brett Webb, File No. redacted, 10/27/2009, Filed by: Bethel Poston

DEA Report of Investigation, Arrest, Search, and Seizer: Douglas Dodd, File No.'s KC-090007/G6/10–0011/G6-10-0011/G6-10-0011, Dated: 10/27/09, 10/29/2009, 11/04/2009, 06/02/2010, Filed by: redacted

DEA Report of Investigation, Acquisition: UPS parcel, File No. redacted, Dated: 10/28/2009, Filed by: S/A Michael Davis

DEA Report of Investigation, Arrest, search, and seizer: James LaPointe, File No. redacted, Dated: 10/29/2009, Filed by: S/A Michael Davis

Pre-Sentence Investigation Report, Douglas Dodd, 09/16/2010

Transcript of US v. James LaPointe, Case No. 3:09-CR141, 07/13/2010

Transcript of Lance Barabas's Sentencing, U.S. District Judge Leon Jordan, Case No. 3:09-CR141, 08/26/2010

Transcript of Douglas Dodd's Sentencing, U.S. District Judge Leon Jordan, Case No. 3:09-CR141, 09/21/2010